Folens

endorsed by
edexcel

GCSE PE

For EDEXCEL

2nd Edition
Julie Walmsley

Acknowledgements

p.10 © Action Plus; p.11 © Action Plus; p.12 © Action Plus; p.14 © PA/Empics; p.15 © Action Plus; p.17 © Corbis; p.18 © Action Plus; p.22 (top, middle, bottom) © PA/Empics; p.23 © Action Plus; p.24 © PA/Empics; p.26 (left) Courtesy of Kellogg; p.26 (right) © PA/Empics; p.27 © Action Plus; p.29 (top) Alamy/Adrian Sherratt; p.29 (bottom) © PA/Empics; p.30 © Action Plus; p.33 © PA/Empics; p.35 © Action Plus; p.37 (top left) Courtesy of Blackpool FC; p.37 (top right, bottom) © PA/Empics; p.39 (left, right) © PA/Empics; p.40 © PA/Empics; p.42 © PA/Empics; p.45 © iStockphoto.com/bbossom; p.47 © PA/Empics; p.47 Logo used with permission of the Youth Sport Trust. www.youthsporttrust.org; p.50 © Action Plus; p.51 © Action Plus; p.52 Logo courtesy of Sport England; p.53 Logo courtesty of Marylebone Cricket Club; p.54 © iStockphoto.com/negaprion; p.55 Logo courtesy of Sainsbury's; p.58 © Action Plus; p.59 © Action Plus; p.61 (top) © Action Plus; p.61 (bottom) © PA/Empics; p.62 (top, middle, bottom) © PA/Empics; p.64 (top left, top middle, top right, bottom left, bottom middle) © Action Plus; p.64 (bottom right) © PA/Empics; p.65 Sipa Press/Rex Features; p.70 (top left, top middle, bottom left) © Action Plus; p.70 (top right, bottom right) © PA/Empics; p.71 © PA/Empics; p.73 (left, right) © PA/Empics; p.74 © PA/Empics; p.80 © iStockphoto.com/technotr; p.81 © Action Plus; p.82 Alamy/Danwar Productions; p.83 © PA/Empics; p.86 © iStockphoto.com/Lighthousebay; p.89 (top left, bottom) © PA/Empics; p.89 (top middle) © Action Plus; p.89 (top right) © Rex Features; p.93 (left, right) © PA/Empics; p.95 (top, bottom) © PA/Empics; p.96 © PA/Empics; p.97 © iStockphoto.com/photoGartner; p.102 © Action Plus; p.115 © PA/Empics; p.119 Alamy/Bon Appetit; p.120 © iStockphoto.com/Sportstock; p.121 (top) © PA/Empics; p.121 (bottom) © Action Plus; p.126 (top) © Trishcreations. Image from BigStockPhoto.com; p.126 (left, right) © PA/Empics; p.127 © PA/Empics; p.128 © PA/Empics; p.129 © PA/Empics; p.130 (left, middle left, right) © PA/Empics; p.130 (middle right) © Action Plus; p.131 © Action Plus; p.134 © Action Plus; p.136 © Action Plus; p.137 (top) © Action Plus; p.137 (bottom) © PA/Empics; p.138 © Action Plus; p.141 (top, bottom) © Action Plus; p.142 (top) © Action Plus; p.142 (middle, bottom) © PA/Empics; p.144 (left, middle, right) © PA/Empics; p.145 (top, bottom) © PA/Empics; p.148 (left, middle left, middle right, right) © PA/Empics; p.149 (top, bottom) © PA/Empics; p.150 © PA/Empics; p.151 (top, top middle, bottom middle) © PA/Empics; p.151 (bottom) © Action Plus; p.152 © PA/Empics; p.159 © Corbis; p.160 (top) © iStockphoto.com/damaianty; p.160 (bottom) © iStockphoto.com/ChristianAnthony; p.161 SPL/Paul Rapson; p.163 © Action Plus; p.166 © PA/Empics; p.171 © Action Plus; p.172 (top, bottom) © PA/Empics; p.176 SIU/Science Photo Library; p.177 © iStockphoto.com/Sportstock; p.181 (left) © Rex Features p.181 (top, bottom right) © PA/Empics; p.181 (bottom left) © iStockphoto.com/Birgitte Magnus; p.185 (left, right) © Action Plus; p.186 © iStockphoto.com/Sean Locke; p.187 © E.J. Camp/Corbis; p.188 (top left, bottom left, bottom right) © PA/Empics; p.188 (top right) © Action Plus; p.190 (top, bottom) © Action Plus; p.191 (top) © Action Plus; p.191 (bottom) © PA/Empics; p.192 © Action Plus; p.193 (top, bottom) © PA/Empics; p.196 © Action Plus; p.197 © PA/Empics; p.202 (top left, top right) © Action Plus; p.202 (top middle, bottom left, bottom middle, bottom right) © PA/Empics; p.203 (left) © Action Plus; p.203 (middle, right) © PA/Empics; p.205 (top, right) © Action Plus; p.205 (left) © PA/Empics; p.207 © PA/Empics; p.208 (top left, bottom left, bottom right) © PA/Empics; p.208 (top right) © Action Plus; p.209 (left, right) © PA/Empics; p.212 © PA/Empics; p.213 © iStockphoto.com/alexxx1981; p.214 (left, right) © PA/Empics; p.220 © Action Plus; p.221 © PA/Empics; p.222 © PA/Empics; p.223 (left) © Action Plus; p.223 (right) © weberfoto/fotolia; p.225 © PA/Empics; p.227 © PA/Empics.

© 2009 Folens Limited, on behalf of the author.

United Kingdom: Folens Publishers, Waterslade House, Thame Road, Haddenham, Buckinghamshire HP17 8NT.
Email: folens@folens.com   Website: www.folens.com

Ireland: Folens Publishers, Greenhills Road, Tallaght, Dublin 24.
Email: info@folens.ie   Website: www.folens.ie

Editor: Rosie Parrish
Text design: Design by Form (www.form.uk.com)
Layout: Planman
Picture researcher: Thelma Gilbert
Illustrations: Planman
Cover design: Design by Form (www.form.uk.com)

The websites recommended in this publication were correct at the time of going to press, however, websites may have been removed or web addresses changed since that time. Folens has made every attempt to suggest websites that are reliable and appropriate for student's use. It is not unknown for unscrupulous individuals to put unsuitable material on websites that may be accessed by students. Teachers should check all websites before allowing students to access them. Folens is not responsible for the content of external websites.

For general spellings Folens adheres to *Oxford Dictionary of English,* Second Edition (Revised), 2005.

First published 2009 by Folens Limited.

ISBN 978-1-85008-399-3   Folens code FD3993

Contents

Introduction

The content of this book covers the theory of the GCSE PE for Edexcel specification for both the Short Course and the full GCSE:

Unit 1   The theory of Physical Education
Section 1.1 Healthy, active lifestyles
Section 1.2 Your healthy, active body

It also provides some guidance for:

Unit 2   Performance in Physical Education
Section 2.2 Analysis of performance

Section 2.1 relates to the practical performance and is therefore not covered in this book.

The content of Section 1.1 supports the GCSE Short Course. The content of Sections 1.1 and 1.2 support the full GCSE. Analysis of performance is required for both the Short Course and the full GCSE.

Section 1.1 requires students to build up their knowledge of physical education and physical activity and understand the bearing they have on a balanced, healthy, active lifestyle. This will include:

- understanding how and why people decide to take part in physical activity
- building knowledge and understanding of fitness and exercise
- understanding and knowledge of personal health and well-being.

Knowledge developed should relate to performance in physical activity.

Section 2.2 requires students to gain knowledge and understanding of the working body in relation to performance, including the cardiovascular, muscular and respiratory systems.

Unit 1 is assessed externally through an examination:

- The exam for the GCSE Short Course is an hour long and contains multiple-choice, short-answer and longer-answer questions. The total mark available is 40.
- The exam for the full GCSE is an hour and 30 minutes long and contains multiple-choice, short-answer and longer-answer questions. The total mark available is 80.

For both the GCSE Short Course and the full GCSE, Unit 1 provides 40 per cent of the maximum total mark for the course. Unit 2 provides the other 60 per cent of the total course mark.

The book's layout

This book is set out so that it matches the Edexcel specification for GCSE PE. The headings of each of the sections relate directly to the specification. Topics with a large amount of information are split into separate a and b sections. If you work your way carefully through this book you will cover everything that the awarding body requires of you. To help you further, the material is presented in small, easy-to-digest chunks that are broken down using frequent sub-headings.

There are many photographs, illustrations and diagrams used to give you a visual way of remembering the work. Each photograph has a caption bringing your attention to the main point so that the link with the information is unmistakable. There are also numerous learning features built into this book.

Topics

At the beginning of each section you will find a list of all the topics you will learn about in that section. Each topic is numbered, which is especially useful when you are revising, as it will be quicker to find relevant information and to check you know all of the points you are supposed to.

What you will learn about in this topic:

1 — What constitutes a healthy, active lifestyle
2 — The benefits of participating in physical activity
3 — Physical activity relieving stress and tension
4 — How physical activity stimulates the individual

Tasks

Each section involves completing a series of numbered tasks. Completing tasks involves referring to the work just read or discussed in class. Tasks need to be recorded in your own workbook or file.

By keeping your workbook up-to-date with completed tasks, the work recorded will build up into your personal revision document. It is important that when you are working, information you write down can be read easily when you refer back to it. Take care to make your words legible.

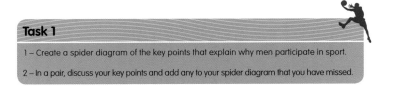

Task 1

1 – Create a spider diagram of the key points that explain why men participate in sport.

2 – In a pair, discuss your key points and add any to your spider diagram that you have missed.

Active challenges

Active challenges are thought-provoking tasks, which often involve working with a partner. Completing these challenges will open your mind to the section being worked on and give you the chance to engage verbally with the topic.

Active challenge

With a partner, make a list of sporting activities that require cardiovascular fitness.

Use the length of time of the activity to help your choices.

Spider diagrams

Spider diagrams are quick and easy to understand. They are an excellent way of recording and remembering the main points of a topic.

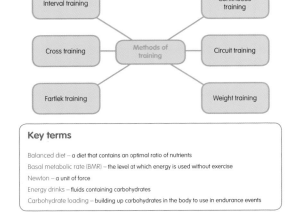

Key terms

Wherever there are words in **bold** in this book they will be found in the key terms boxes. These boxes indicate important words for you to remember together with their definitions.

Key terms

Balanced diet – a diet that contains an optimal ratio of nutrients
Basal metabolic rate (BMR) – the level at which energy is used without exercise
Newton – a unit of force
Energy drinks – fluids containing carbohydrates
Carbohydrate loading – building up carbohydrates in the body to use in endurance events

Summary

At the end of each section there is a summary that rounds up the essential information that you need to remember from the topics covered. It acts as a short collection of the ideas that are the most important to the section. When revising, the summaries can be used as a starting point to remind you of the main ideas. You can then add to them with more detailed information from memory or by re-reading the text.

Summary

There are many social, physical and mental benefits to leading a healthy, active lifestyle. A person in the habit of regular exercise can benefit from their healthy lifestyle. Physically, the body and its systems can increase in fitness and be able to meet the pressures of a more demanding environment. A stronger body and stronger systems could increase life expectancy. Personal development can come about through the challenges of exercise: a person may develop determination, courage and a positive attitude as a result of taking up exercise; in turn, this may spill over into general life and positively affect a person's confidence. Cooperation, teamwork and friendships can also develop from being a member of a group, club or team.

Glossary

Many words that you come across in this book are explained in the glossary. When you come across a word and you are unsure of its meaning, look it up in the glossary.

C

Carbohydrate loading building up carbohydrates in the body to use in endurance events.

Cardiac muscle only found in the heart, never tires.

Detoxify removing poison from.

Diaphragm muscle that divides the chest cavity from the abdominal cavity.

Dislocate joints moved out of their normal arrangement.

Index

The index at the back of this book helps you to find a particular subject quickly. The index gives you a page reference and should take you to one or more places in the text where the subject occurs.

Exam questions

At the end of each section there are a series of examination-style questions for you to answer. They will include multiple-choice, short-answer and longer-answer questions, matching the types of questions you will meet in the final exam.

For all questions, look carefully at the key words being used and what you are being asked: how, what, which, where, when? Always think logically through the question.

Exam questions

Multiple-choice questions

1. (a) Which of the following describes circuit training?

    ☐ A This method of training involves times of work followed by times of rest

    ☐ B A series of exercises, completed for a certain amount of time, after one another

    ☐ C Exercising, often running, varying time, distance and effort

    ☐ D Involves shifting weight to increase the strength of muscles, using a programme of repetitions and sets
    (1)

    (b) Which of the following describes interval training?

    ☐ A This method of training involves times of work followed by times of rest

    (c) Which method of training is a triathlete most likely to use?

    ☐ A Cross training

    ☐ B Weight training

    ☐ C Circuit training

    ☐ D Fartlek training
    (1)

    (d) Fartlek training depends on varying:

    ☐ A The people in the training session

    ☐ B The sports played

    ☐ C The weights lifted

    ☐ D The time, distance and effort in the session
    (1)

Multiple-choice questions

Multiple-choice questions are worth one mark per correct answer. There are two types of multiple-choice question:

Questions using maths

1. The correct target zone for an endurance athlete is 120 to 160 bpm. How old is the athlete?

   ☐ A 15

   ☐ B 20

   ☐ C 25

   ☐ D 40
   (1)

This question requires you to:

- Know how to work out the maximum heart rate (220 – age).
- Know what the target zone is (60 to 80 per cent of the maximum heart rate).
- Be able to work out and recognize the target zone in the question.

You can tackle this question by trial and error:

Option A:
220 – 15 = 205 divided by 100 x 60 = 123
220 – 15 = 205 divided by 100 x 80 = 164

Option B:
220 – 20 = 200 divided by 100 x 60 = 120
220 – 20 = 200 divided by 100 x 80 = 160

Option B is the correct one so you may want to stop there, but there should be enough time to double-check by working out the other options to make sure of your choice.

Questions requiring a choice made from knowledge and value judgement

2. Which of the following gives the **most** important reason for wearing the correct clothing when taking part in physical activity?

   ☐ **A** It gives you the opportunity to look good

   ☐ **B** It gives you a psychological advantage over the opposition

   ☐ **C** It reduces the chance of injury

   ☐ **D** It is in the rules of the practical activity

   (1)

This question requires you to:

- Know the reasons for wearing correct clothing.
- Recognize that the word 'most' is in bold because it is important.
- Make a value judgement on what the 'most' important reason is.

Option A is the weakest alternative.
Option B may give an edge competitively and is more important than A.
Option C is more important than A and B.
Option D is more important than A and B but it is not more important than C. So the correct answer is C.

Short-answer questions

Short-answer questions can be worth between one and four marks each. There is usually one mark given per correct idea or response. These questions often give a leading sentence which require a single word, a list of words or a few sentences on a single idea.

3. Each of the following statements refer to health-related exercise components.

   (a) Which component of fitness does a badminton player depend on when they reach for a shot?

   (b) When voluntary muscles are used for long periods, which component of health-related exercise is required?

   (c) Which health-related exercise component relates to calculating body weight and what percentage is fat, muscle and bone?

   (3)

This question requires you to:

• Understand the components of health-related exercise.
• Know the difference between the components of health-related exercise and skill–related fitness

(a) The key word is 'reach'. This relates to joints and range of movement and so relates to flexibility.

(b) The key words are 'long periods' and 'voluntary muscle'. The answer will include endurance as you have to work out if it is muscular or cardiovascular. As the question relates to 'voluntary muscle' then it must be muscular endurance. If the question had been about the entire body then it would have been about the heart and lungs and so the answer would have been cardiovascular endurance.

(c) The key words are 'body weight' and 'percentage'. This question is looking at how the body weight is made up (or composed) in relation to fat, muscle and bone. You need to have learnt the correct term for this, which is body composition.

Longer-answer questions

Longer-answer questions can be worth up to six marks. The question can be set out with an opening sentence giving the subject and the key ideas to focus on. Instructions will be given to tell you what to do.

4. Jenny plays netball. She is in the school team and wants to improve her skills of the game and general fitness. She is learning about circuit training and thinks this can help her improve her play.

   Jenny plans a six-station circuit of her own:

   Station 1 – chest passing against a wall
   Station 2 – dribbling a ball between cones
   Station 3 – aiming a tennis ball at a target on the wall
   Station 4 – shooting into a netball post
   Station 5 – serving a shuttle into a target area
   Station 6 – playing bounce passes against a wall

   Evaluate Jenny's circuit taking into account the circuit's strengths, weaknesses and what can be done to improve it.

   (6)

This question requires you to:

- Apply your knowledge of circuit training.
- Decide what the strengths of the circuit are. For example, it involves three netball skills activities so three different skills are addressed.
- Decide what the weaknesses of the circuit are. For example, it does not involve any fitness stations or activities not related to netball.
- Decide how you would improve it. For example, by involving fitness stations relating to the skill of the game such as, sprinting between cones to help speed over short distances and change of direction, step ups to strengthen leg muscles and bench lifts to strengthen arms.

There are six marks available so, with three areas to comment on, work on earning two marks for each group of comments.

You and the exam

You could view the exam as a competition to get a better mark than students nationwide who have chosen to take this exam. So give yourself the best chance! If you are absent from any lessons, it is up to you to catch up on any work missed. Gaps in work are gaps in knowledge. Students who have completed all of the work will give themselves the best chance of success.

1.1 ～ Healthy, active lifestyles

1.1.1 Healthy, active lifestyles and how they could benefit you

What you will learn about in this topic:

1 — What constitutes a healthy, active lifestyle
2 — The benefits of participating in physical activity
3 — Physical activity relieving stress and tension
4 — How physical activity stimulates the individual

1 — What constitutes a healthy, active lifestyle

People become involved in **physical activity** for different reasons. A young person with talent will make their choice for completely different reasons than those of a young mum with a toddler or a recently retired person. However they start in sport, the routes and pathways to involvement in physical activity are wide and varied with key influences coming from many directions. Living a **healthy, active lifestyle** involves the individual making choices. These include:

- taking part in physical activity
- eating a balanced diet
- avoiding harmful substances
- sustaining friendships
- having the ability to concentrate.

2 — The benefits of participating in physical activity

For people who seek a healthy, active lifestyle, the benefits to their long-term **health** can be enormous, helping their **social**, **physical** and **mental** well-being.

The World Health Organization (WHO) defines health as: "A state of complete mental, physical and social well-being, not simply the absence of disease or infirmity."

Physical well-being relates to what changes happen to the body because of activity. Mental well-being relates to how your approach and attitude changes due to activity. Social well-being is to do with how well you relate to others.

Social benefits of exercise

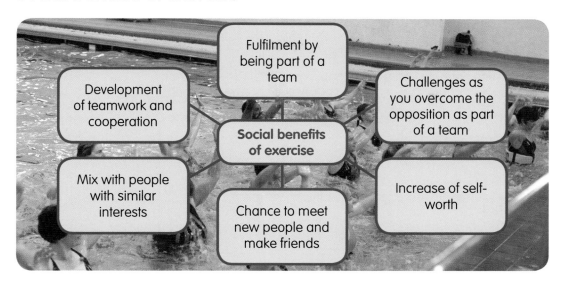

Development of teamwork and cooperation
Choosing a team or group activity relies on the individual's development of personal qualities.

Situations may arise in group situations where certain demands may be put on its members. For example:

- being able to listen to instructions and carry them out
- being able to give instructions for others to carry out
- being able to think quickly for the good of the group
- changing and relaying a change of strategy
- being able to encourage others to change what they are doing or to work harder.

Whatever the situation, cooperating and working for the whole group is necessary for success.

Fulfilment by being part of a team
Pursuing a physically active hobby may give a person the opportunity for regular exercise and so a healthier lifestyle. It can also fill a gap in their life that work and family cannot. The activity chosen and the people they mix with may be such a change to their everyday experiences that they add a new dimension to their life.

Challenge as you overcome the opposition as part of a team
A person may start a sport as a novice performer, happy to learn new skills within a club, as part of a team. As their ability develops their confidence may grow in such a way that they desire competition and are confident to enter competitive events. This may develop further so they want to compete against other clubs.

For some individuals clearly set out goals and targets lead the performer through to higher levels of competition. Some people have the ability, desire and application to represent their local area, county and ultimately their country in their chosen sport.

Increase of self-worth
A good performance can lead to gaining the respect of peers. As a person learns, develops and applies their knowledge in an activity, personal confidence increases. Fellow players and peers also see this development: a good performance may earn respect for such achievements and further increases the feelings of self-worth and popularity.

Chance to meet new people and make friends
Joining a group, club or society enables a person to increase the number of people they know and so increases the possibility of friendships being made.

Mix with people with similar interests
When people are in a team or a club for a particular activity there is a common interest. This provides an opportunity to share and develop ideas on a common theme in a social environment.

Key terms

Physical activity – any form of exercise or movement. Physical activity may be planned and structured or unplanned and unstructured (in PE we are concerned with planned and structured physical activity, such as a fitness class)

Healthy, active lifestyle – a lifestyle that contributes positively to social, physical and mental well-being, and that includes regular physical activity

Health – a state of complete mental, physical and social well-being, and not merely the absence of disease and infirmity

Social – to do with the community and society

Physical – of the body

Mental – of the mind

Physical benefits of exercise

In order for any physical activity to be of value to a person's physical **fitness**, it must meet the **FITT** requirements:

Frequency – taking part in physical activity between three and five times a week
Intensity – during these sessions the heart rate must be raised to above 60 per cent of its maximum (maximum heart rate = 220 – age)
Time – the heart rate should be raised to this level and sustained for more than 20 minutes
Type – the type of exercise should suit the sport and individual.

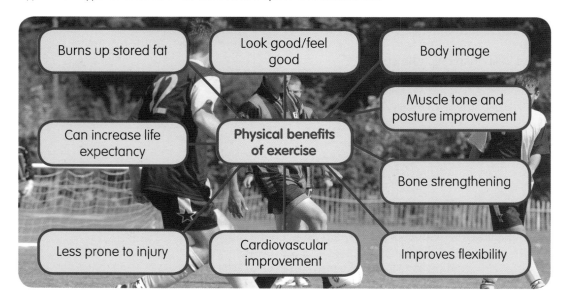

Burns up stored fat

Exercise will put extra demands on the body. In turn, body fat will be burnt off, ultimately changing the shape of the person. Exercise at the correct level burns calories and as long as the dietary intake remains the same, a person should lose weight with the extra activity.

Look good/feel good

The effect of fat burning and the improvement it has on the shape of the body can make a person feel good about themselves.

Body image

The changes to the body shape and the body's condition will not only change the person's feelings towards themselves but can affect the opinions of others towards them too.

Muscle tone and posture improvement

With regular exercise the muscles become toned: this is a tightening of the muscles in a state of readiness to work. The more muscles are toned the more they can do their job properly, which in turn can improve posture. Depending on the type of training programme, the shape and size of the muscle will begin to develop. Many people want greater muscle definition. 'Dynamic posture' can directly relate to the athlete in action and the application of correct technique.

Bone strengthening

Vigorous physical exercise stimulates the uptake of calcium to the bones. In young people this helps to build bone mass and in older people reduces the loss of bone mass. Bone mass density (BMD) is important as it reduces the risk of osteoporosis. Regularly exercising can strengthen the bones as long as the effort gradually increases. There are two ways this can happen:

1. Impact – through the gravitational force of weight bearing exercises such as vigorous walking and jogging at the point of 'footstrike' (when the foot contacts the ground) apply here.
2. Muscular pull – as muscles are attached to bone, those bones attached to the muscles involved in the exercise will be strengthened. Exercises such as rowing and weight training are examples of strengthening bone in this way.

A gymnast uses muscular pull in balances such as handstands and impact during landings such as during a tumble routine, and so has a high BMD.

A swimmer performs muscular pull without loading and therefore has a good BMD, but not as high as a gymnast.

A weight trainer uses muscular pull and the stronger they are the greater their BMD. Weight training is a great way to increase BMD in the hip and spine.

Improves flexibility

Generally, the more a person exercises at suitable levels, the more readily the body is able to reach the demands of the exercise, making their movements more efficient. The body is able to perform tasks more efficiently with training and performers are able to reach their outcome with less effort. Training muscles and joints will increase strength and flexibility.

Cardiovascular improvement

The result of regular training on the heart and lungs improves the transport of blood around the body making the body more effective and efficient. This allows a person to work more efficiently for longer. As the heart becomes stronger it can pump more blood with each beat. So, as you become fitter, the heart pumps enough blood but with fewer beats. Therefore, a fit person has a slower heart rate.

Less prone to injury
When exercise is carried out regularly the body begins to respond to the activity. The body may become stronger, more enduring and flexible. As a result, the body can work harder without becoming tired or breathless. With less fatigue and a stronger body, there may be less chance of injury.

Can increase life expectancy
When involved in physical activity, the stress a person may feel in everyday life is forgotten for a time. This can have a positive effect on the functioning of the heart and so stress-related illnesses may be reduced, increasing the life expectancy of the person.

Research carried out by the Department of Medicine at the University of Dundee came to the following conclusions: 'Older people with better health habits live healthier for longer' and 'Regular physical activity in old age can rejuvenate physical capacity by 10–15 years.'

Task 1

1 – Study the information on physical benefits of participating in sport and physical activities.
2 – Create a spider diagram of all the reasons, including ideas of your own.

Use the Internet to find further information. Select a search engine and then type in 'Physical activity' as a starting point.

Active challenge

With a partner, discuss what physical effects exercise has had on your body.

Mental benefits of exercise

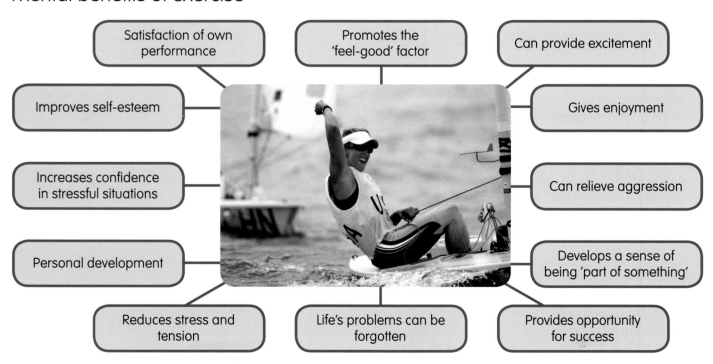

- Satisfaction of own performance
- Promotes the 'feel-good' factor
- Can provide excitement
- Improves self-esteem
- Gives enjoyment
- Increases confidence in stressful situations
- Can relieve aggression
- Personal development
- Develops a sense of being 'part of something'
- Reduces stress and tension
- Life's problems can be forgotten
- Provides opportunity for success

Satisfaction of own performance

A person may take up physical exercise later in life for the first time since school or be a long-term regular exerciser. Whatever the circumstances, targets for development can be set so progress can be made. The satisfaction of reaching a higher standard through hard work, determination and effort can be the feeling that keeps a person continuing with exercise.

Promotes the 'feel-good' factor

The improvement to general body shape and posture can result in people feeling more positive about themselves. The fact that they have worked hard and got results increases their feeling of self-worth.

Can provide excitement

Some activities are attractive because they are exciting to perform. Skiing, climbing, skateboarding and BMX track racing are all examples of sports that attract people because of the thrill and adrenalin rush they provide.

Gives enjoyment

There are various reasons why a person enjoys an activity: it can be the physical challenge, the tactical battle to outwit an opponent, or the fun of playing as a team to achieve success. There is a sport suitable for everyone and those who seek exercise can usually find one they enjoy that satisfies them.

Can relieve aggression

Some activities are extremely competitive. These activities can act as a release valve for aggressive behaviour, possibly making a person's general life calmer.

Develops a sense of being 'part of something'

Many people look for physical activities that are team-, society- or club-based. By doing so they automatically become integral members of a group and so part of that unit. A sense of belonging follows, satisfying the personal needs of the individual.

Provides opportunity for success

The challenging situations set by physical exercise can be the draw for a person's participation. Reaching a goal or winning an event can have a positive effect on a person, which encourages future participation. Many clubs arrange internal and/or external competitions. The competitive approach needed in some sports can link to qualities needed in everyday life. In the relatively safe environment of sport, a competitive, personal characteristic may develop that could help effectiveness at work.

Successes in sport can lead to a positive and successful work life.

Life's problems can be forgotten

Having a hobby, especially one which is physically demanding, is something to look forward to, and when taking part in a sport or activity a person deals with a new set of challenges; this can take their mind off problems in their daily life.

Reduces stress and tension

Regular physical activity reduces the risk of anxiety and stress. Walking, cycling and even housework can all have a positive effect. People who take part in physical activity have a chance to socialize, increase their confidence, achieve goals and forget their own worries and stresses.

Personal development

Starting a new interest can extend the knowledge of the individual. New tactics, skills, strategies and safety factors may have to be learnt. As skills develop, personal pride in the new achievement is felt and so pleasure and satisfaction result.

Increases confidence in stressful situations

As challenges become more demanding, greater resilience and application are required from the individual. As the new demands are met, a person's confidence will grow, safe in the knowledge that future demands will be met and overcome as before.

Improves self-esteem

Doing well and improving in a physical activity can enable a person to think favourably of themselves, thereby improving their **self-esteem**.

Active challenge

With a partner, link reasons for taking part in physical activity to the following people:

- a retired person
- a young mum
- a young, talented games player.

Task 2

1 – Read the sentences below on health reasons for participating in physical activity.

a. My skills have improved in basketball and I have made the local county team; this makes me proud of my achievements.

b. Despite my training sessions getting harder, I seem to be able to keep working for longer without tiring.

c. I have met many new people since I joined the sports club.

d. My pulse rate per minute is reducing; this means my heart is becoming more efficient.

e. The rush of skiing downhill at my maximum speed, is what I really enjoy.

f. I play right defender in the team; the right midfield player and I work well together in matches and we have a laugh after the game too.

2 – Copy out the table below in your workbook and write out each sentence under their correct heading: either 'physical', 'social' or 'mental'.

Physical	Social	Mental

3 — Physical activity relieving stress and tension

Serotonin can be referred to as the 'molecule of happiness'. It controls many different functions in the human body including appetite, sleep, memory and mood. Increasing exercise levels is the most effective way of increasing levels of serotonin in the body. Not only are levels increased during exercise, but serotonin continues to be produced by the body for several days after the activity as well, helping to improve a person's energy and mood.

Regular physical activity also helps to reduce the risk of anxiety and stress-related illnesses. Walking, cycling and even housework can all have positive effects on a person. People who take part in regular activity have more of a chance to socialize, achieve personal goals and increase their confidence. They also have a chance to forget any worries and problems they have by focusing on something else.

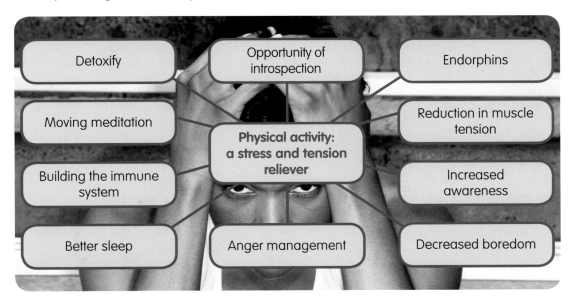

Detoxify — Opportunity of introspection — Endorphins — Moving meditation — **Physical activity: a stress and tension reliever** — Reduction in muscle tension — Building the immune system — Increased awareness — Better sleep — Anger management — Decreased boredom

Detoxify
In stressful situations brain signals are activated, hormones are released and nutrients are converted to energy. Some body systems speed up, such as the cardiovascular system; others slow down, such as the gastrointestinal system. Exercise allows the body to **detoxify** by returning to the homeostasis (the balance of the internal environment) faster and reducing the impact of the stress.

Opportunity of introspection
Exercise provides an escape from daily pressures, giving time to recharge energy levels and become **introspective** (thoughtful). It can also provide time for reflection, to sort out what is important and problem solve creatively.

Endorphins
Endorphins increase during exercise over 20 minutes. They can relieve pain, produce a feeling of euphoria and give a positive mood.

Reduction in muscle tension
When stressed muscles contract, they lose their normal muscle tone. Exercise causes a release of energy, allowing them to go back to their normal resting state. This can release **tension** headaches, backache and joint pain.

Increased awareness
Exercise increases a person's awareness of their body such as small changes in breathing patterns, allowing them to recognise if they are becoming worried or stressed.

Decreased boredom

By testing themselves through sport, people are stimulated and excited, learning to take on more stress, which can transfer to coping better with day-to-day living.

Anger management

Research has shown that anger and hostility can progress disease. Exercise provides a socially acceptable way to release negative energy, by releasing anger in a positive way.

Better sleep

Exercise can be effective in helping people get to sleep and to sleep more soundly.

Building the immune system

Fit people fight illness better and recover quicker.

Moving meditation

Exercises requiring repetitive movements (such as yoga techniques) can be responsible for a calm and tranquil feeling through meditation.

Active challenge

Discuss with a partner the types of sports and activities available in your school or local area and the different effects on stress and tension they may have. For example, rugby may provide a socially acceptable way to release anger in a positive way.

4 — How physical activity stimulates the individual

Taking part in a healthy, active lifestyle can stimulate:

- Cooperation
- Competition
- Physical challenge
- **Aesthetic appreciation**
- The development of friendships and social mixing.

Cooperation

If a person joins a club they may not only get the benefit of the physical activity, but also in joining in with the general running of the club too. For example, fixtures have to be arranged, finances have to be managed and facilities have to be maintained. By working together for the good of the club, a person can be a player/organizer/helper, cooperating with fellow members for maximum success.

Competition

Individual and team activities present competitive situations. A person starting a sport will compete at a low level. As skills progress and **competence** develops the desire and motivation to compete at a higher level can increase.

Physical challenge

Certain physical activities can present a person with challenging situations. By seeing problems through, whether individually or as a member of a team, and reaching the set goal, a person can develop courage and confidence.

Rock climbing relies on ultimate cooperation between the climbers.

Aesthetic appreciation

As a performer develops their skills and understanding about an activity they may also learn to appreciate the activity as a whole. A person who understands the difficulties of performing the skills can appreciate the level of skill required, while watching top-class players in action, and the beauty of the event.

The development of friendships and social mixing

With many sports there is often a social side, where groups stay after a game in the clubhouse. By regularly attending these social events, friendships can be formed. Through sporting experiences a person can become more outgoing and confident in the company of others.

Key terms

Fitness – the ability to meet the demands of the environment

FITT – Frequency, Intensity, Time and Type (used to increase the amount of work the body does, in order to achieve **overload**)

Self-esteem – respect for, or a favourable opinion of, oneself

Tension – mental and emotional strain

Detoxify – removing poison from

Serotonin – is released during exercise, improving a person's energy and mood

Introspective – thoughtful or meditative

Endorphins – hormone released during exercise

Aesthetic appreciation – recognition of beauty

Competence – the relationship between skill, the selection and application of skills, tactics, strategies and compositional ideas, and the readiness of the body and mind to cope with the activity. It requires an understanding of how these combine to produce effective performances in different activities and contexts

Overload – Fitness can only be improved through training more than you normally do

Summary

There are many social, physical and mental benefits to leading a healthy, active lifestyle. A person in the habit of regular exercise can benefit from their healthy lifestyle. Physically, the body and its systems can increase in fitness and be able to meet the pressures of a more demanding environment. A stronger body and stronger systems could increase life expectancy. Personal development can come about through the challenges of exercise: a person may develop determination, courage and a positive attitude as a result of taking up exercise; in turn, this may spill over into general life and positively affect a person's confidence. Cooperation, teamwork and friendships can also develop from being a member of a group, club or team.

Exam questions

Multiple-choice questions

1. (a) Which of the following best describes why people take part in sport?

   ☐ **A** Gives enjoyment, encourages friendship, helps pay bills, encourages cooperation

   ☐ **B** Changes diet, gives enjoyment, provides excitement, encourages cooperation

   ☐ **C** Encourages friendship, gives enjoyment, provides excitement, encourages cooperation

   ☐ **D** Provides excitement, encourages friendship, is a training principle, encourages cooperation

   (1)

   (b) Which of the following best describes the social effects of taking part in physical activity?

   ☐ **A** Is a chance to meet others, encourages cooperation, burns fat, can meet challenges with others

   ☐ **B** Become part of a team, can meet challenges with others, encourages cooperation, relieves stress

   ☐ **C** Can meet challenges with others, gives enjoyment, is a chance to meet others, improves flexibility

   ☐ **D** Encourages cooperation, is a chance to meet others, become part of a team, can meet challenges with others

   (1)

   (c) Which of the following best describes the mental benefits of physical activity?

   ☐ **A** Gives satisfaction, gives enjoyment, provides excitement, is a chance to meet others

   ☐ **B** Improves the immune system, provides excitement, improves self-esteem, gives satisfaction

   ☐ **C** Provides excitement, reduces muscle tension, improves self-esteem, gives satisfaction

   ☐ **D** Gives enjoyment, provides excitement, improves self-esteem, gives satisfaction

   (1)

   (d) Which of the following best describes the effects physical activity has on stress and tension?

   ☐ **A** Endorphins released giving positive mood, provides time to recharge energy levels, decreases boredom, burns fat

   ☐ **B** Helps sleep, provides time to recharge energy levels, strengthens bones, decreases boredom

   ☐ **C** Reduces most tension, endorphins released giving positive mood, provides time to recharge energy levels, decreases boredom

   ☐ **D** Helps with anger management, endorphins released giving positive mood, provides time to recharge energy levels, encourages cooperation

   (1)

Short-answer questions

2. What is the following statement defining? 'Any form of exercise or movement; planned and structured or unplanned and unstructured.'

   (1)

3. Participation in sport can be grouped into mental, physical and social benefits. What group do the following statements match with?

   (i) Improves flexibility, allowing for more efficient movement.

   (ii) Can relieve stress, tension and aggression.

   (iii) Provides chances to meet new people with similar interests.

   (3)

Longer-answer questions

4. What are the physical benefits of taking part in physical activity?

   (4)

5. Give **two** reasons why a retired person would take part in physical activity.

   (4)

1.1 ~ Healthy, active lifestyles

1.1.2a Influences on your healthy, active lifestyle: key influences that impact on achieving sustained involvement in physical activity

What you will learn about in this topic:

1 — Cultural influences
2 — Health and well-being influences
3 — Image influences
4 — Influencial people
5 — Resource influences
6 — Socio-economic influences

There are many influences on a person to become involved in physical activity. Some have a great impact and are influential enough to sustain the long-term interest of an individual in sport. These influences include:

- Cultural: age, disability, **gender** and race
- Health and well-being: illness and health problems
- Image: fashion and media coverage
- People: family, peers and **role models**
- Resources: access to, availability of, location and time
- Socio-economic: cost and status

1 — Cultural influences

Cultural influences are those that impact on daily life and are often out of a person's control.

Age

The age of a person may influence their chances of participating in certain activities. There may be age limits for participation or joining of some clubs, such as golf, netball or rugby. Depending on the size of the club, each age group usually has its own section with separate competition and coaching. Guidelines may be set by the sports governing body to help organization and for clubs to meet the needs of groups of different ages.

Young people have many opportunities to take part in physical activity. Schools encourage greater participation by organizing clubs and teams. Outside of school there are many clubs encouraging young people to take part in sport with teams for all age ranges.

As the **trend** for a healthier lifestyle continues, older people realize the need to keep exercising. Although they may be carrying an injury or a health condition, if they are properly educated about the problem and are sensible about how much they take on, they will continue to benefit from exercising.

Older people have the chance to learn new skills as many public and private centres now cater for older age groups. More people are planning for their retirement, but money may still be a problem for the older generation. In some cases, concessions are made for older participants and off-peak times are set aside for them.

Demands for sporting opportunities span all generations.

As the age of the population increases there are more older people that want to keep fit; therefore, more opportunity and publicity of activities for this age group is necessary. There has been a slow increase in the television coverage of the seniors' golf tournaments and the occasional veterans' tennis matches, but more coverage, promoting older people and top-class sport, is necessary if there is to be an increase of older, active sportspeople.

Disability

The Sport for All campaign encourages everyone to participate in sport. The campaign makes all people aware that those with a disability have a need and an ability to participate in sport. Encouragement is given to this group to join in physical activity. They take part in their own groups, or mix with able-bodied people, showing that sport is to everyone's benefit.

Oscar Pistorius is a role model for all those with disabilities.

Established facilities are adapted to accommodate the varied needs of disabled players. Ramps and stairlifts are installed, and changing areas and toilets are modified to make accessibility easier.

Lottery grants for sports facilities have helped usage for the disabled because often, part of the deal for funding is to make sure disabled facilities are in place.

Special groups are formed to help participation, for example, Disability Sport Cymru is focused on sport and recreation opportunities for the disabled in Wales.

Gender

Both males and females are encouraged to participate in most sports. Ideally everyone who

Stereotypes are changing. Here both men and women take part in a yoga class.

has an interest should be able to participate and compete in their chosen activity. However, sometimes there are constraints: some clubs may only offer single-sex teams due to a lack of facilities and qualified coaches, even though popular trends are moving away from gender stereotyping where girls only play netball and boys only play football.

Although most sports are available to both sexes, generally, each sex competes separately. This is for safety reasons, due to the physical differences in size and strength and fair play. Some sports have their own governing bodies for each sex; tennis and golf, for example. Two of the few major sporting events to have male and female competitors in the same event are show jumping and mixed-doubles matches in tennis and badminton.

Active challenge

Use the Internet to research how trends in participation by gender have changed.

Look at the change in popularity of sports in your school and discuss your thoughts in a group.

Men and sport

Boys often start playing sport because they regard the activity as great fun. In the controlled environment of a game situation an activity may provide an outlet for aggression and act as a release valve for youth, energy and enthusiasm. Sport can also provide opportunities to express natural tendencies for competition. Some sports are popular with men due to the nature of the game. For example, rugby attracts some males because it is a physically demanding contact sport.

Activities readily available in a local area may have reputations for success because of good facilities, excellent coaching, social events and the like. These will be well known in the community and so new, young members (attracted by these reputations) will help keep the traditions and the strong continuation of the activity going in the area.

Training for an activity often develops skill, physique and competitiveness in sport and activities are often chosen by men for its physicality.

Men often state that their reason for joining a club is to be part of a team. They enjoy the feeling of togetherness and camaraderie brought about by being in a group of similarly minded people, all working to the same end. Many activities have a social side; teams will often have a clubhouse where everyone can mix after a game. Some clubs still have the tradition of providing a meal after a match for the players. When the speeches are over all the players can have a drink together and this gives the possibility of making new acquaintances and friends. Many clubs often arrange special social events enabling all members and friends to be involved and feel part of the club.

Men often choose a sport for its physicality.

Task 1

1 – Create a spider diagram of the key points that explain why men participate in sport.

2 – In a pair, discuss your key points and add any to your spider diagram that you have missed.

Women and sport

Women have a different mix of reasons from men for participating in physical activity.

Some women enjoy the competitiveness of a team game. To be part of a group with similar interests and the same aim gives a sense of belonging. The popularity of ladies' hockey and netball teams is a result of this.

Often the sports most attractive to women are those with less body contact with other players. These can include netball, gym, dance and racket sports.

Many women enjoy less competitive physical activities such as aerobics or weights. These activities involve great amounts of effort but do not require aggression geared towards others. What is required, especially in weight training, is self-determination to overcome the resistance of the weights. The emphasis of these activities is on the effects they have on the shape of the body. The effects on the body – keeping a balanced weight/height ratio – may make a woman feel more physically attractive.

Although aerobics and weights are more individual activities in nature, there is still scope for meeting other people with similar interests such as through a group aerobics session.

Women wanting to participate in physical activity often choose activities that will maintain their feminine image.

For young girls, the pressure from peers not to take part in exercise can prevent them from taking part at all; here the need to remain popular in a group outweighs the desire for exercise.

Women often enjoy less competitive sports such as dance.

The trends in participation in sport continue to vary. The different nature of the activity and its accessibility affect the amount of young people who become involved.

Participation of girls aged 2 to 11 years in sport out of school time at least once in the past year

	1994	1999	2002
Games	85%	86%	88%
Team games	71%	78%	76%
Invasion games	58%	32%	67%
Football (including five-a-side)	35%	46%	46%
Netball	29%	32%	28%
Basketball	19%	26%	28%
Striking games	53%	58%	54%
Cricket	22%	27%	24%
Rounders	45%	48%	46%
Volleyball	14%	15%	16%
Racket sports	64%	59%	64%
Tennis	51%	46%	53%
Badminton	31%	29%	31%
Table tennis	25%	20%	27%
Golf (all types)	19%	20%	22%
Swimming activities	84%	81%	83%
Dance and ice skating	53%	48%	52%
Dance classes	27%	25%	32%
Ice skating	36%	32%	34%
Gym and trampolining	13%	13%	16%

Source: MORI published in 'Young People and Sport' report by Sport England 2003.

Active challenge

Ask all of the girls in the class about the sport and exercise activities they participate in by creating a survey.

Once you have collected all of your survey data, prepare a bar chart and analyse your findings.

Women and top-level sport

Women's opportunities in sport are steadily increasing and becoming more financially rewarding. There is now greater representation for women in the national authorities. The Sports Council supports women's participation in sport and has ways in place to raise levels of achievement. More governing bodies are recognizing women's place in their sport.

In 1972, the Women's Football Association (WFA) was formed, supporting female talent for the game. The Women's Sport Foundation (WSF), founded in 1984, also pioneers the female cause, working hard to increase media coverage and raising the awareness of top-class women's sporting success. Events such as the Women's Rugby World Cup show women playing the game at its highest level of skill, helping it to become more popular. There are increasingly more opportunities for women to have careers linked with sport in the media. This may be a first career or an occupation taken up after competitive life is over. On a local level, many sports centres make time during the day for women's activities. They may also provide crèche facilities to help as many women as possible to take part.

More women's sports are being televised, raising the profile of those activities. Sports such as the Women's FA Cup final, WTA tennis, golf, aerobics and rhythmic gymnastics are regularly televised for Sky viewers.

The spectacle of women's sport is increasing; with that comes better sponsorship, media coverage and prize money (although prize money is generally still lower than that for men). The golfer Michelle Wie competed in a 2008 event on the men's tour at the Legends Reno-Tahoe Open, in America. She followed in the footsteps of Annika Sorenstam and Laura Davies who have also cut across the male/female divide of the past.

In recent times, companies are more ready to use high-profile, successful women to advertise their products. Kelly Holmes' double Olympic success in 2004 made her extremely desirable as a person to promote a company's product.

Success on the track promotes a successful image for a product.

By sponsoring the Women's Open Golf Tournament the IT company Ricoh raises its profile and can, as a result, increase the popularity and participation in that activity.

Task 2

Using Olympic winner Rebecca Adlington as an example, write down why a company would want to use her for promotional purposes.

Use the following ideas to help you:

- What efforts has she had to make to achieve her state of fitness?
- What has she achieved?
- Where has she achieved it?
- What does her success mean to the country?
- What are her personal qualities?

Both the company and women's sport can benefit from associations:

- The women used give a wholesome image to the product being advertised.
- The women are seen as role models to look up to and emulate. This in turn can encourage people to lead a healthy lifestyle, including healthy eating and exercise.
- The activity associated with the woman is brought to the public eye. The effect can make that activity more popular.

Current trends hope to make the majority of sports accessible to all groups. These trends have allowed women to access a broader range of sports such as less bans on women taking part in certain activities. For example, athletics has seen women's pole vault added to their competition list in recent years.

Media images of fit and healthy women can influence female participation and the popularity levels of exercise. Activities such as aerobics and weight training, which focus on body shape and lifestyle, are increasingly popular with women and can be accessible at both public and private gyms.

The swimmer Rebecca Adlington won two gold medals at the 2008 Olympics for Great Britain.

Task 3

1 – Look in the sports pages of a variety of media, such as newspapers, magazines, the Internet, and so on.

2 – Collect news items to do with women in sport and write a short report on your findings.

Promoting women in sport

There have been many campaigns and programmes promoting women in sport. These have included a wide range of participants from young novice to top-level coach.

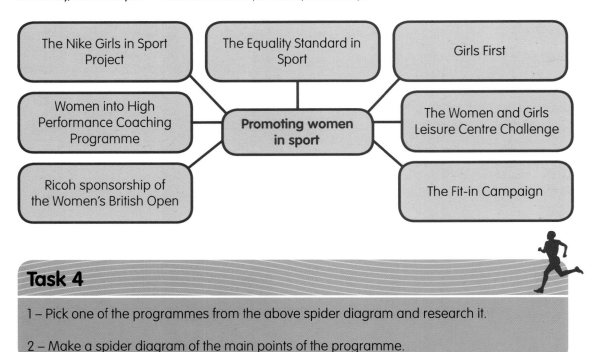

Task 4

1 – Pick one of the programmes from the above spider diagram and research it.

2 – Make a spider diagram of the main points of the programme.

Race

Many ethnic minority groups enjoy taking part in sport but live in poor areas. These areas have very few facilities for sport and so the opportunity to participate is reduced. For greater participation, financial issues relating to disposable income and facilities available need resolving for a difference to be made.

There are also sporting prejudices that exist, implying that certain races are less adaptable to particular activities. African-Caribbeans are said to be less successful at swimming, and the physical make-up of Asians is said to cause them to injure easily despite the fact that many Asians are successful in sports.

A survey exploring sport and ethnicity in England was carried out by Sport England in 1999/2000. It found that women who classify themselves as Black Caribbean (34 per cent), Black African (34 per cent), Indian (31 per cent), Pakistani (21 per cent) and Bangladeshi (19 per cent) participate regularly in sport or active recreation less often than the national average (39 per cent). One reason for this may be that their home and family commitments are put first and there is little time for them to participate in sport as a result. Extra provision in the community for childcare could release time for exercise and leisure pursuits.

Increasing and sustaining involvement in physical activity
Clubs and groups can help to increase and sustain involvement in physical activity by ethnic minorities by:

- making all who come to the club feel welcome
- making everyone feel secure when participating
- making public their intention to prevent racism
- making the procedure for complaints easy and straightforward
- showing images of people from different races involved in sport facilities
- encouraging people from all backgrounds to have roles in administration, decision making and coaching.

Efforts are made so that all feel welcome at clubs.

2 — Health and well-being influences

Sustained involvement in physical activity can have a bearing on health and well-being:

Weight control gives more energy, staving off fatigue.

Exercising can be an outlet for stress and anger, relieving mental pressures.

Exercising with others can lead to friendships, making a person feel good.

Increasing fitness makes it easier to meet the demands of the environment.

Bones become stronger and less susceptible to damage and osteoporosis.

The body becomes better equipped to prevent or deal with injury.

The heart becomes bigger and stronger, reducing the risk of heart disease.

Ligaments become stronger, reducing joint injury.

Cardiovascular fitness increases as the heart pumps more blood per beat, so works more efficiently.

The body's immune system is improved so can fight off disease and infection better.

Quicker recovery from physical exertion.

Arteries become larger and more elastic, leading to reduced blood pressure.

Tendons become stronger, reducing muscle injury.

Active challenge

Prepare a talk on how sustained physical activity can reduce illness and health problems. Deliver your talk to the class.

3 — Image influences

Fashion

Sports clothing is often worn as a fashion item, irrespective of whether the wearer participates in the sport or not. For example, a person might wear a replica football shirt of their favorite team or follow what their sporting role model is wearing. Trainers, for instance, are regularly worn as everyday shoes due to their comfort and style.

The popularity of an activity can change quickly as particular trends in sports fall in and out of fashion. For example, during Wimbledon week more people may be seen using local tennis facilities inspired by what they are seeing on the television. A more long-term effect can come about by a national side doing well in a major tournament, which causes an increase in popularity in that sport, and may encourage local authorities to fund new facilities.

If a minority sport begins to receive greater coverage on the television, this can lead to an increase in its popularity. In recent years snooker has gained in popularity, perhaps due to the coverage of the top personalities within the sport, thereby inspiring and attracting youngsters to the game. A sport can also decline in popularity with less people taking part; squash has taken such a downturn in recent years. But courts in local sports centres, rather than remaining unused, are being adapted for trendier activities such as aerobics and yoga.

The image of an activity can come from several areas including personal experience through joining in, spectating at an event or from media coverage. If these influences show the particular sport in an appealing way – successful, wholesome, exciting – then sustained involvement may result.

Media coverage

Sport uses different forms of media to bring itself to the widest possible audience. For example, each newspaper has a sports column, there are programmes and whole channels on television and radio devoted to sport and the Internet provides access to many websites devoted to specific sports and events.

The different forms of media include television, radio, press (newspapers, magazines and specialist publications) and the Internet.

Task 5

1 – Copy the media and sport spider diagram shown on page 30 into your workbook.

2 – Add the names of television channels, newspapers, magazines and websites that have connections with sport to each category.

Types of television broadcast

TERRESTRIAL   Terrestrial television includes BBC1, BBC2, ITV, Channel 4 and Channel 5 (free to air channels). All televisions can receive these channels providing they have an aerial to pick up the signal. If you own a television you must have a television licence. BBC programmes are financed by revenue from television licence sales, whilst the independent channels pay their way by advertisements during and at the end of programmes shown. Certain programmes may even be sponsored by particular products, which are seen at the beginning, breaks and end of the programme.

The competition between terrestrial and satellite television companies is such that the Independent Television Commission (ITC) has to organize the allocation of sporting broadcasts between them as they feel that some sporting events are of major importance and should be available to everybody. This prevents the wealthier satellite companies buying up all the best sporting events. As a result, there are some sporting events that are protected by the ITC so that terrestrial television can broadcast them. These sporting events make up two groups: group A and group B. Events in group A are legally bound to have the rights of their live coverage on the free television channels. Those in group B can be shown on satellite or digital television as long as there is provision made for highlights and delayed coverage for terrestrial television. There are strict guidelines for group B events concerning regulations on the length of the highlight coverage and how long after the live event it can be transmitted. Protecting sports events in this way guarantees that traditional events are available in some way to the free to air channels.

Group A events (Live coverage protected)	Group B events (Secondary coverage protected)
The Olympic Games	Cricket Test matches played in England
The FIFA World Cup	Non-finals matches at Wimbledon
The FA Cup Final	The Rugby World Cup (not the final)
The Scottish FA Cup Final (applies to Scotland only)	Six Nations Rugby Tournament Matches (matches involving home countries)
The Grand National	The Commonwealth Games
The Epsom Derby	The IAAF World Athletic Championships
The Wimbledon Tennis Finals	The Cricket World Cup (limited to the final, semi-final and any matches involving UK teams)
The European Football Championship Finals	The Ryder Cup
The Rugby League Challenge Cup Finals	The Open Golf Championship
The Rugby World Cup Final	

Active challenge

1 – With a partner, decide on changes to the group A and group B lists you would make so that a variety of sports of your choice could be seen on terrestrial television.

2 – State why you have made your changes.

The following are positive effects of coverage on terrestrial television:

- Keeps people informed of new trends and current players.
- Particular sports get exposure on television with improved quality of coverage.
- Increased technology aids decision making such as playbacks and ProZone.
- Pundits can help increase people's appreciation of sport through their professional opinion and experiences.
- The BBC licence fee helps to fund more channels and therefore extends their sports coverage.
- New events can be seen.
- Enhances development of sport.
- Seeing the sport on television may encourage participation.
- The more the sport is seen on television then the more supporters it may attract.
- The more coverage there is of a sport in the media, the easier it may be to attract sponsors, making more money available to that sport.
- People become familiar with sports personalities who can become positive role models.
- Money from broadcast bids goes directly to the sport.
- Coverage of disabled sportspeople in events such as the Paralympics brings about an awareness of the needs of others and how sport can be undertaken by all.

Task 6

1 – Choose six of the positive effects of media coverage on terrestrial television.

2 – Put them into full sentences with examples.

The following are negative effects of sports coverage on terrestrial television:

- Major sports have most of the coverage to the detriment of minority sports.
- Can discourage watching sport live as it's more convenient to sit in comfort at home.
- Small incidents on the field of play can often be exaggerated and sensationalized.
- The director of viewing controls what is watched.
- Television directors control how the sport is put across.
- The channel can put its own slant on a subject.
- Excessive coverage can affect interest.
- Subtle rule changes to sports may occur to increase the appeal to television spectators, such as the tiebreak rule in tennis.
- Replays can undermine officials and umpires.
- Extra pressure is put on sports stars on both performance and demands for interviews.
- Demand to see a performer can affect their privacy.

SATELLITE TELEVISION AND SPORT   Subscription television was first transmitted into homes by BSkyB (British Sky Broadcasting Group PLC) in 1989 and has completely changed the way broadcasting operates.

Broadcasters can be privately owned companies such as Virgin Media, owned by Richard Branson, or publicly owned companies such as the BBC. Digital broadcasting is done via television, such as on satellite, cable and Freeview channels. Electronic broadcasting is done via the Internet: most broadcasts from terrestrial and digital broadcasts are also available on the Internet.

For companies to gain the right to broadcast particular events that are not on the group A list, each has to make a bid for the rights to do so. The successful bid, which is largely based on the amount of money offered, earns exclusive rights to that sporting event. The more popular the sport, the more expensive it is to buy the rights.

There are several specialist sports channels provided by Sky, broadcasting a wide variety of sports for all tastes. Eurosport is a sports channel showing a variety of events taking place in Europe. Setanta, an Irish-based broadcaster, now has rights to show major and popular sporting events such as premiership and international football, boxing and golf.

The coverage includes a wide variety of activities, including those that have yet to make their mark in Britain. This gives people the chance to see a sport for the first time and possibly become interested enough to participate in it.

Viewers are also offered chances to watch sports events interactively. These facilities give viewers a variety of choices when watching sport, which include different matches to watch, a choice of commentary, access to player profiles and the ability to view the match using a different camera angle. The new options provide greater freedom and give detailed information to the viewers, which can increase their interest in and knowledge of the sport.

If a person subscribes to Sky they are eligible to watch pay-per-view events whereby they pay a certain amount of money to receive the event. Boxing is one of the main sports that are broadcast in this way. Setanta is available to Sky customers on a monthly 'top up' basis so extra sports channels can be viewed. Here the companies feel that there will be such a demand to see same events that they can make money by showing it in this way.

Des Lynam is one of the sports anchors on the Setanta Sports network.

Task 7

Write a paragraph on how terrestrial and subscription television differ.

Cable and satellite broadcasts have had a major influence on watching sport. Although there is greater airtime and a wider variety of sports, it is only available to those who can afford to pay a monthly subscription.

The following are positive effects of sports coverage by cable and satellite television:

- Greater coverage of minority sports (Sky's Extreme Sports Channel broadcasts an of average 18 minority sports per week).
- Makes a wider variety of sports more accessible.
- Helps increase the funding for sport.
- Heightens the profile of sport and so can attract interest and sponsorship.
- Increased depth of coverage for major sports; some football clubs even have their own channel, such as Manchester United and Celtic FC.
- Can encourage participation by stimulating interest, thereby encouraging people to take part themselves.
- More live sport can be viewed by more people.

Cable and satellite have similar negative affects as terrestrial television such as, it discourages live watching, sensationalizes incidents in play and the viewing is controlled by the director, but there are also specific negative effects associated with this coverage.

The following are negative effects of sports coverage by cable and satellite television:

- Some networks may have the traditional gender pundits and presenters matched with a sport. Reinforcing stereotypes in this way may give the impression that the sport is unavailable to certain sections of people and therefore doesn't encourage participation.
- Matches can be rescheduled due to the best broadcast day for the network; this often happens to premiership football coverage.
- The start time of a match can change so it goes out at the optimum time for the network.
- Traditional events have gone to Sky – only subscribers can see Welsh football and live test cricket matches from 2006.
- Sport can suffer from over-exposure as people tire of the saturation of coverage.

Sometimes the influence of television coverage is not so black and white. A person may see an event on television and as a result be so motivated that they go to see it live; on the other hand, they may think why go out of the home when television gives the best view and they can watch it in the comfort of their own surroundings?

The impact of television coverage of sport has been both positive and negative. Terrestrial television has had its share of sport reduced by Sky, as it cannot pay the same amount of money to buy the rights to broadcast particular events.

Types of television broadcast

The various methods used by the media help improve people's understanding of sport and current affairs, popularize personalities and provide sports' entertainment. Each form of media employs a series of experts (past players, pundits, presenters and journalists) to give their judgements, opinions and views on the sport in question. By broadcasting sport in a variety of ways television may influence people to pursue an activity.

Television programmes can be classified as informative, educational, instructive and entertaining. This reflects the general content and aims of the programme and many programmes contain a combination of these different elements.

INFORMATIVE PROGRAMMES   News, news bulletins and sport update programmes, together with Ceefax and Teletext services, are all in the informative programme group. They are based on facts, intending to give the viewer more information about a sport, event, club or performer. They are designed to give the public updates on results, future events and current issues regarding a sport or activity.

EDUCATIONAL PROGRAMMES   Educational, schools and skills programmes are productions dealing with coaching and helping people learn about the skills, tactics and strategies of a game or activity. Sometimes, school programmes will suggest ways for further development and give information of where to take up an activity in the area, helping to encourage an increase in its popularity. Some broadcasts are documentary-based and are concerned with the facts of an event or activity, such as the history of a sport, for example. For some people, knowing more about a sport is interesting and increases their understanding of the game.

INSTRUCTIVE PROGRAMMES   This type of coverage is closely linked with educational programmes, but is mainly interested in teaching the viewer about a specific sport. They appeal to a specialist market interested in a particular activity. Some programmes mix the type of coverage shown and include an entertainment and instructive element. The broadcasting of cricket test matches, largely under the heading of entertainment, have a 'master/super class' section in the lunch break, where experts and coaches relay coaching points, instructing young players on how to improve their technique. This part of the programme would fall under the informative title, but does give advice on how to improve technique and can encourage players to put the advice into action.

Seeing how Lewis Hamilton started in racing may encourage others to do the same.

ENTERTAINING PROGRAMMES   These programmes are designed for enjoyment, such as highlight programmes and celebrity quiz shows. They can also include coverage of live matches and special events. For some, the drama of a game can be entertainment enough, but the addition of the commentary gives greater information and insight and can enhance the appeal even more. To add to the entertainment, a series of presenters, pundits and experts are employed to give their opinion on the event. Expert commentators, who have often competed at the highest level themselves, give in-depth views, which aim to be accurate and factual. Those currently involved in the sport can give up-to-date information on the issues relevant at the time. Live coverage matches are cheap to produce and attract large audiences even when broadcast off-peak.

For example, Manchester United has such a following that it produces its own programmes, broadcast on its own channel. This gives fans up-to-date information on players, the club and fixtures.

Highlight programmes, showing the events of the day, pick out the best of the action in the time they have available. Here the audience where sees exactly what the director wants them to see. This is usually the best of the action and any contentious moments too (particularly in football). However, these isolated incidents can be over-sensationalized by the panel of experts, becoming more talked about than the play itself.

Sports quiz shows have high ratings on television. This can be due to the popular personalities on the show attracting audiences where the quiz seems secondary to the antics of the personalities. The appeal to the public may be that they see respected sportspeople having fun and making people laugh. Guest appearances of current, popular sportspeople can attract a bigger audience as people want to know more about, and have greater access to, their sporting role models.

Task 8

Write two sentences on each of the four types of television broadcast describing what effect each type could have on the viewer or listener and participation in physical activity.

Radio, press and the Internet and sport

Radio   Radio broadcasts regularly produce specialist sports programmes. These include coverage of live matches, discussion programmes and informative programmes. There is little rivalry between radio and television, as television regards itself as far more popular. Radio is therefore allowed to broadcast all live sporting events. There are several channels devoted solely to sport and news, including Five Live, Talksport and BBC Radio Four's coverage of the cricket test matches. Cricket enthusiasts take their radios to matches so that they can hear the commentary whilst they are watching the live match. Some people watch an event on television with the sound down, whilst listening to the radio commentary.

Press   The back pages of most newspapers are devoted to current sporting news. Each newspaper employs journalists and photographers to gather up-to-the-minute information about matches and events for publication in the morning press. With this form of media the reader sees the match through the eyes of the journalists, who are able to put their opinions forward and influence the reader.

Sports magazines devoted to the specialized reader are an expanding market, the most popular subject being football. These publications contain entertaining, instructive and informative articles on events and players.

The following table highlights the growing number of readers of specialized sports magazines.

Circulation of leading sports magazines.			
Title	**Sport**	**Issues actively purchased**	**Total average net circulation per issue**
Match	Football	110,779	113,049
Runner's World	Running	87,029	88,567
Angling Times	Fishing	50,947	51,006
Rugby World	Rugby	45,377	48,381
Shoot	Football	30,885	35,830
Cycling Weekly	Cycling	26,786	27,609

Source: ABC data between January 2007 and December 2007.

Active challenge

Some papers differ in the extent of coverage of different sports. In a small group, discuss why you think this is.

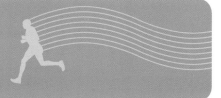

INTERNET This is the newest and quickest-developing form of media. The Internet provides a way to access up-to-date information about sports, events and personalities for those with access to an on-line computer. (It is worth remembering that some websites remain unchanged for a long time, so they may not be that current, but generally there is a note at the end of the website saying when it was last updated.) Many sports governing bodies, major clubs and smaller teams provide a website for those interested to learn more about them. The Internet also provides an advertising vehicle for retailers. Sports goods can be bought and sold quickly and easily using this service.

Up-to-the minute club news is available on club websites.

Live coverage brings sport to the majority of people.

4 — Influential people

People who are in regular contact with each other, whether in person or via the media, can have a great influence on participation in physical activity. Family traditions and support, what friends find popular and seeing role models physically active can all have a bearing on what and how much physical activity a person may carry out.

Family

Parents have a great influence on their child's participation in sport. Youngsters who grow up in a family that has had good sporting experiences can be encouraged to follow the same interests. Their parents' enthusiasm, interest and enjoyment, experienced through the activity, can often be enough to start the appeal.

If a child is introduced to an activity at an early age and regularly participates in it, sport is seen as a usual part of life. It follows that the youngster could regard sport as part of their lifestyle and may keep taking part when they get older and are able to make more decisions for themselves.

Some parents use club membership not only to develop their children's physical skills, but their social ones too. By regularly meeting at a club to train and compete, the child mixes with youngsters of their own age, with others who have similar interests and are often in the presence of similar-minded adults, providing role models to emulate.

Some families have a tradition in certain sports. Jamie and Harry Redknapp, father and son, are both connected to professional football.

A family may be keen on a particular activity because of family traditions passed on through generations. In this instance, family pride and experience are added to the benefits of the pursuit.

Active challenge

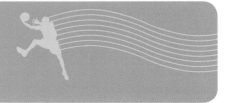

With a partner, think of any examples you know of where there are different generations taking part in the same sport or even at the same time.

A role model provided by a family member may be an inspiration to copy. Their lifestyle shows a healthy, social, active and happy life brought about by their involvement in sport. This way of life could be appealing to the young, so they aim to pursue happiness in the same way and take up physical activity. A relative could have been extremely successful in a sport and so a younger nephew or niece may want to try to emulate their victories for themselves.

Many families provide financial backing so their child can pursue their interest. Lack of funds can inhibit some participation, but for those families who can find the money, they make a commitment to support their child for as long as the youngster is interested. To fund a child's participation parents often need to find money for:

- kit
- subscription fees
- equipment
- travel costs
- joining fees.

Parents often take on the task of taking children to and from training and competition venues. This duty comes with a certain financial cost, but also involves dedication by the parent, who often has to devote a large amount of their own time to their child's activity.

Some dedicated parents will also adapt their child's diet to support training and competition. Although there are only a small percentage of families who do this, they recognize the need for the correct type of diet needed for success.

Task 9

1 – Search the Internet for any reports on the increase of participation in sports by children.

2 – Print out the reports as evidence of your search.

3 – Using the reports, produce a short summary of your findings.

Peers

Peers are people of a similar age. They can be in the same class, same year group or at a different school. Peers can sometimes have a great influence on their friends, also known as 'peer pressure'. If a peer group takes part in a physical activity or sport, they could influence others to join in too.

Starting an activity with a friend can be easier than going alone to a sports centre or club. The same can be said of joining in a new leisure interest in a group situation. Going with others can be more fun and can give confidence to the group or to an individual to go again.

Role models

There are many role models in sport; their following can be due to a combination of their sport skill, personality and lifestyle. As there is more coverage of their play and everyday life in the media, these people can become trendsetters in their sport and can shape the attitudes and behaviour of their fans – whether good or bad. Top-class sportspeople not only encourage people to participate in a sport and possibly play in a certain way, but can also influence lifestyle choices on and off the sports field. Role models don't have to be players, people may also want to emulate high-profile officials.

A clean-cut image on and off the field can give a football player role model status.

People who are good at their job and are successful can often become role models.

Active challenge

Choose two sporting people in the public eye. Make a list of the positive ways they have influenced you and your participation in sport.

5 — Resource influences

Many factors influence participation in physical activity. Where a person lives can have a great deal of impact on what activities are undertaken because of what transport links exist and what resources are available.

Resources available

The provision of indoor and outdoor facilities depends on many factors. All areas of the country would like excellent local facilities, but providing these would not be financially or practically viable. There are many issues taken into consideration when deciding on new facilities.

The funding to increase or improve facilities can come from different sources: the government may set aside money in their annual budget, lottery funding may meet part of the cost, or an individual may personally finance a team.

Whether it is privately or publicly funded, the aim is to have as many people use the facilities for as much of the time as possible. When deciding on a site for a new facility the expected use and demand of the facilities has to be worked out as enough people should be available in the area to make full use of it.

Access

Where facilities for certain activities are good, there may be a greater chance that more people will participate. The greater the involvement, the better the possibility of a higher standard of sports play, which then attracts more players and coaches. In small communities, there may be an interest but not enough people living locally to make the facilities viable. Unless transport is available to towns with established clubs, the opportunity to play is lost.

Location

The location of facilities is very important; certain sites naturally lend themselves to various activities. Outdoor pursuit centres can be situated where there are hills, rivers, lakes and forests suited to the particular activities involved. The beautiful countryside of North Wales is popular for mountaineers as it provides challenges for all abilities and has excellent facilities catering to the activities. Plas y Brenin, in Snowdonia, is the National Mountain Centre for Wales where such activities take place.

In locations where the demand for an activity is high, but the natural environment doesn't lend itself to the activity, then the conditions can be created artificially. For example, in London the Castle Climbing Centre meets the needs of the local community by providing indoor climbing walls.

An indoor climbing wall at the Castle Climbing Centre in London.

Time

The amount of free time available greatly affects a person's involvement in physical activity. There may be several short periods of time in the week when a person can pursue an activity, which could lend itself to being a member of a leisure club, for instance. People who have blocks of days of work then blocks of days of rest have more of an opportunity to regularly take part in activities that require overnight stays, such as mountaineering expeditions.

6 — Socio-economic influences

Socio-economic status

National data is collected on how much people participate in sport in their leisure time. National statistics divide the country's population into nine socio-economic categories, depending on how they earn their living – this is called the National Statistics Socio-economic Classification (NS-SEC). The table on page 41 shows the percentage distribution of participation in these groups.

It shows that, in the main, the higher the classification category, the more likely you are to participate in sporting activities.

Adults aged 16+									England 2002
Active sports, games and physical activities	National Statistics Socio-economic Classification (NS-SEC)								
	1.1	1.2	2	3	4	5	6	7	8
	Large employers & higher managerial	Higher professional	Lower managerial & professional	Intermediate	Small employers & own account workers	Lower supervisory & technical	Semi-routine	Routine	Never worked & long-term unemployed
Rugby	0.8	0.7	0.5	0.2	0.1	0.3	0.2	0.3	0.3
Table tennis	1.8	1.8	2.0	1.2	1.1	0.9	1.5	0.2	1.1
Golf	9.5	8.4	6.1	4.2	4.9	3.6	1.8	1.7	0.0
Tennis	3.1	4.0	2.7	1.8	1.7	0.5	0.8	0.5	1.0
Fishing	1.1	1.1	1.2	1.5	2.5	2.3	1.6	1.5	0.8
At least one activity	89.1	88.9	84.2	72.7	74.0	72.0	64.6	59.9	53.5
Base (all adults)	*858*	*1131*	*3068*	*1051*	*1266*	*1607*	*1646*	*1628*	*317*

Sports, games and physical activities. Participation rates in the 12 months before interview by National Statistics Socio-economic Classification (% of respondents).

Source: From 'Participataion in Sport in England' report by Sport England 2002.

The categories suggest that those who are classed as large employers and in higher management generally tend to participate in physical activity to a greater extent than those in other groups. Certain activities are more popular with particular sections of the population, for instance, fishing is more popular with small employers than the higher management group.

Task 10

Study the NS-SEC table and answer the following questions:

a. Which is classification 8's most popular activity?
b. In which activities are classification 1.2 the highest participants?
c. Of all the activities, which is the most popular with group 6?
d. Which group participants the least in rugby?

Cost

In order to participate in most sports there needs to be a certain financial commitment. Some sports are relatively cheap to sustain. For example, the major essential for running is a good quality pair of running shoes and you're off! Other activities are more technical, complicated and expensive to complete so taking part in them often requires membership of a club. Being a member of a gliding club allows a person to enjoy the activity but not necessarily own a glider, or an airfield! There are sports that are just too expensive for most people to finance individually and membership of a club is the only way to take part. For example, anyone can play indoor bowls, but they have to be a member of a club in order to use the rink, or in order to sail a particular class, a person would have to became a member of a sailing club to join a crew.

Task 11

Think about different types of physical activity. Make three lists of activities:

- requiring less than £150 to take part in
- requiring between £151 and £300 to take part in
- requiring more than £300 to take part in.

> A person can take part in sport at different levels. Football can be a 'kick around' in the park or belonging to a team with a team kit, proper football boots and actual goal posts!

For a lot of people an amount of disposable income is necessary to finance a physically active pursuit. If a person wants to keep taking part over a long period of time then there needs to be a plan in place to cover the cost: money for joining fees and annual subscriptions, equipment will need replacing, new innovations may be made in the sport and equipment needs updating to keep competitive.

For Rhys Jones to climb safely, there is an initial expense of buying high-quality mountaineering equipment. For a time, only transport costs will be necessary, but as equipment is used and eventually wears out it will need to be replaced.

Task 12

1 – Choose five different activities.

2 – For each of the activities, list the expenses that each may incur in order for a person to regularly participate.

Key terms

Gender – male or female

Role model – a person looked to by others as an example to follow

Cultural influences – established way of living of a particular group

Trend – fad or fashion of the moment

Summary

Many factors influence participation. These factors can relate to:

• the sport – its appeal, nature and popularity
• the person – their influences, interests and personality
• circumstances – finance, location and tradition of the area.

For some people a good start in sport with pleasant experiences to look back on can be the key to a life that includes physical activity. Others realize when they are older what the benefits of exercise (and possibly competitive/outdoor adventurous situations) can bring.

Exam questions

Multiple-choice questions

1. The following statements relate to key influences. Decide which combinations are correct.

    (a) Statement 1: A key influence impacting on participation, associated with resources, is location.

    Statement 2: A key influence impacting on participation, associated with resources, is peer pressure.

    ☐ **A** Both statements are true

    ☐ **B** Statement 1 is true, Statement 2 is false

    ☐ **C** Statement 1 is false, Statement 2 is true

    ☐ **D** Both statements are false

    (1)

    (b) Statement 1: A key influence impacting on participation, associated with the image of an activity, is fashion.

    Statement 2: A key influence impacting on participation, associated with the image of an activity, is media coverage.

    ☐ **A** Both statements are true

    ☐ **B** Statement 1 is true, Statement 2 is false

    ☐ **C** Statement 1 is false, Statement 2 is true

    ☐ **D** Both statements are false

    (1)

    (c) Statement 1: A key influence impacting on participation, associated with people, is socio-economic status.

    Statement 2: A key influence impacting on participation, associated with people, is family.

    ☐ **A** Both statements are true

    ☐ **B** Statement 1 is true, Statement 2 is false

☐ **C** Statement 1 is false, Statement 2 is true

☐ **D** Both statements are false

(1)

2. The availability of resources can influence participation. Which of the following best describes this category?

    ☐ **A** Public transport, family influences, facilities in the locality, time available

    ☐ **B** Facilities in the locality, road links, role model influence, time available

    ☐ **C** Road links, public transport, facilities in the locality, time available

    ☐ **D** Time available, road links, public transport, cost of the activity

Short-answer questions

3. There are many influences impacting on involvement in physical activity. Name **two** influences that are linked with cultural factors.

    (2)

4. Give the name of a terrestrial television broadcaster.

    (1)

5. What is the name for programmes that can be bought by viewers from satellite companies as a one-off event?

    (1)

Longer-answer questions

6. People start taking part in physical activity at different stages of life. For example, a retired person may take up physical activity late in life.

    Make a detailed list of the key factors that can impact on an individual's participation in sport.

    (6)

7. What difficulties may a disabled person encounter when participating in sport?

    (4)

1.1 ～ Healthy, active lifestyles

1.1.2b Influences on your healthy, active lifestyle: opportunities, pathways and initiatives for involvement in physical activity

What you will learn about in this topic:

1 — Opportunities to be involved in physical activities in a variety of roles
2 — The sports participation pyramid
3 — Initiatives providing opportunities for involvement in physical activity

1 — Opportunities to be involved in physical activities in a variety of roles

Many opportunities exist for becoming and remaining involved in physical activities. Being a sports performer is the obvious way, but there are also other roles too. For most sports in England there is information on how to get involved in a sport in all roles on specific sports websites.

Roles in sport include:

Performer

Coaching

Sports leader

Volunteer

Official

Performer

The pathways a young performer learns and progresses by can have a clear structure and can include the following:

- their school provides teaching of fundamental sports skills
- their school develops skills by providing opportunities to join clubs and teams
- a club provides training to compete and enter local and district events
- a club provides opportunities to gain regional and local participation status
- a club provides opportunities for selection for international representation.

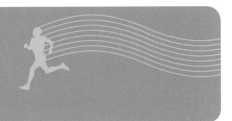

Active challenge

With a partner, choose a sport and look on the Internet to find the sport's official website. Look at the pathways a player goes through to reach international honours.

Sports leader

Sports Leaders UK is a registered charity. It provides the opportunity to gain qualifications and develop core skills and competencies in sporting activities. Groups are run in the local area, using schools, community halls or wherever is suitable for running practical and theory sessions. The nationally recognized awards help develop essential personal skills such as confidence, motivation, communication and teamwork. The practical aspect of the awards can equip the candidate with lifelong skills of self-management and leadership.

The qualifications can act as a stepping-stone for employment as well as helping individuals to develop character and personality.

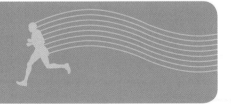

Active challenge

Look on the website www.sportsleaders.org to find out about the organization's core values and the different qualifications available.

Volunteer

For sports clubs to continue to run they need to be organized efficiently. The jobs associated with running a club are wide and varied. In most cases players double their contribution to the club by taking on another role. Volunteers such as these are often vital to keep the club in existence. When a person takes on a job they can draw on their life skills to help with the role. For example, a banker or accounts clerk may well be comfortable taking on the role of club treasurer.

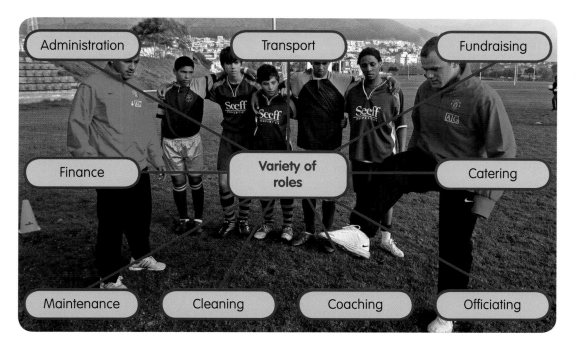

Official

In 2007/08 the Youth Sport Trust funded training for young people aged 16 to 19 to officiate at sports such as athletics, volleyball, swimming, gymnastics, badminton, table tennis, fencing, judo and disability sports.

The aim of this training is to give young people skills to help at local events, national events, such as the UK School Games, and major events alongside top officials.

The following partners are involved:

- National Governing Bodies of Sport
- School Sport Partnerships
- Competition Managers.

The national governing bodies of sport design courses for people interested in becoming officials in their chosen sport. Each pathway is different according to the nature of the sport.

Active challenge

Look on the Internet and find the pathway a person needs to follow to become a football referee.

Coaching

sports coach UK is a charitable organization concerned with coaching. They have set up the UK Coaching Framework, a structure for planning and implementing a comprehensive system to support children, adults and players and athletes with skilled coaches. Players at all stages will be supported so that by 2016 the framework becomes a world-leading example.

The framework links:

- the governing bodies of each sport
- the four Home Country Sports Councils:**Sport England**, sportsscotland, the Sports Council for Wales and the Sports Council for Northern Ireland
- UK Sport
- Skills Active
- Youth Sport Trust

The objectives are to help sports improve their coaching, see coaches play a key role in increasing sport participation and improving sporting performances, and help build a clear career structure for coaches. This will give a lasting legacy, with coaching being recognized as a professional career.

"Implementation will create world class coaching expertise from grassroots to elite…the vital role coaches play in introducing people to sport, helping them to realise their potential, and spotting and nurturing our stars of the future."

(Sport England, UK Coaching Framework)

2 — The sports participation pyramid

The sports participation pyramid shows the structure of progression in sport. It clearly identifies the different groups of performers involved at each level and the pathways for them to progress to a higher level, working from the bottom upwards.

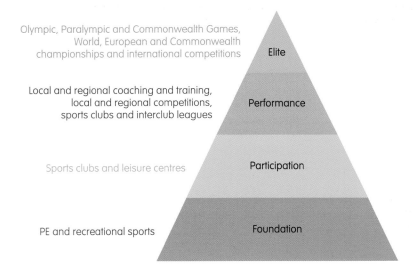

For example:

- Foundation – students at school taking part in sport
- Participation – people taking part in sport in their free time, such as extra curricular activities
- Performance – performer receiving local and regional coaching and training, and enters local competitions and leagues
- Elite – top-class, elite performers taking part in international competitions.

To make sport development succeed, so that the performance and elite stages are achieved, The Sports Council for Wales identified the following as areas to be addressed:

• Increasing club and governing body membership.
• Increasing numbers of volunteers.
• Increasing numbers and improving standards of coaches.
• Increasing numbers of trained officials (such as referees).
• Increasing numbers of administrators at all levels of sport.
• Better access to better facilities.
• Appropriate competition.
• Talent is identified and developed.
• Better access to support services (such as sports science).

Each sport has its own pathways planned. The Football Association (FA) has created a player pathway using the participation pyramid. They want everyone, whatever their age, background, culture, ability or gender, to have a chance to find a way to play the game. They have data on 38,000 clubs in every area of England, helping people to find a club in which to play. The FA have identified what is needed at the foundation level, the elements needed for participation and performance all the way through to elite at the top of the pyramid pathway. They have put in place links for players to progress in this chosen sport. The FA has also created pathways for different roles within the game: if a person wants to be a volunteer, coach or referee the Association shows them how.

Task 1

1 – Look on the Football Association website www.thefa.com and find 'Links for players'.

2 – Find information about your nearest club.

3 – Identify football academies and centres of excellence for boys and girls.

3 — Initiatives providing opportunities for involvement in physical activity

The government has invested £978 million, over a four-year period, to develop and deliver the PE, School Sport and Club Links (**PESSCL**) strategy. The aims of this strategy are to increase the number of 5 to 16 year olds taking up opportunities for sport and remaining involved throughout their lives. The plan is for 85 per cent of schoolchildren in this age range to receive a minimum of two hours of high-quality PE and school sport each week. Sport England is providing funding for national and community schemes so that by 2010 children can have the opportunity to take part in their two-hour entitlement.

Task 2

Look on the website www.teachernet.gov.uk and find out two or more facts about:

• Club Links
• Gifted and Talented
• Sporting Playgrounds
• Swimming

The PESSCL strategy involves nine links:

1. Sports colleges
- Promote excellence in PE
- Involve families
- Link with sports bodies and communities
- Share resources
- Develop and spread good practice
- Provide a structure for careers in sport and physical education

2. School sport partnerships
- Partnerships with other groups aiming to enhance sporting opportunities
- Aims to create greater involvement

3. Professional development
- Improve teaching quality, raise attainment and increase amount of sport undertaken
- Increase understanding of how PE can help whole-school improvement
- Increase understanding of PE's role in supporting healthy lifestyles and physical activity
- Encourage innovation so all needs are catered for and achievement is enhanced
- Develop cross-phase work to enhance progress

9. Step into Sport
- Involves Youth Sport Trust, Sport England and Sports Leaders UK
- Aimed at 14 to 19 year olds
- Enables starting and continuing leadership and volunteering through sport
- Increasing junior and community leadership awards

4. QCA's PE and School Sport (PESS)
- The Qualifications and Curriculum Authority (QCA) who maintain and develop the curriculum examinations, tests and assessments in schools in England realize the role PE in school sport has to play on the individual and the school
- Guiding how to improve PE in schools
- Outlining the impact good school sports has on many areas of school life

8. Club Links
- Increase children's membership of sports clubs

7. Gifted and Talented
(divided into four areas)
1 Benchmark excellence – help for schools to achieve the required standard
2 Talent identification – show schools how to recognize talent
3 Provision for talented athletes – help talented athletes to develop core skills
4 Support for talented athletes – train teachers and young people in lifestyle management and performance planning

6. Sporting Playgrounds
- Colour zoning primary school playgrounds so all children can enjoy the space in their own way

5. Swimming
- Swimming charter – provides guidance on encouraging more children to swim
- Swimming and water safety websites give practical ideas on how to swim safely and well
- Swimming top-up schemes – supports children leaving primary school who have not yet learnt to swim to learn and enjoy the activity

PESSCL

SHROPSHIRE TOUR

School sport partnerships

Schools sport partnerships can create a positive experience of taking part in a sporting activity. Teachers, students, coaches and club members can all be involved in bringing physical activity to the whole community. The different events allow for progress in performance, leadership and organization.

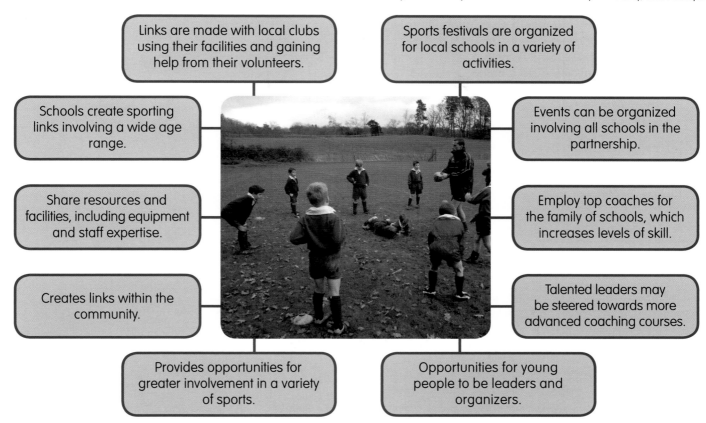

Links are made with local clubs using their facilities and gaining help from their volunteers.

Sports festivals are organized for local schools in a variety of activities.

Schools create sporting links involving a wide age range.

Events can be organized involving all schools in the partnership.

Share resources and facilities, including equipment and staff expertise.

Employ top coaches for the family of schools, which increases levels of skill.

Creates links within the community.

Talented leaders may be steered towards more advanced coaching courses.

Provides opportunities for greater involvement in a variety of sports.

Opportunities for young people to be leaders and organizers.

Sport England

Sport England is responsible for delivering the government's sporting objectives. They believe in the power of sport and the way it can change people's lives and aim to create opportunities for everyone throughout their lives. Sport England's key aims are to create:

- Active communities leading to greater independence of individuals.
- Healthy communities contributing to more integrated health and social care.
- Sustainable communities.

Sport England supports local authorities in their planning process. They give advice on what facilities should be provided, where they should be and how to maintain them.

Start, Stay, Succeed initiative

Sport England made a commitment to creating opportunities for people to pursue their sporting interests and set out the following objectives:

- Start – improve the health of the nation by increasing participation in sport with a focus on certain priority groups;
- Stay – create a network of accredited clubs, sports facilities, volunteers, coaches and competitions so people will continue to be involved in sport in various roles;
- Succeed – talented performers have the chance to be successful due to the appropriate and available opportunities being presented to them.

Following the success of the Start, Stay, Succeed initiative, Sport England launched a new strategy in June 2008 which aims to help all people, irrespective of their age or ability, to take part in sport in their community. The new Grow Sustain Excel initiative aims to:

- Grow –increase the number of participants in physical activity;
- Sustain –keep people involved in physical activity once they have started
- Excel –increase the number of talented performers through the opportunities provided by the national governing bodies.

Task 3

Look on the Internet and find out more about Sport England's Start, Stay, Succeed initiative and the new Grow Sustain Excel strategy.

Local facilities

The different levels of facilities around the country support the structure of encouraging involvement, progression and a lifelong active lifestyle. Following a particular sport in a local area often begins in school. A school's facilities are increasingly available for use by the public after school hours, making the most of the amenities for the community.

Schools often have links with local organizations. Either students already have a connection with a local club or a teacher can recommend a promising player to join the local team to further their talents. For some, less competitive and more leisure participation is desired; here the local sport centre provides a wide range of activities for all interests.

Sport centres aim to provide and encourage the community to take part in an active lifestyle. They can make their facility more accessible by arranging their sessions and pricing structure in different ways according to the target group. These changes can be made in a variety of ways:

- special users – sessions for a certain type of user, such as women, juniors and pensioners
- discounts – for pensioners, the unemployed and under 16s
- crèche facilities – so parents can take part
- starting a club – increasing interest by having clubs based at the centre.

Private clubs can also encourage more people to play by:

- holding open days – events encouraging people to 'have a go' at the activity
- school visits – going into schools to show the sport off
- organizing trips to events – to show the sport at its best, whichcan lead to more people taking part
- advertising – letting people know they are there.

Centres of Excellence

There are **Centres of Excellence** all around the country, catering for various activities and skill levels. By developing Centres in different parts of the UK more people are given the chance to participate, use top-class facilities and potentially have the opportunity to show off their talents. By developing top-class facilities, potentially catering for the best performers, better quality coaches and volunteers can often be recruited.

Strong links are in place between local communities and Centres of Excellence. The MCC (Marylebone Cricket Club) is the controlling body for cricket. In 2005, it announced that it would be supporting six University Centres of Cricket Excellence:

- Cambridge
- Durham
- Loughborough
- Cardiff/Glamorgan
- Leeds/Bradford
- Oxford.

These universities have close links with their communities. They offer a chance to participate in many sports and invite all levels to take advantage of their facilities including young and disabled players. Many sports will be available including swimming, bowling and hockey.

Active challenge

With a partner, look on the Internet for other Centres of Excellence in the UK. Find out how both the community and top-class performers will be catered for.

The National Sports Centres

The **National Sports Centres** are available for local communities as well as elite athletes. Collectively the centres offer participation in different ways:

- Clubs can be based at these centres.
- The public are able to pay and play.
- Courses are available and organized.
- Facilities are available to hire.

The diagram on the right highlights National Sports Centres in the UK.

Active challenge

Choose a sport and work out, using the Internet, the pathways a player might take to move from novice to elite athlete.

Use the following headings to guide you:

- School
- Area
- National
- Club
- County
- International

Say what part Sport England plays in this process.

Key
1 English Institute of Sport, Sheffield (EISS)
2 Lilleshall National Sports Centre
3 Plas y Brenin, the National Mountain Centre
4 Bisham Abbey National Sports Centre
5 National Water Sports Centre, Nottingham
6 Stoke Mandeville Stadium, the National Centre for Wheelchair Sport

Active challenge

With a partner, decide what facilities there are in your area.

Youth Sport Trust

The Youth Sport Trust (YST) is a registered charity, which aims to support and develop young people's physical education and opportunities in sport. They aim to help young people by:

- attempting to increase enjoyment and participation in school sport
- helping to provide the chance for greater variety of experience in PE at all levels
- providing the best teaching, coaching and resources possible
- helping young people to live a healthy, happy life.

TOP Programme

TOP Programmes are available for ages ranging from 18 months to 18 years and aim to provide the best opportunities that PE and sport have to offer. All are encouraged irrespective of age, disability or gender. Teachers, coaches and volunteers are also supported through the scheme. Up to and including the Sainsbury's TOP Activity, the schemes focus on personal physical activity. TOP Link and beyond supports young people to develop their organizing and leadership abilities.

- TOP Tots (18 months to 3 years)
- TOP Start (3 to 5 year olds)
- TOP Play (4 to 9 year olds)
- Sainsbury's TOP Activity (7 to 11 year olds)
- TOP Link (14 to 16 year olds)
- TOP Sports ability (all age groups)
- TOP Resources

Young people can express themselves through various activities as part of the Sainsbury's TOP Activity programme.

At each stage from the school-based volunteering scheme, TOP Link programme, there are progressive awards to be achieved:

- 11 to 14 years: Sport Education – Sport Leaders UK (SLUK) Young Leaders Award
- 14 to 19 years: Sport Diploma Level 2 – Vocational qualifications including Young Ambassadors, BTEC and National Governing Bodies Introductory Leadership Awards Levels 1 and 2
- 16 to 19 years: Sport Diploma Level 3 – Vocational qualifications including MA and BTEC, International Baccalaureate, National Governing Bodies coaching/official Awards and SLUK Levels 2 and 3.

Active challenge

1 – Look on the website of the Youth Sport Trust and find out more about the TOP Programmes. Prepare a report on your findings. You may choose to look at one of the TOP Programmes and prepare your report on that one programme alone.

2 – Share your report with others.

TOP LINK – STEP INTO SPORT (SIS)   This scheme gives experience to young people to be leaders in a variety of ways and run festivals of sport and dance. It is a plan for all 11 to 16 year olds and provides a pathway to leadership (Sports Leaders UK Awards – SLUK) and volunteering. It includes work in PE lessons, on-school site activities and off–school site activities. The involvement includes taking on different roles such as:

- coach
- official
- team manager
- event volunteer
- administrator
- young ambassador.

By being involved, the Youth Sport Trust recognizes the scheme's value to young people:

- It gives empowerment and voice to young people
- It develops personal learning and thinking skills
- It encourages people to makes a positive contribution to the community
- Key skills prepare young people for life
- Success increases self-esteem and pride
- Respect is gained for their efforts
- It provides pathways into employment.

ACTIVE KIDS PROGRAMME   A person may donate collected Active Kids programme vouchers from Sainsbury's, to the school, Scout or Guide group of their choice. The school or group may then redeem them for sports equipment. Sainsbury's also have partnerships with Premier Rugby and English Basketball allowing students to go and see matches and be inspired to take part.

Key terms

Sport England – non-departmental public body, operating under Royal Charter, responsible for sport in England

PESSCL – PE, School Sport and Club Links, a strategy linking PE, school sport and clubs

QCA – Qualifications and Curriculum Authority developing and modernizing curriculum, assessments, examinations and qualifications

Sport centres – providing sport facilities for the community

Centres of Excellence – centres offering use of facilities to all levels in a variety of sports, but also concentrating on one sport taking it to the highest level

National Sports Centres – headquarters for particular sports, providing facilities for the public, aiming to provide the best facilities for the success of elite athletes

Summary

A person often becomes involved in sport by becoming a player, but there are many other roles that can involve people in an activity. Clubs require volunteers at all levels and with different skills to keep them functioning effectively. Sport England, in association with other bodies, has created a framework to help people of all ages and backgrounds in their various roles in sport. Training, advice and guidelines exist to keep people positively involved, improve their health and encourage development of skills and give opportunities to talented athletes to excel.

The government leads the way by creating legislation for increased participation and a healthy and active life for the population. Their decisions influence schools, local sporting facilities and Centres of Excellence both in a local area and nationally.

The different types of examination linked with Physical Education can provide tangible proof of success in that area and help with future employment.

Opening the doors of schools, local facilities and large centres for sport creates many pathways for participation. By opening the Centres of Excellence and the National Sports Centres to all users, more people have the chance to use the best facilities and follow in the footsteps of elite athletes.

Exam questions

Multiple-choice questions

1. **(a)** There are many roles a person can take up directly associated with sport. Which of the following best describes these range of roles?

   ☐ **A** Coach, volunteer, official, grounds person, treasurer

   ☐ **B** Player, fixtures secretary, manager, coach, painter, official

   ☐ **C** Leader, coach, administrator, spectator, farmer

   ☐ **D** Volunteer, official, coach, lawyer, player

   (1)

   (b) Volunteers are often essential for the day-to-day running of a sports club. Which of the following includes all volunteer types?

   ☐ **A** Caterer, officiator, administrator, coach, gardener

   ☐ **B** Fundraiser, sales advisor, officiator, administrator, coach

   ☐ **C** Fundraiser, caterer, officiator, administrator, coach

   ☐ **D** Officiator, administrator, shop keeper, coach

   (1)

2. Read the following statements on the sports participation pyramid and decide which option is correct.

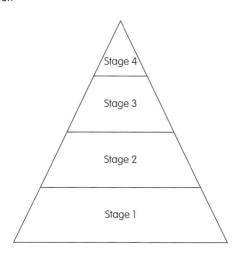

(a) Statement 1: Stage 3 is the performance stage.

Statement 2: Stage 3 is where people regularly take fitness classes.

   ☐ **A** Both statements are true

   ☐ **B** Statement 1 is true, Statement 2 is false

   ☐ **C** Statement 1 is false, Statement 2 is true

   ☐ **D** Both statements are false

   (1)

3. The initials PESSCL stand for:

   ☐ **A** PE and School Sport Club Links

   ☐ **B** PE, School Sport and Confidence Links

   ☐ **C** PE, Social Sport and Club Links

   ☐ **D** PE, School Sport and Club Links

   (1)

Short-answer questions

4. What is the name of the scheme initiated by the Youth Sport Trust aiming to increase lifelong enjoyment and participation in sport?

   (1)

5. How does Sport England help local authorities with their sports planning?

   (1)

Longer-answer questions

6. Sport England set up an initiative called Start, Stay, Succeed. What did it aim to do?

   (3)

7. How does Sport England cater for top-class facilities but also ensure a healthy and active lifestyle for the public?

   (3)

1.1～Healthy, active lifestyles

1.1.3 Exercise and fitness as part of your healthy, active lifestyle

What you will learn about in this topic:

1 — An explanation of the terms health, fitness and exercise
2 — The relationship between health, fitness and exercise and how they impact on performance
3 — Components of health-related exercise
4 — Components of skill-related fitness

1 — An explanation of the terms health, fitness and exercise

Health

Health is not merely the absence of illness or disease. For you to be classed as healthy you need to have developed each of the following components:

• physical well-being
• mental well-being
• social well-being.

Physical well-being

Mental well-being

Health components

Social well-being

Fitness

Fitness can be defined as the ability to meet the demands of the environment.

Because everyone has their own natural fitness level, everyone will have different requirements to maintain their own minimum level of fitness. If the demands of the environment become greater, the body can be trained to meet those demands.

Every sporting activity requires a different level of physical fitness ability. Some activities depend on the development of only a few of the health components; others need a combination of all three.

Exercise

Exercise is the participation in an activity that requires physical effort which exerts your muscles in order to sustain or improve your health and fitness. To maintain a level of general fitness you should try to:

- Exercise three to five times a week.
- Increase your **heart rate** to above 60 per cent of your maximum heart rate.
- Keep your heart rate raised for no less than 20 minutes in each session.

> To calculate your maximum heart rate, subtract your age from 220. For example, 220 – 16 = 204 beats per minute (bpm); 60% of this maximum heart rate is 122 bpm.

2 — The relationship between health, fitness and exercise and how they impact on performance

In order to be healthy you have to be physically fit. But as well as exercising in order to develop the physical health component, you also need to be socially and mentally well adjusted in order to be healthy. If the social and mental components are lacking or underdeveloped you could still be physically fit, but not classed as healthy.

- Fitness is to do with the physical component, so your body may be functioning at a peak but the other aspects of health may not be present.
- The mental component is to do with how well you concentrate, think things through and approach life.
- The social component is to do with how well you interact, cooperate and deal with other people.

Your general health is the basis on which to train harder. Someone who trains specifically for a sport has to 'raise the bar' of their state of good health and go beyond this level in order to keep improving their performance.

Professional footballers such as Ashley Cole continually train in order to improve their skills and fitness, which improves their health too.

The effects of lack of exercise on physical performance

Weight increase
If more calories are taken in than are burned off, the result is weight gain. The effect on performance is that extra weight can increase fatigue as there is more fat to shift; fat takes up more space than muscle so the extra bulk may also get in the way and restrict flexibility. Following the guidelines for calorie intake can help a person keep the right balance.

A lack of exercise may cause an initial decrease in overall body weight, as muscle weighs more than fat. For performers who do not have a tendency to put on muscle and are relying on weight in their sport, such as forwards in rugby, this can be a disadvantage.

Less flexibility
If joints are not regularly moved to their full range then the ability to move them to their fullest extent will be lost. For example, this could inhibit a person rotating their arm in a tennis serve or kicking a ball in football.

Become breathless sooner
The body loses the ability to work for long periods of time without becoming breathless. A person will reach **anaerobic** capacity (VO_2 maximum) sooner.

Aerobic capacity reduced
The body's ability to exchange gases efficiently reduces. A person will find that a lack of exercise prevents the body from working for long periods without tiring as the **aerobic** capacity is reduced. As a result, not enough oxygen reaches the working muscles so fatigue sets in. This is due to the insufficient transportation of oxygen to the working muscles making the muscles tire, reducing skill levels and eventually preventing muscle contraction.

Loss of strength
Reduced stress on muscles allows them to become flaccid and weak. This gives rise to the saying 'use it or lose it'!

Task 1

For each of the effects of lack of exercise on physical performance, give a detrimental effect they would have on a sporting example. Choose a different sport for each effect.

3 — Components of health-related exercise

Health-related exercise is activity undertaken with specific focus on improving the bodily systems in order to improve a person's health.

Each sporting activity uses its own combination of health-related exercise components. Some activities depend on the development of only a few of these components; others need a combination of all of them.

Cardiovascular fitness

The cardiovascular system deals with the heart and blood vessels of the body so it is important to have good **cardiovascular fitness**. The good condition of the cardiovascular system allows for efficient transportation of blood to the necessary parts of the body in order that the body can meet the extra demands of exercise.

In training, if the cardiovascular system is not fit then the ability to keep working is reduced and so the required skill level is less likely to be reached. In competition, fatigue and breathlessness would prevent a person playing to the required standard or even continuing the activity in some instances.

To exercise effectively for any length of time, without tiring or becoming less efficient, requires the training of the **cardiorespiratory** system. The better the heart and lungs work, the more efficiently the body gets oxygen to the working muscles and removes waste products from the body.

Marathan runners like Emma Archer and Melanie Ellis need good cardiovascular fitness to transport oxygen to their working muscles.

Active challenge

With a partner, make a list of sporting activities that require cardiovascular fitness.

> Use the length of time of the activity to help your choices.

Muscular strength

Muscular strength is the muscle's ability to apply force and overcome resistance. Muscular strength can be measured by its ability to lift the maximum weight possible in one attempt. In itself, muscular strength can be used to overpower an opponent. A player who can combine strength with speed can create power, which is especially useful when playing a forehand drive down the line in tennis, in order to pass an opponent at the net, for instance.

Having poor strength may prevent a player shooting with the required amount of power to beat a goalkeeper. In contact sports, such as judo, a weak player gives little resistance to an opponent with muscular strength.

Jo Calzaghe uses his muscular strength to overpower Bernard Hopkins.

Active challenge

1 – Make a list of sporting examples requiring muscular strength.

2 – Compare your list with another class member and combine your ideas together.

> Look at the skills of the activity you have chosen, such as, jumping high for a ball shows leg strength.

Muscular endurance

Muscular endurance is the muscle's ability to work over long periods without tiring. The development of muscular endurance requires light to moderate exercise over long periods, whereas developing muscular strength needs short bursts of maximum effort. To execute actions with the correct technique and least likelihood of injury relies on the joints having good flexibility and muscles that can control the movement of these joints safely.

Muscular endurance is essential for long-distance events such as 10,000m racing. The body is able to keep working for a long time without tiring and so has more chance of winning.

Good muscular endurance prevents Jody Cundy's body tiring quickly.

Flexibility

Flexibility is the ability of the joint to move through its full range. Controlled use of the full range of movement available at a joint can allow for the execution of the correct technique, improving performance and lessening the risk of injury. Where resistance to a force is necessary, the muscles must be strong enough to prevent overextension beyond the fullest range. For example, players in a rugby scrum must have muscles strong enough to prevent overextension of their shoulders.

Louis Smith needs to move his joints through the full range to be effective.

Body composition

Body composition is the ratio of bone, muscle, connective tissue and body fat that makes up the body, so plays an important part in the effectiveness of the performer. There is an ideal body shape for each activity (somatotype is explained in detail on page 130). Athletes can improve their shape by:

- controlling their diet and choosing the correct combinations of food
- eating the right amounts of food
- the amount of exercise completed.

Timmy Murphy has a small frame and a minimal fat component, ideal for his sport.

Active challenge

With a partner, decide on examples where flexibility and body composition can be seen in the sporting environment.

Look at the size and shape of the performers and the movements required to succeed.

Key terms

Exercise – a form of physical activity done to maintain or improve health and/or physical fitness

Heart rate – the number of times the heart beats each minute

Anaerobic – 'without oxygen'. If exercise is done in short, fast bursts, the heart cannot supply blood and oxygen to muscles as fast as the cells use them

Aerobic – 'with oxygen'. If exercise is not too fast and is steady, the heart can supply all the oxygen muscles need

Cardiovascular fitness – the ability to exercise the entire body for long periods of time

Cardiorespiratory – to do with the heart and lungs

Muscular strength – the amount of force a muscle can exert against a resistance

Muscular endurance – the ability to use voluntary muscles many times without getting tired

Flexibility – the ability of the joint to move through its full range

Body composition – the percentage of body weight which is fat, muscle and bone

Summary

A healthy person has a good balance of mental, social and physical well-being. Fitness relates to the physical attributes of the person and how well they adapt to the demands of the environment in which they function. These surroundings can be their everyday environment or in connection with sport.

The development of the components of health-related exercise has a direct effect on a player's ability to complete the skills successfully and so achieve favourable results.

4 — Components of skill-related fitness

There are six **skill-related fitness** components, which can be improved through training: they are all skills that can applied to everyday activities, but specifically sports. The elements being improved will depend on the particular sport being performed, as each activity will have a different combination of these components to accomplish for effectiveness. To be effective in competition or performance, the following components should be adapted to the needs of the particular sporting activity:

1. **Agility**
2. **Balance**
3. **Coordination**
4. **Power**
5. **Reaction time**
6. **Speed**

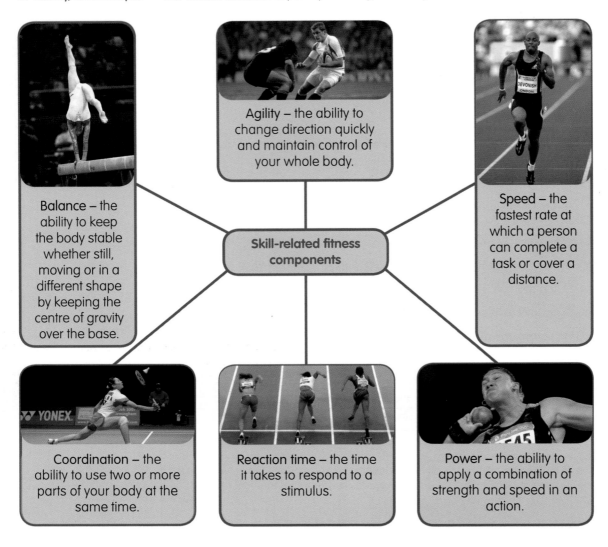

Balance – the ability to keep the body stable whether still, moving or in a different shape by keeping the centre of gravity over the base.

Agility – the ability to change direction quickly and maintain control of your whole body.

Skill-related fitness components

Speed – the fastest rate at which a person can complete a task or cover a distance.

Coordination – the ability to use two or more parts of your body at the same time.

Reaction time – the time it takes to respond to a stimulus.

Power – the ability to apply a combination of strength and speed in an action.

How performance is linked with skill-related fitness

Performance is the action or process of performing a task. A good performance relies on each of the skill-related fitness components coming into play at the right time and to the right degree. For example, as a ball is struck in rounders or cricket, the reaction time, coordination and power of the shot should be such that it avoids the fielders and results in a score. In an invasion game the winners will have often been able to demonstrate the components when necessary and in a more efficient way than the opposition.

Identify the relative importance of each component to different sporting activities

Sporting activities rely on different combinations of skill-related fitness. For example, some activities rely heavily on only one or two components, such as sprinters who reply on reaction time and speed, whereas hurdlers rely on a combination of these components throughout their event:

Reaction time – to be out of the blocks first.

Speed – to make it to each hurdle quickly.

Power – to make take-off before the hurdle.

Coordination – using all limbs in unison to clear the hurdle.

Agility – to clear the hurdle efficiently.

Balance – to land, keeping the body stable after clearing the hurdle, and resume the running phase.

Task 2

1 – Choose a sport and identify an action within it.

2 – Link the components of skill-related fitness to the skill required for that action.

Use the hurdler example above to help guide your answer.

How health-related exercise can be affected by skill-related fitness

Health-related exercise components can have a bearing on the effectiveness of skill-related fitness.

Cardiovascular fitness
Having good cardiovascular fitness allows a sportsperson to keep working at a high level throughout an event with oxygen being transported efficiently to the working muscles and waste products removed from them. This allows the muscles to remain agile so contract in a controlled manner. This leads to quicker reactions and the ability to apply power to a performance.

Muscular strength
Muscular strength allows a performer to play a shot powerfully, combining power and speed to flex and control the muscles to keep the body balanced.

Muscular endurance
Muscles can continue to work over long periods of time without tiring, allowing a performer to execute skills accurately and effectively throughout the whole length of a game. Having well-developed muscular endurance will allow a performer to control movement appropriately so remain coordinated and balanced.

Flexibility
Being flexible allows a performer to be agile and move their joints in all positions necessary in order to complete a performance, enabling them to move quickly and in a controlled manner. Being able to move the joints through their full range will help with movement: the correct action can be performed with greater speed, improved agility and greater power.

Body composition

The amount of muscle, bone and fat on a sportsperson can have a bearing on agility, balance and speed.

Task 3

Give a sporting example of how each of the components of health-related exercise affects the skill-related fitness components.

Key terms

Skill-related fitness – physical fitness that is related to health, which can change depending on an individual's exercise habits

Agility – the ability to change the position of the body quickly and to control the movements of the whole body

Balance – the ability to retain the body's centre of mass (gravity) above the base of support with reference to static (stationary), or dynamic (changing), conditions of movement, shape and orientation

Coordination – the ability to use two or more body parts together

Power – the ability to do strength performances quickly (power = strength x speed)

Reaction time – the time between the presentation of a stimulus and the onset of a movement

Speed – the differential rate at which an individual is able to perform a movement or cover a distance in a period of time

Summary

The components of skill-related fitness are associated with sport as they identify certain abilities that are directly related to sporting situations. The more accomplished a person is at these components, coupled with their ability to adapt them to the intensity of competition, the more likely it is that success will follow. Each different sport requires the development of a certain combination of these areas for success.

Exam questions

Multiple-choice questions

1. **(a)** Health is:

   ☐ **A** The ability to meet the demands of the environment

   ☐ **B** Working towards improving all areas of the body

   ☐ **C** A state of complete physical fitness and calmness

   ☐ **D** A state of physical, mental and social well-being

   (1)

   (b) Fitness is:

   ☐ **A** Being able to exercise properly, three to five times a week

   ☐ **B** The ability to meet the demands of the environment

   ☐ **C** Following a training programme for a particular sport

   ☐ **D** A form of training to improve health and fitness

   (1)

2. The following statements relate to health-related exercise. Decide which combination is correct.

   (a) Statement 1: Flexibility allows the joints to move to the full range available.

   Statement 2: Muscular endurance relies on full movement at a joint.

   ☐ **A** Both statements are true

   ☐ **B** Statement 1 is true, Statement 2 is false

   ☐ **C** Statement 1 is false, Statement 2 is true

   ☐ **D** Both statements are false

   (1)

   (b) Statement 1: Muscular endurance allows the muscles to work over long periods without tiring.

   Statement 2: Muscular strength is still needed late in a game and relies on the muscles contracting and relaxing efficiently.

   ☐ **A** Both statements are true

   ☐ **B** Statement 1 is true, Statement 2 is false

   ☐ **C** Statement 1 is false, Statement 2 is true

   ☐ **D** Both statements are false

   (1)

Short-answer questions

3. Name **two** sports that rely on **muscular endurance**.
   (2)

4. What does the following definition describe? 'The resulting skill-related fitness component that combines strength and speed in an action'.
   (1)

Longer-answer questions

5. This question is about flexibility.

   (a) Choose a sporting activity that requires flexibility.
   (1)

   (b) Give **two** examples for your chosen activity describing the actions that require flexibility.
   (2)

6. What is the difference between muscular strength and muscular endurance?
   (2)

1.1～Healthy, active lifestyles

1.1.4a Physical activity as part of your healthy, active lifestyle: training principles and goal setting

What you will learn about in this topic:

1 — The principles of training
2 — Components of the FITT principles
3 — Reversibility
4 — The value of goal setting
5 — Working SMART

1— The principles of training

Principles of training are the rules to follow when undertaking physical activity programmes to improve fitness. Each person has a different reason for exercising. It may be for leisure, competition, professional or personal pride. A person trains to improve **performance**. When the principles are applied, improvements in cardiovascular and respiratory condition, fitness, strength, endurance and skill might be expected.

Task 1

1 – Write down a definition of the principles of training.

2 – Write down the reasons why training principles are important to the performer.

3 – What considerations do you think should be made when creating a training schedule?

There are several principles of training, each influencing the training of the performer in a different way. Good training takes into consideration all of the principles and their effects on the body. They are essential to the planning of a **systematic training** programme so that an individual can improve their fitness. The main principles are **progressive overload**, **specificity**, **individual differences/needs** and **rest and recovery**. The FITT principles (Frequency, Intensity, Time and Type) are other significant components affecting fitness development.

Progressive overload

The principle of progressive overload involves having the body work at a greater rate than normal and then gradually increasing the stress on the body, as it adapts to the exercise training levels.

Exercising at the same degree of difficulty all the time will:

- in the short term only maintain current fitness levels
- in the long term, as the training starts to change your body tolerances, have no effect on improvement.

An athlete's body needs to be gradually and systematically put under slightly more pressure to continue to improve. To improve muscular strength the muscles should work harder than normal, by shifting greater weight. When these levels of stress are easily dealt with then the stress should be slightly increased.

The need to increase the amount of difficulty of the exercise gradually is reflected by the ease with which the task is completed. For cardiovascular improvement the same amount of exercise will not bring the pulse rate into the **target zone**. After about five to six weeks there may be a need to change the programme. The resting heart rate also indicates improvement: as it decreases, it shows how much fitter a person is becoming.

Whether a person is training for muscular endurance or muscular strength, their aim is to train between 60 and 80 per cent of their maximum heart rate. This is the target zone. As people get older the threshold of training decreases. Working at 50 per cent of their maximum heart rate will often have a positive effect on their cardiovascular fitness.

The point where exercise is demanding enough to have an effect on the body is called the threshold of training.

Gradually increasing the duration of a training session applies the principle of progressive overload.

The cardiovascular system works to take up oxygen so that the body can function. The total amount of oxygen needed is called the oxygen uptake, also known as the VO_2. As the intensity of the exercise increases there is a greater demand for more oxygen to produce energy. Although there is more demand, there is a limit to the amount of oxygen uptake and this is called the **VO_2 maximum** (VO_2 max). A simple indicator of when a person reaches a level between 60 and 80 per cent of their maximum work rate is that they will be unable to talk to another person, as they will have little breath to do so.

Specificity

The principle of specificity requires an understanding of the needs of the game or event. For example, a goalkeeper will include lots of reaction work in their training. When applying this principle the activity is usually practised at the pace required in the sport. If a person trains too slowly then their skills will only be reproduced at the slower pace and the action will be unable to match the requirements of the game. At a school practice for your team, if you repeat the skills slowly then when you get to the game the other team may be quicker than you are. So, speed up your practices!

The actions in training should copy the actions used in the game. If a person needs good leg strength, simply making them strong may not be enough. A cyclist will train their legs, whilst cycling, in a different way from a long-distance runner: both need muscular endurance, but the method of training is different. In order to become a better swimmer a person needs to spend most of their time in the water!

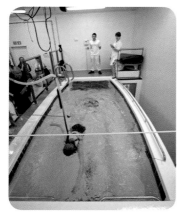
Swimming training.

Cycling training.

Running training.

Weight training.

Tennis training.

Individual differences/needs

The principles of progressive overload and specificity show the way in which the body is affected by the degree and type of exercise undertaken. If these basic rules are to be adhered to, each stage should be followed and planned carefully. As everyone's fitness level differs, systematic training must take into account the individual differences/needs of the performer. An understanding of body systems is vital: knowing the existing capabilities of the heart, lungs and muscles sets the degree of difficulty of the training plan. For training to succeed, the degree of difficulty or intensity is set at a personal level. Setting the demands and intensity of the exercise at the right level ensures it is safe for the performer. If the demands are set too low there will be no improvement; if too high, injuries may occur.

Top-class athletes have a final competition in mind. Their training process is systematically planned so they reach a peak of performance to coincide with that event.

Rest and recovery

For training to be effective there should be a balance between exercise and rest and recovery. Damage and injury can result if recovery phases are not planned and incorporated into a training programme. Rest and recovery gives time for restoration of:

- energy-producing enzymes in muscle fibres
- stores of carbohydrates in muscle cells
- hormonal balance and immune systems.

Recovery allows the muscles to become stronger as they increase in muscle proteins, increase energy stores and enzymes helping to improve the lactic acid threshold. Eating carbohydrates just after the training session and then more within the following two hours not only adds to the energy stores but helps the muscle proteins become restored too.

Recovery can be monitored by using the Orthostatic Heart Rate test. This test requires a stopwatch. It is conducted as follows:

- Rest for 15 minutes after your training session.
- Take your resting pulse and record (reading 1).
- Stand up.
- Fifteen seconds later, take your pulse again and record (reading 2).
- Calculate the difference between the two pulse readings and record the results.

Should the difference between the two readings be greater than 15 to 20 beats, the athlete is unlikely to be recovered from the training. Possible adjustments should be made to the session in order to allow for recovery.

Overtraining results in poorer results from performance and training. It increases the risk of injury and illness and decreases the desire to exercise.

- Inability to concentrate
- Lack of flow and rhythm to movement
- Overanxious, depressed and sensitive
- Personality changes occur including being irritable and quarrelsome
- Can become demoralized before and during competition
- Inability to keep to the usual tactics

Signs of overtraining

- Loss of acquired skills
- Reduced powers in strength, endurance and speed
- Greater recovery time required
- Feelings of inhibition and insecurity and fear of competition
- Giving up when difficult situations arise, particularly towards the end of a competition

Planning the training year helps to highlight specific aims so that peak performance can be reached by the performer for a certain event or competition. Planning reduces the risk of overtraining and involves:

- designated times for rests, giving adequate time for recovery between training sessions
- applying a variety of types of training and session content to keep motivation up
- varying the way the same muscles are exercised, but keeping the same effect.

Key terms

Performance – how well a task is completed

Systematic training – planning a programme for an individual as a result of the effect of previous training

Progressive overload – to gradually increase the amount of overload so that fitness gains occur, but without potential for injury

Specificity – matching training to the requirements of the activity

Individual differences/needs – matching training to the requirements of an individual

Rest – the period of time allotted to recovery

Recovery – the time required for the repair of damage to the body caused by training or competition

Target zone – the range within which an individual needs to work for aerobic training to take place (60 to 80 per cent of the maximum heart rate)

VO_2 maximum – the maximum amount of oxygen used in one minute per kilogram of body weight

2 — Components of the FITT principle

FITT stands for Frequency, Intensity, Time and Type and all must be taken into consideration when undertaking a training programme. Combining these four targets, a person may achieve the minimum level of fitness, or by adapting them further and increasing the intensity, a person can train to a higher level.

Frequency

Frequency is the number of times exercise is undertaken per week. The more times a person exercises the more often their body is put under stress. Three to five times a week is the recommended number of times exercise should be repeated to reach the minimum level of fitness. However, top-class sportspeople have to train a lot more frequently than this if they are to achieve results good enough for their aspirations.

But remember, the body also needs time to recover from training. Training very hard, every day, may be harmful even for a top-class athlete.

Intensity

Intensity is the level of difficulty of the exercise. For instance, when considering cardiovascular fitness your pulse rate can show you how intensely you are working.

Exercising three to five times per week is recommended for fitness. The sessions should be intensive and long enough to reach the target zone for at least 20 minutes.

Working in a target zone of 60 to 80 per cent of the maximum heart rate is the level where fitness will usually increase. When training for strength the intensity is calculated in the same way. A person trains within the target zone by finding the maximum weight they can lift and working to 60 to 80 per cent of that weight. As the amount of weight lifted increases with training, this adds to the intensity.

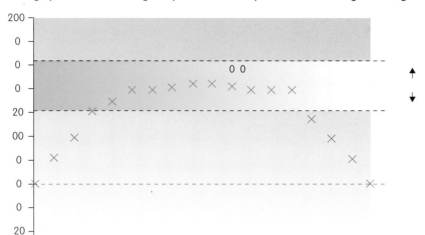

A graph to show the changes in pulse rate of a 16 year old when training in the target zone.

Time

Time relates to how long an exercise session lasts. The length of the session benefits the performer if they reach 60 per cent of their maximum heart rate (MHR). Working the body between 60 and 80 per cent of the MHR exercises the body in the target zone.

Type

Type refers to the variety of training that a performer undertakes in order to prevent boredom. By changing the types of training, the performer is more likely to remain interested and motivated to work hard and perform to the best of their ability. For example, footballers will work on their skills and tactics, but a session may include a different activity such as a modified rugby game, helping general skills of speed, reaction time and agility, but adding variety and interest to the session.

After the warm-up, exercising regularly for 20 minutes at 60 to 80 per cent of the maximum heart rate will increase the body's fitness.

Task 2

Write three sentences for each of the FITT principles.

F = Frequency
I = Intensity
T = Time
T = Type

3 — Reversibility

Just as the body will increase in strength, tone and skill with exercise, it will lose them without it. This is called **reversibility**. The body needs to be stressed to maintain and increase strength. After an injury or illness, an athlete may have lost their strength and skill. Although a person can quickly improve their endurance capability, it can be lost three times faster than it can be gained. Remember, if you don't use it you lose it!

4 — The value of goal setting

Goal setting is important to the performer. By setting out staged and achievable goals a coach/teacher can keep the performer motivated. Having knowledge of the phases shows the way forward and keeps the athlete focused on the task, reducing the possibility of boredom.

Goals can keep the performer working hard, giving a better chance to improve fitness and skills. Reaching a stage and then moving on signposts the athlete's physical progress.

Goals can mentally prepare the performer for an activity or competition. Each stage may train the individual in a way that grooms them for a more challenging situation so when it arrives the person can handle the conditions, taking them in their stride, without them affecting their level of performance.

Reaching goals indicates the progress of training. It shows how the performance is developing in relation to the structured time settings and points out the need for changes to the training.

Knowing the stages gives an element of control to the performer. As each stage is reached and passed the athlete can see the progress and rather than worry about their ability, can be confident that development is on track. Athletes, for instance, gain much confidence when they reach a personal best time or distance in training.

A committed athlete trains in all weathers, focusing on their long-term goal.

Short- and long-term goals

The difference between short- and long-term goals is time. Short-term goals are achievable sooner than long-term goals. In order to achieve a long-term goal, short-term goals must be met first. So smaller achievable targets are reached which will eventually bring the long-term goal nearer. Often in sport the goals are time-specific, due to the fact that the long-term goal may have a particular date set to it, like an athletics event or a major tournament.

Short-term goals
These are often set in training programmes and can act as incentives to train hard. They can work as a signpost indicating whether the performer is on target for success.

There may be several different levels to a short-term goal. For instance, an athlete may have the following stages:

- train hard to achieve a good distance that qualifies them for an event
- they may win that event
- they then may be selected for the county team.

Long-term goals

These targets are often the culmination of several training programmes and can possibly lead to a competition or final event. There are two types of goals in sport:

1. outcome goals, which are linked to results of performance in competition; and
2. performance goals that are concerned with previous performances.

Long-term goals may include:

- beating a personal best performance
- making a round of a competition previously not reached
- running for the country
- being selected for the Olympics.

Task 3

For a sport of your choice, list the short- and long-term goals needed for success.

5 — Working SMART

Goals need to be SMART. When planning goals they should focus on five points:

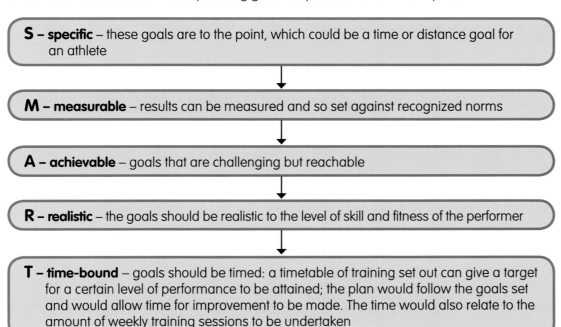

S – specific – these goals are to the point, which could be a time or distance goal for an athlete

M – measurable – results can be measured and so set against recognized norms

A – achievable – goals that are challenging but reachable

R – realistic – the goals should be realistic to the level of skill and fitness of the performer

T – time-bound – goals should be timed: a timetable of training set out can give a target for a certain level of performance to be attained; the plan would follow the goals set and would allow time for improvement to be made. The time would also relate to the amount of weekly training sessions to be undertaken

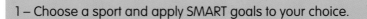

Task 4

1 – Choose a sport and apply SMART goals to your choice.

2 – List how each point would apply to that sport.

3 – List two main targets you have for a particular sport and in sentences, describe how SMART applies to them.

Key terms

FITT – training principles consisting of Frequency, Intensity, Time and Type

Minimum level of fitness – the resulting fitness level when someone exercises over a period of weeks including three to five sessions of 20 minutes, raising the heart rate to between 60 and 80 per cent of its maximum

Reversibility – any adaptation that takes place as a consequence of training will be reversed when you stop training

Goal setting – series of phases setting out achievable targets for progress

SMART – Specific, Measurable, Achievable, Realistic and Time-bound goals

Summary

People deciding to train need to think carefully about the type and intensity of the exercise they are to do. Age, ability, gender and experience will all influence the type of programme suitability. A clear awareness of the reason for training will influence the type of activities in the programme. The more serious the athlete, the greater intensity the exercise will be. Any part of the body exercised, if done so at the correct intensity, will develop. When increasing strength, the shape and size of the muscles change. It is important that an athlete develops the type of strength needed for the activity and exercises both sides of their body equally so that their shape stays as symmetrical as possible. Applying the principles of training is vital for maximum success.

Injury may cause training to stop, reversing the effects of training. Muscles will atrophy (lose their strength and reduce in size).

Rest and recovery phases are important in the programme. These phases allow the athlete's body time to recuperate and so maintain a high level of performance.

Goal setting keeps the athlete focused and motivated during training. It provides stages of achievement until the opportunity to fulfil the long-term goal is reached. Working SMART focuses on the specific needs of the athlete.

Exam questions

Multiple-choice questions

1. (a) Progressive overload is:

   ☐ A Matching the exercises to the activity

   ☐ B The degeneration of the muscles after exercise has stopped

   ☐ C Working the body harder than normal and then increasing the intensity gradually

   ☐ D Allowing the body to recover to maintain a high level of performance

   (1)

   (b) Specificity is:

   ☐ A Allowing the body to recover to maintain a high level of performance

   ☐ B Matching the exercises to the activity

   ☐ C The degeneration of the muscles after exercise has stopped

   ☐ D Working the body harder than normal and then increasing the intensity gradually

   (1)

   (c) The letters in FITT stand for:

   ☐ A Fitness, Intensity, Time and Type

   ☐ B Frequency, Intensity, Training and Type

   ☐ C Frequency, Intensity, Time and Training

   ☐ D Frequency, Intensity, Time and Type

   (1)

   (d) The reason for goal setting is to:

   ☐ A Optimize performance, join in as many sports as possible, control anxiety

   ☐ B Optimize performance, keep to the exercise plan, control anxiety

   ☐ C Know where to score, keep to the exercise plan, control anxiety

   ☐ D Optimize performance, keep to the exercise plan, know how to find a sport you like

   (1)

   (e) SMART stands for:

   ☐ A Sport, Measurable, Agreed, Realistic, Timed

   ☐ B Specific, Meaningful, Agreed, Realistic, Time-phased

   ☐ C Specific, Measurable, Achievable, Realistic, Time-bound

   ☐ D Specific, Measurable, Agreed, Realistic, Timed

   (1)

Short-answer questions

2. Which principle refers to the undoing of the effects of training as a result of training stopping?

   (1)

3. Between what percentages of the maximum heart rate does the heart need to beat to work at the target zone?

   (1)

Longer-answer questions

4. There are recognized training principles. One of them is progressive overload. What is meant by progressive overload when training for an active lifestyle?

   (2)

1.1 ~ Healthy, active lifestyles

1.1.4b Physical activity as part of your healthy, active lifestyle: assessing fitness and developing an exercise programme

What you will learn about in this topic:

1 — PAR-Q
2 — Methods of training
3 — Understanding the exercise session
4 — Using the principles in an exercise programme
5 — Health-related component testing
6 — Heart rate and exercise

1 — PAR-Q

PAR-Q stands for Physical Activity Readiness Questionnaire. Taking part in physical activity should suit most people, but for a small number of the population, getting active may be inappropriate for their physical condition. In these cases, answering a PAR-Q can be the first step to assessing personal suitability and readiness for exercise. The questions ask about your doctor's previous comments on your condition, including:

• heart trouble
• chest pains
• feeling faint or dizzy
• blood pressure
• bone or joint problems
• effects of exercise on bones and joints
• any physical reasons known why an active programme should not be followed
• age and present activity levels.

If any answers relate to problems then seeking the opinion of a doctor and taking their advice on suitable exercise and exercise levels is the next step.

2 — Methods of training

There are many **methods of training** open to the performer. Each method works the body differently. The reason for training and the type of activity being trained for will steer a performer to a particular training method. When training over a long period, varying the methods used will reduce the risk of overuse injury and keep the athlete interested and fresh for each session.

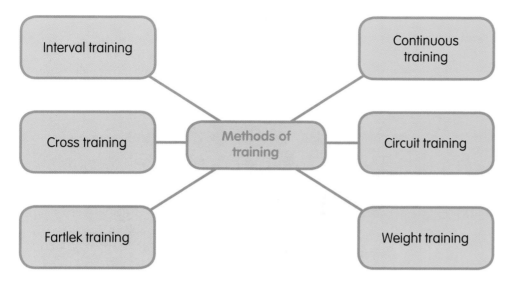

For each of the training methods you will learn about:

- the training method
- what the training develops
- how the method works
- the exercises involved
- how the training principles apply.

Interval training

About the method
Interval training involves times of work followed by times of rest.

What the training develops
This method can be adapted to develop different types of fitness. Short bursts of pace, using anaerobic respiration, needed by sprinters, uses short interval training. Prolonged moderate to hard pace, using aerobic respiration, needed in middle-distance running events, uses long interval training.

Interval training is suited to individuals working on their own, small groups of people and larger numbers, like teams of players. Many sportspeople can benefit from interval training. The sessions can be adapted to practise the skills used in a particular game. Whether a sprinter, swimmer, footballer or netball player, interval training can be adapted to the specific sport.

Athletes use interval running to improve their workload. Interval running involves:

- periods of running fast, followed by
- periods of slower jogging allowing recovery.

Lactic acid builds up during the run phase and a state of **oxygen debt** (the amount of oxygen taken in during activity above that which would have been taken in ordinarily) is reached by the athlete. During the recovery phase, of slow jogging, the heart and lungs work hard to pay back the oxygen in order to breakdown the lactic acid. As a result of the stresses of the training:

- the heart is strengthened
- more capillaries are formed
- more oxygen can be taken up, which helps to break down the lactic acid.

The result is improved performance of the cardiovascular system especially.

The work is intensive and should be performed with accuracy and at competition pace. The times of rest allow performers to regain energy so they do not become too tired and can no longer carry on training. The times of work are repeated to form repetitions. Four or five repetitions make up a set. There may be four or five sets in a session.

Interval training is made up of repetitions and sets.

The table below shows an example of an interval training activity for hockey/football.

Complete four sets of the following in the time limit	Complete four sets of the following in the time limit for return
6–10 seconds dribble and shoot	60–120 seconds jog, return and rest
6–10 seconds dribble and shoot	60–120 seconds jog, return and rest
6–10 seconds dribble and shoot	60–120 seconds jog, return and rest
6–10 seconds dribble and shoot	60–120 seconds jog, return and rest

Task 1

1 – Choose a game or event that can be adapted to interval training.

2 – Work out a set of skills and exercises that could be used in a training session for your chosen activity.

3 – Set out your work in a table like the example above.

How the method works

Interval training can be adapted to different types of athlete and event as the working periods copy those in the event. The rest periods allow time for recovery in the same way that there would be quieter times during a game.

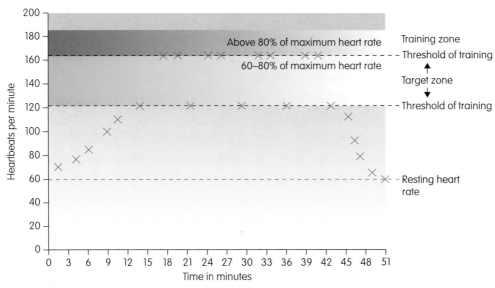

A graph to show the change in pulse rate of a 16 year old during interval training.

Long Interval Training   Work time is 15 seconds to three minutes. Games players and middle-distance athletes benefit from this type of training. The training copies the events in the need for bursts of maximal effort within the 15 second and three minute time spans. Even the best athletes cannot work at full pace for longer than 60 second periods so, when using this method, performers work at 80 to 90 per cent of their maximum heart rate in their training zone.

> A four minute 1500m runner could use interval training in the following way:
>
> Repeat 10 x 60 second 375m distances with two minutes rest between each run.

The resting times match the working times so the longer the athletes work the longer they rest. The resting times are important to enable a performer to recover and continue the session. When working in larger groups it is more difficult for everyone to keep together due to the longer time limit and the variation in ability.

Short Interval Training   This training works on short bursts of maximal effort. The working times may be as short as 15 seconds. The performer aims to work all out for the whole of this time. Sprinters and racket sport players use this method to match the short bursts of maximum effort used in their events. A sprinter goes all out to reach the line as fast as possible and a squash player hits the ball with a burst of maximum effort. Due to the effects of the intensive effort on the body, rests of two minutes are necessary. In this time, the body has a chance to recover enough to carry on training.

The exercises involved

You will have used interval training in school already. Shuttle runs, dribbling relays, lay up shot drills and swimming 25m are all examples of exercises used for interval training. In a games or athletics lesson, you will have used shuttle runs. As you complete your shuttle run, that is one repetition. You rest while your teammates complete their's. You may complete four repetitions before you are stopped; these repetitions make up a set. The teacher may give you another chance to complete the shuttle run after resting and so you will have then completed two sets.

Swimming, athletics and many games, such as football, use interval training. Here, Joleon Lescott practises his dribbling skills.

How the training principles apply

As the periods of work and rest imitate the game, the principle of specificity is applied. To keep the performer improving when using interval training, the principle of progressive overload is used. There are several ways to do this:

- the amount of recovery time may shorten and the pace you would work at competitively is increased
- the intensity or difficulty of the work may increase; this could be increasing the distance covered or amount of time run
- the number of repetitions or sets completed may increase.

Task 2

1 – Choose a sport.

2 – Design a 30-minute interval training session for that sport.

> If designing a session for long interval training, include five repetitions and four sets. If using short interval training, use more repetitions and sets.

Continuous training

About the training method

Continuous training exercises the body at a moderate rate, keeping the pulse at a constant level above the **training threshold** (between 60 and 80 per cent of the maximum so working in the target zone).

What the training develops

This training works the body aerobically and keeps the pulse at a moderate to high rate. Its effect is to improve the cardiovascular and respiratory systems. It can be adapted for both the health and fitness performer and the top athlete.

Running at different intensities has different effects:

- 60 per cent of the maximum heart rate for 60 minutes or more burns fat: is good for joggers.
- 60 to 70 per cent of the maximum heart rate for 45 to 90 minutes burns glycogen and fat, improves cardiovascular system (increases capillaries): is good for marathon runners.
- 70 to 80 per cent of the maximum heart rate for 30 to 45 minutes burns glycogen, improves cardiovascular system (increases capillaries): is good for 5km to marathon distances.

Increasing the intensity further works the body anaerobically but can only be carried out for shorter periods of time, helping with lactic acid tolerance.

How the method works

After a gradual warm-up, the person training works their body at a moderate level throughout the session. The heart rate is above 60 per cent of its maximum but below 80 per cent. By keeping in this zone the work is aerobic and can carry on for a long time.

Continuous training suits a person who is training for the first time or returning to exercise after a period of non-activity, such as after injury. A person who specializes in

The use of a variety of machines, such as rowers, treadmills and exercise bikes, can adapt to continuous training.

long-distance events can use this type of training out of season to maintain a good level of cardiorespiratory fitness. At the start of the season, continuous training can act as a gentle way to re-establish the cardiorespiratory levels. To begin with, the work is moderate, but can be adapted to be harder at a later time.

A graph to show the change in pulse rate of a 16 year old during continuous training.

Graph with y-axis labelled "Heartbeats per minute" (0 to 200) and x-axis labelled "Time in minutes" (0 to 51). Annotations include: "Above 80% of maximum heart rate" (Training zone), "Threshold of training", "60–80% of maximum heart rate" (Target zone), "Threshold of training", and "Resting heart rate".

The exercises involved

The types of activity that suit this training include cycling, swimming, exercise classes (aerobics), running and jogging. Many sports centres and gyms have specialized machines that adapt to continuous training. Treadmills, exercise bikes, rowing machines and steppers all lend themselves to this type of training. The activities are a good way of developing general fitness and can be adapted to suit both individuals and groups of people. If running is the exercise chosen, then it is inexpensive to start: changing the place of training is easily arranged to add interest to the session.

How the training principles apply

After several training sessions, the body will have adapted to the strains of the exercise.

Marathon runners use continuous training within their training programme.

Checking the pulse rate during exercise will show if it is in the 60 to 80 per cent zone, showing that the heart has become stronger as a result of the exercise. The speed of the exercise should be increased, in order to get the pulse rate into the target zone so the training continues to have an effect on the performer.

For the more advanced performer, greater stresses and demands are made on their body. By keeping in the training zone of 80 to 90 per cent of their maximum heart rate and working for 15 to 20 minutes, the training will be effective. An endurance athlete, such as a marathon runner, would use this method as part of their training programme.

Task 3

1 – Write six facts about continuous training.

2 – How can the training method be adapted for beginners and more competitive performers?

Think about: how hard the body works, what effect the exercise has on the heart, what types of activity can adapt to this method and who would use this method of training.

Circuit training

About the training method
Circuit training is a series of exercises, completed for a certain amount of time, after one another.

What the training develops
Circuit training can be useful in different ways. Depending on how the circuit is set up, it can develop power, strength, flexibility and endurance. At a basic level, it can improve the general fitness of the heart and lungs as long as the rests in between the activities are kept short. It can be adapted to incorporate skills for a particular game. Top-class performers, however, do not benefit much from circuit training, as it does not allow them to achieve a high enough level of skill.

Circuit training can develop aerobic and anaerobic respiration. When using large muscle groups at each station (moving the whole body), aerobic respiration is in operation and this will develop the cardiovascular system. If exercising small muscle groups (such as the biceps and triceps) in turn at the stations, this is anaerobic respiration, which builds strength.

How the method works
A circuit is made up of several activities. Each activity is given its own space in the gym or sports hall; this space is called a station. Each activity is completed as many times as possible, these are called repetitions. There is a set time for each activity; this is usually between 30 and 60 seconds. In this time as many repetitions of the activity are performed as possible. When all exercises at each station are completed, the circuit is finished. By repeating the circuit or adding exercises, the session increases in intensity. For general fitness the sequence of exercises works different muscle groups at each station. Whether a beginner or not, three circuits is usually enough.

Circuit training can be used in different ways. For example, working in pairs, one person performs the activity whilst the other counts and records their partner's score. The roles are then swapped and the activity repeated: this is good for beginners as there is plenty of recovery time. Another activity relates to targets. At each station a training card is used, showing several different levels with different numbers of repetitions required to achieve that level. Each performer is either allocated a card or chooses the level at which to work. If the target is reached within the stipulated time the performer rests and waits at the station for the remaining time. This variation requires the performer to be aware of their ability, which will influence the chosen level of performance. The performer can increase the intensity by working at a higher level when the circuit is repeated. The final activity, the pyramid circuit, involves the performer taking different amounts of time to complete each station: the first station round is to be completed in 30 seconds, the second round in 20 seconds and the final round in 10 seconds. This variation suits fit and experienced athletes as the intensity of repetitions is increased.

A graph to show the change in pulse rate of a 16 year old during circuit training.

Above 80% of maximum heart rate — Training zone

Threshold of training

60–80% of maximum heart rate

Target zone

Threshold of training

Resting heart rate

Heartbeats per minute

Time in minutes

The exercises involved

Circuit training can be adapted to different sporting activities by including exercises that can be repeated and match the skills of the chosen sport. If an activity requires a dominance of leg strength then more stations can include exercises working the lower limbs: skiing would suit such adaptation.

How the training principles apply

A circuit can be set for individual needs. Each person doing the circuit can have their own targets but completing the circuit three times would be the minimum target. The third circuit is the one when a person's fitness will be visible. This means that beginners and fitter people can work at the same time because they can work within the same time limits, but they each complete a different number of repetitions. Completing a circuit can be competitive and motivate people to work harder and achieve more repetitions. Even with inexpensive equipment, a successful general fitness circuit can be set up.

Circuit training in school.

Active challenge

Cover the numbered list below without reading it. With a partner, study the circuit training illustration on page 85 and try to name some of the exercises in the circuit. Make additions to the list of exercises from your own experience.

1. Step-ups
2. Skipping
3. Sit-ups
4. Bench lifts

5. Bench astrides
6. Leg raises
7. Push-ups
8. Squats

9. Star jumps
10. Shuttle runs

Task 4

1 – List the advantages and disadvantages of circuit training.

2 – Look again at the circuit training illustration. Change four exercises from general fitness to skills using a named sport.

3 – How can a circuit be adapted to progressive overload?

> Choose skills from a sport. Are the skills able to be repeated in the same way? Place them in the circuit.

Weight training

About the training method
Weight training involves shifting weight to increase the strength of muscles, using a programme of repetitions and sets.

What the training develops
A person setting up a weight training programme needs to think about the following questions: what is the reason for doing the training? Is it for aerobic (endurance) or anaerobic (strength) development? Which parts of the body are to be exercised? The answers to these questions will shape the whole programme.

Weight training machines are always set up and fully adjustable.

Weightlifting can develop different types of strength. Lifting lighter weights many times develops muscular endurance so uses aerobic respiration. This way of adapting weight training can help a person who is rehabilitating after injury. By moving light weights, the muscles gradually get used to working and taking weight again in a safe and controlled way. This adaptation to the method would also suit long-distance athletes.

Lifting heavy weights with few repetitions develops strength and power. This will build up strength, increase muscle size and use anaerobic respiration. Long jumpers, javelin throwers and sprinters would use this adaptation.

Lifting medium to high numbers of repetitions and shifting medium to high weights builds strength and increases the size of the muscles and uses aerobic respiration. Rugby players would benefit from this combination.

Lifting maximum weights in a single repetition builds strength. A shot-putter would benefit from this combination. This uses anaerobic respiration.

Rest and recovery times are essential for a weight lifter. The length and frequency of the sessions have a bearing on the effort applied:

- the athlete's weight – a heavier athlete usually lifts heavier weights
- the athlete's condition – strength of the muscles
- whether large or small muscle groups are used – small muscle groups can require more recovery time
- the loads shifted in the session – different loads can require different recovery times; heavier loads take longer to recover from
- the type of strength developed – whether endurance or strength training (an aerobic or aerobic); aerobic work takes longer to recover from

Usually two days' rest is needed between sessions, especially when muscular endurance is the type of strength being developed, as it takes this long for glycogen levels to be restored.

The time for recovery allows:

- energy reserves to be replenished in the muscles
- muscle tears to be repaired
- tissue to be regenerated
- water loss to be replenished.

How the method works

A weight training session relies on good testing to find the correct level of intensity at which to work. Keeping to the planned number of repetitions and sets is important for a safe, appropriate training session. Often, the space and equipment used for the sessions is shared by others, so some coordination and flexibility in the order of the exercises may be necessary.

When organizing a weight training programme:

Number of exercises – the usual range is between 8 and 12.

Assess – the performer's strength and fitness. Once the maximum a person can lift is known, the programme can start to develop.

Safety factors – use of straps, adjustments to the seats, setting the correct weight and correct technique are essential for safe weight training.

Review – when the body has adapted to the stresses of the programme, changes are made. The strength of the performer is re-tested. If the programme has been set at the right level, the performer will have increased in strength.

Repetitions – complete 12 to 17 repetitions at 60 to 70% of maximum lifting ability for an anaerobic beginner. Use many repetitions for lighter, aerobic work.

Weights – light for aerobic (endurance) heavier for anaerobic (strength and size).

Rest between sets – about two minutes.

New programme – changes are made to the programme. As a result, a combination of weights, repetitions and sets increases slightly.

Number of sets – a beginner might complete one set for anaerobic, building up to two sets after two weeks. More repetitions are completed for aerobic training.

Training to get the best results – speed of exercise for greatest benefit: lifting and lowering takes two seconds for greatest benefit.

Number of sessions per week – three to four sessions every other week should show an improvement with up to 48 hours between each session.

Examples of weight training cards:

% of maximum lift	Repetitions
60%	17
65%	14
70%	12
75%	10
80%	8
85%	6
90%	5
95%	3
100%	1

Good for beginners.
Complete one set of above.
After three weeks, increase sets.

Weight training repetitions – the performer works through the card from 60 to 100 per cent in a session. (If 160kg is the maximum weight a person can lift then 60 per cent is 96kg, so the 96kg lift is repeated 17 times.)

Lift 70% of max.
Eight repetitions
Three sets completed

Good for beginner.
Level of effort required means weights are lifted properly.
Little risk of injury.

Simple sets – the performer works at the same intensity throughout the session completing three sets of eight repetitions.

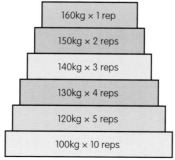

Pyramid sets – the performer starts at the easiest weight, working their way to heavy weights, but with fewer repetitions.

The exercises involved

There are two ways of training:

MACHINE WEIGHTS Using machines can be a safer way of weight training. They are technically designed to move in the correct way and are adjustable for different sizes of user. They are safe as they are steady and do not vary position apart from the designed range. However, this also has the effect of not training the stabilizing muscles that may be needed for a sport. Machine weights usually have supports and belts to make sure the body is prepared in the correct position to shift the weight. They are always set up, so are ready to use. Users starting a weight training programme find them easy to work. One drawback is that extra weights cannot be added to the machines: this limits their use for the advanced performer.

The following photos show examples of machine weights.

Seated leg extensions.

Hamstring curls.

Bicep curls.

FREE WEIGHTS Free weights can be used in a weight training programme. The use of such weights is specialized and needs lots of training so that the performer works safely. Many top sportspeople use free weights. A person training with heavy weights must always use a spotter; this is a person who helps steady the performer and is ready to catch the bar or assist if the performer is struggling.

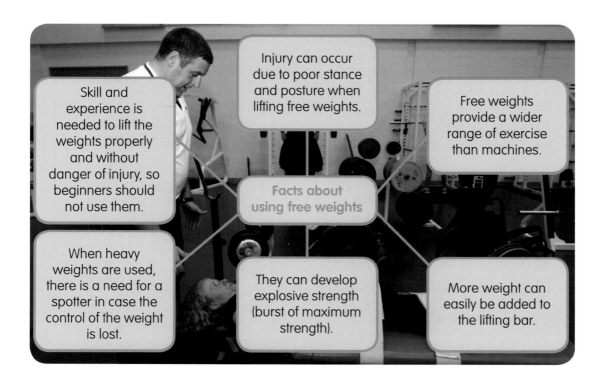

Skill and experience is needed to lift the weights properly and without danger of injury, so beginners should not use them.

Injury can occur due to poor stance and posture when lifting free weights.

Free weights provide a wider range of exercise than machines.

Facts about using free weights

When heavy weights are used, there is a need for a spotter in case the control of the weight is lost.

They can develop explosive strength (burst of maximum strength).

More weight can easily be added to the lifting bar.

How the training principles apply

With both types of weight training method, regular training improves the muscles' ability to move the weight. As the body adapts, the progressive overload and FITT principles are applied and the weights, repetitions and sets are gradually increased. This allows improvement of the muscles to continue. Lifting 60 to 80 per cent of the maximum weight a person is able to lift will keep the performer within the target zone. Each session should last for no longer than 45 minutes.

A weight-training card helps the performer to train safely and see progress.

Name:	Personal trainer:		Date programme started:	
Visits	1 2 3 4 5 6 7 8		9 10 11 12 13 14	
Warm-up option	Jog 5 mins	Cycle 5 mins	Easy row 5 mins	Stepper 5 mins
Then:	Stretches	Arms/shoulders	Legs/hips	Abdominals
Exercise	Starting point	Progression 1	Progression 2	Progression 3
Tricep pulldowns				
Squats				
Hip flexors				
Lateral pulldown				
Hamstring curls				
Hip extensors				
Bench presses				
Seated leg extensions				
Cool-down options	Walk/jog 5 mins	Easy cycle 5 mins	Easy row 5 mins	
Finish with stretches				

Task 5

1 – What makes each weight-training session different?

2 – How do free weight training sessions compare to machine weight training sessions?

> The training principles change in the sessions. When comparing each type, think of the special features each method has.

Fartlek training

About the training method

Fartlek is a Swedish word meaning 'speed play'. **Fartlek training** involves exercise, often running, varying in time, distance and effort.

What the training develops

Due to the changes of intensity of the exercises, Fartlek training works on both aerobic and anaerobic fitness so the athlete becomes increasingly capable of meeting the changes of pace in a competition or game.

How the method works

Speed, distances covered and the amount of time spent exercising change. In general, the session has work of varying intensity taking place over a minimum of a 20-minute period. Fartlek can be an introduction to interval training and sometimes both can be combined to form a programme of exercise, owing to their similar content.

This method of training would suit a games player. The type of exercise should be adapted to suit the movements in a game. The speed will vary and the direction of movement should vary too. Players in most games will backtrack and change direction so running backwards and slalom running will be important factors to include.

The content of the session is flexible. Therefore, the repetitions in the sessions are made different to add interest to the training. Rest periods or less strenuous exercise gives time to recover so training can continue. For example, in a 45-minute session:

0–15 minutes	Warm-up Sprint 10 seconds on flat Jog on flat Sprint 10 seconds uphill Jog/walk downhill then on flat Run 150m on flat for one minute Jog Sprint 80m on flat
15–35 minutes	Jog Sprint 20m uphill Jog downhill then on flat Sprint 10 seconds on flat Jog/walk uphill Jog/run downhill then on flat Sprint 10 seconds uphill Jog/run downhill then on flat
35–45 minutes	Cool-down

The exercises involved

Sprints, jogs and runs make up the session. These may have times set for them or may be for a certain distance. The session can be continuous with periods of intense work followed by easier work, which gives the body chance to recover. Sometimes the session can include periods of complete rest.

In Sweden, where this method originated, athletes use the surrounding hills and forests to train in. Many areas large enough to run in can be used to vary the training session such as in a park, at the beach and in the countryside. Fartlek training can be adapted to running, cycling and swimming.

How the training principles apply
The FITT principle adapts to keep the performer improving.

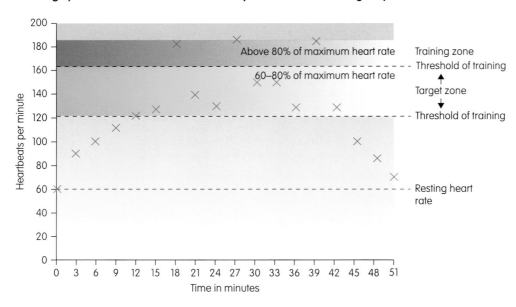

A graph to show how the heart rate of a 16 year old rises and falls regularly in a fartlek session.

Task 6

Devise your own Fartlek training session using the terrain in your local area. The session should last for 20 minutes.

Remember, the session should have a warm-up and a cool-down.

Cross training

About the training method
Cross training combines different methods of training and is adaptable to a variety of situations.

What the training develops
Each activity improves different muscle groups giving a wide range of development for the body.

How the method works

By changing the activity, parts of the body are able to rest and this prevents overuse injury. The variety of sessions can make training more interesting. Cross training can be adapted to suit individuals: a person may choose to run, play a game or do some aerobics work.

Cross training can be used for developing general fitness, but also serious triathletes would use this method so all aspects of their event were developed. This method allows individuals to work on their own or in a group. For those working in a group, as the activities change the groupings can change (which can widen the number of people a person knows as they train with a different group for each activity). Weather does not stop training as the sessions can be changed: an indoor session can be completed instead of an outdoor one.

James Willstrop, a top British squash player could follow a cross training programme as part of his training plan.

A graph showing pulse rate changes in a 16 year old using continuous training as part of a cross training programme.

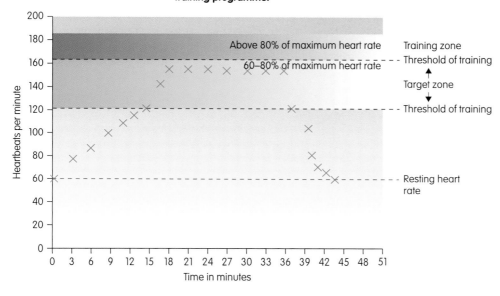

A graph showing pulse rate changes in a 16 year old playing football for 30 minutes, as part of a cross training programme.

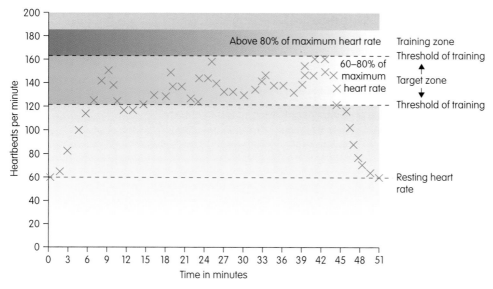

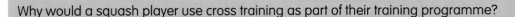

Task 7

Why would a squash player use cross training as part of their training programme?

The exercises involved

Exercises for cross training include running, swimming, cycling, a chosen game and aerobics.

How the training principles apply

Like the other methods of training, the FITT principle can be applied. As the performer adapts to the training, the sessions are gradually made harder, so that further progress can be made.

Task 8

Write three statements a person may make about the each of the following training methods:

a. Fartlek training **b.** Continuous training **c.** Cross training

> Make their statements about the nature of the methods, which sportspeople would use them and any advantages or disadvantages there might be in using them. You could use speech marks as though the person is actually saying the statements.

Key terms

PAR-Q – Physical Activity Readiness Questionnaire

Methods of training – interval training, continuous training, circuit training, weight training, Fartlek training, cross training

Interval training – mixing periods of hard exercise with rest periods

Oxygen debt – the amount of oxygen consumed during activity above that which would ordinarily have been consumed in the same time at rest (this results in a shortfall in the oxygen available)

Continuous training – aerobic exercising, at a moderate to high level, with no rests

Training threshold – the boundaries of the target zone

Circuit training – a series of exercises completed in order and for a certain time

Weight training – progressively lifting heavier weights or lifting weights more often to improve strength

Fartlek training – 'speed play', changing speed, distances and times of exercise in the same session

Cross training – using different training methods in the same session

3 — Understanding the exercise session

An exercise session consists of a:

- warm-up – preparing the body for work
- main activity – the activity, match or competition
- cool-down – preparing the body to return to rest.

Warm-up

A warm-up should precede any physical activity, whether training or competing. Although there are definite phases to all warm-ups, they should be relevant and appropriate to the sport in question. Sport-specific warm-ups are essential, each has its own skills, techniques and actions so that appropriate muscles and parts of the body are prepared for hard work.

Reasons for warm-up:
1. Gradually increases the heart rate to nearer the working rate.
2. Gradually increases body temperature to nearer the working rate.
3. Gradually moves the muscles and joints in ways that will be used in the competition.
4. Introduces skills to be used in the competition.
5. Increases intensity so that the body is prepared for competitive speed.
6. Systematically working through the routine will prepare the performer's mind for the competition – this may give them a better start than the opposition.
7. Allows players to work in small groups in the way they will in the game.

The following types of movement should be included in a warm-up:

- pulse raisers
- stretch and flexibility phase
- skills and intensive exercise phase.

PULSE RAISERS   Pulse raising activities aim to gradually raise the heart rate and warm up large muscle groups. Activities can include jogging, side stepping and bouncing on the spot.

STRETCH AND FLEXIBILITY PHASE   The stretch and flexibility phase eases the muscles and joints into positions appropriate to the activity. These can be static, assisted and/or dynamic.

Athletes using static stretches ease the muscle gradually into the stretched position and hold it there for 10 seconds. Assisted stretching is when the action is helped by pushing against another person or a wall. A specialized way of stretching is often used in gymnastics and football.

A warm-up precedes all intensive work, whether training or competing.

A coach using PNF stretching.

Here, the coach helps the performer by pushing the limb and so stretching the joint further. These are called proprioceptive neuromuscular facilitation (PNF) techniques. These should only be undertaken by an expert and with great care.

Dynamic stretches are the most complex to perform. Care needs to be taken as injury can occur if these are misused. The athlete moves into the stretch position and 'bounces' the muscle. This starts at half pace for two to three repetitions and gradually increases to full speed. These movements are used when the event or activity needs rapid, explosive movement.

Flexibility exercises increase the mobility of the joints of the body – rotating shoulders and hips, for example. Each joint should be given some time, although certain sports may need some joints warmed more than others.

After the pulse raisers, static stretches should follow in a warm-up.

SKILLS AND INTENSIVE EXERCISE PHASE   The skills and intensive exercise phase of the warm-up contains slow stretching of muscles beyond normal position, which are held for short periods of time.

Including basic skills related to the sport in the warm-up can help coordination in the game. The exercises gradually increase in intensity. If the sport includes times when bursts of pace are necessary then, at the end of the warm-up session, some short sprints can be included. By warming-up, a person will increase their awareness and reaction time ready for the game. Preparing the body will increase the level of work the person is capable of producing in the event. Note that professional football teams have set warm-ups, which they perform on the pitch before a match.

Main activity

The warm-up leads to the main activity. This can be a training session, skills session or a competition, match or performance. Once the body systems are trained they become fit enough to complete the skills practiced. When the body is pushed to the limit in competition, the skills can be put to the test without breaking down because of inadequate fitness levels.

Cool-down

There are two phases to the cool-down: gentle aerobic and stretching. After the main activity, the body is given the chance of gradually returning to its resting state; the gentle aerobic cool-down helps to do this. In this phase the heart has a chance to gradually slow down and the muscles to relax. By completing a cool-down, the heartbeat reaches its resting rate sooner; this is called the recovery time. The heart, therefore, does not have to work too hard for longer than it needs to. The speed of the recovery rate is influenced by several factors:

- The older a person is, the slower the recovery rate will be.
- If the exercise is new, then the new stresses will be harder to recover from.
- How 'in shape' the performer is: the fitter a person is, the quicker the recovery.
- Women tend to recover more slowly than men.

Like the warm-up, there is no set time for a cool-down. By keeping the blood circulating it does not have the chance to 'pool' or collect in areas of the circulatory system; this prevents light-headedness.

Gentle stretching stops the build-up of lactic acid in the muscles and so prevents immediate cramp and aching and soreness the following day (known as DOMS – delayed onset muscle soreness). Stretches in a cool-down should be held for about 30 seconds and should concentrate on the muscles used in the event. Freestyle swimmers will concentrate on cooling down their arms; runners will stretch their legs. A controlled, restful cool-down can have a calming effect on a person after the excitement of a competitive match.

Gentle jogging helps the body to slow down gradually, preventing blood pooling.

Task 9

1 – Give three reasons why a warm-up helps a performer.

2 – List three types of exercise that would be included in a warm-up.

3 – Draw a spider diagram of the main points and reasons for a cool-down.

4 — Using the principles in an exercise programme

What is a Personal Exercise Programme?

A Personal Exercise Programme (PEP) is a series of exercises put together for a particular person. The exercise sessions follow all the guidelines of the principles of training to make them safe and suitable for the performer. To be effective, the PEP should be performed regularly and over a period of weeks. There will come a time when the programme is physically too easy to have an effect on the performer. This can happen in about week five or six of the programme. At this stage, reviewing the programme is necessary. By applying the principles of training, the programme may be made more demanding.

Link the PEP with the effects of exercise

The following diagram shows how the PEP develops. It always starts with individual needs and capabilities, moving on to the planning, performing and then to the reviewing. The review of the programme is most important if progress is to continue to be made. Retesting the individual will show how their body has adapted to the programme. Increasing the FITT principle according to the results will ensure further progress.

Look at the individual and consider:

- Test results of health-related exercise and skill-related fitness components
- Cardio results (resting heart rate)
- Respiratory results (VO$_2$ max)
- Body composition (how much of the body is fat, muscle and bone?)
- Which exercises they prefer
- Whether they like training on their own or in a group.

Plan and perform the programme, choosing from a variety of training methods:

- Interval
- Continuous
- Circuit
- Weights
- Fartlek
- Cross.

Devising a PEP

Review programme by applying the FITT principles of training:

- Increase how many times individual trains – frequency
- Increase the intensity
- Increase time exercising
- Vary the type of exercise.

What is the purpose of the PEP?

- General health
- Sport-specific
- Rehabilitation
- Strength improvement
- Flexibility
- Muscular endurance.

A personal exercise programme can be adapted to help a person:

- achieve health-related exercise components
- improve skill-related fitness.

The following guides should be followed to achieve an improved fitness level:

- three to five sessions a week
- at least 20 minutes duration
- heart rate above 60 per cent of maximum.

Active challenge

Design your own proforma to record your weekly physical activity.

For the serious athlete the PEP should be more demanding. The principles of training will be applied to the programme and the related activity to a greater intensity.

Task 10

1 – Using the ideas from the above spider diagram, write your own action plan of how a PEP should be organized.

2 – Devise your own PEP using your knowledge. Record your strategy in writing.

5 — Health-related component testing

There are two types of health-related component testing:

1. Health-related exercise testing
2. Skill-related fitness testing.

Health-related exercise testing

Cardiovascular endurance testing

Having strong and efficient heart and lungs will help a player keep working hard throughout a game without losing breath and lowering performance. The Harvard Step Test and Cooper's 12-minute run test are two other methods of measuring cardiovascular endurance. These tests use pulse and frequency rate as the indicators of fitness.

COOPER'S 12-MINUTE RUN TEST This test uses pulse rates as an indicator of cardiovascular fitness as it measures the athlete's endurance capabilities.

Equipment needed

- Athletics track
- Marker cones
- Recording sheets
- Pen
- Stopwatch

How it works

1. Athletes run for 12 minutes.
2. They cover as much distance as they can.
3. Marker cones are placed around the track to aid in measuring the distance covered.
4. Walking is allowed but performers are encouraged to push themselves as hard as they can.
5. The distance covered is recorded for each athlete.

Cooper's 12-minute run test results table for adult males	
Rating	**Distance (metres)**
Excellent	>2700
Good	2300–2700
Average	1900–2300
Below average	1500–1900
Poor	<1500

Active challenge

Find the Cooper's 12-minute run test on the Internet and then write out the protocol for administering the test.

HARVARD STEP TEST   This test uses pulse rates as an indicator of cardiovascular fitness as it measures the athlete's endurance capabilities.

Equipment needed

- Standard gym bench
- Recording sheet
- Pen
- Stopwatch
- Assistant

How it works

1. Athlete steps up onto gym bench once every two seconds for a period of five minutes (150 steps).
2. Help with keeping to the pace may be necessary.
3. One minute after the test take pulse and record = Pulse 1.
4. Two minutes after test take pulse and record = Pulse 2.
5. Three minutes after test take pulse and record = Pulse 3.
6. Calculate the result by applying the following equation:

$$\frac{30{,}000}{\text{the sum of the three pulse readings}}$$

Normative data for the Harvard Step Test					
Gender	Poor	Below average	Average	Above average	Excellent
Male	<55	55–64	65–79	80–90	>90
Female	<50	50–60	61–75	76–86	>86

Source: McArdle W.D et al; Essentials of Exercise Physiology: 2000

Task 11

1 – Choose an appropriate sport.

2 – Using the sport you have chosen, answer this question: what is good cardiovascular endurance?

3 – Give two examples of how good cardiovascular endurance improves the performance of the activity.

The difference between muscular strength and muscular endurance

Muscular strength and muscular endurance are similar, but not the same. Strength is the ability to shift a weight and muscular endurance is the ability to shift weight repeatedly, or over a long period of time. When an activity takes place over a long period it uses muscular endurance; for short, explosive events muscular strength is necessary. Team games use a combination of both types.

Muscular endurance testing

Performers working for lengthy periods need muscular endurance so they can keep their skill level high throughout the game.

TREADMILL TEST There are several different treadmill tests which evaluate muscular endurance. One such test is the Bruce Treadmill VO_2 test.

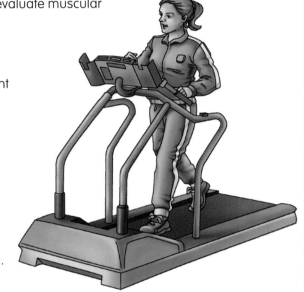

Equipment needed

- A treadmill with speed and gradient adjusters
- Stopwatch
- Record sheet
- Pen
- Assistant

How it works

1. The assistant starts the stopwatch.
2. Treadmill starts at 2.74 km and at a ten per cent gradient.
3. At certain times the speed and gradient are increased (see table below).
4. The athlete runs on the treadmill until exhausted.
5. Assistant stops the stopwatch when the athlete stops running.
6. The time is recorded.

Treadmill Test timings

Stage	Time (in minutes)	Speed (km per hour)	Gradient (%)
1	0	2.74	10
2	3	4.02	12
3	6	5.47	14
4	9	6.76	16
5	12	8.05	18
6	15	8.85	20
7	18	9.65	22
8	21	10.46	24
9	24	11.26	26
10	27	12.07	28

Another test for muscular endurance is the press-up test.

Active challenge

Find the press-up test on the Internet and write out the protocol for its administration.

Muscular strength testing

Muscular strength is the muscles' ability to apply force and overcome resistance.

HAND GRIP STRENGTH TEST The hand grip dynamometer measures the force generated by the performer's hand in one grip action. This is an easy test to administer and is used as a measurement of general strength.

Equipment needed

- Hand grip dynamometer
- Record sheet
- Pen

How it works

1. Adjust the hand grip dynamometer to the size of the performer's hand – this is important as the accuracy of the adjustment will affect the results.
2. Performer grips the dynamometer with dominant hand.
3. The arm hangs by the side with dynamometer in line with the forearm.
4. Maximum grip strength is applied without any swinging of the arm.
5. The performer has two attempts for each hand result.
6. Best results are added together and divided by two to reach a score.

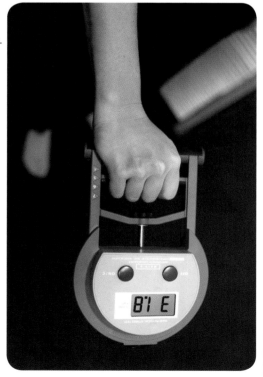

A hand grip dynamometer with the performer's arm by their side.

Hand grip strength test results		
Rating	**Male (kg)**	**Female (kg)**
Excellent	>64	>38
Very good	56–64	34–38
Above average	52–56	30–34
Average	48–52	26–30
Below average	44–48	22–26
Poor	40–44	20–22
Very poor	<40	<20

Flexibility testing

Players need to move their joints to their full range without hurting themselves. In football, tackling effectively needs flexibility. The sit and reach flexibility test is the most common test for flexibility.

SIT AND REACH FLEXIBILITY TEST

Equipment needed

- Indoor area
- Wooden block or bench
- Measure

How it works

1. Person sits, straight-legged, with feet touching the start of the measuring block.
2. They reach forward and place their hands on the block to be measured.
3. If they reach as far as their toes this measures 0cm, beyond their toes is +0cm and if it is not as far as their toes it is –0cm.
4. A recorder measures the distance along the block that the hands reach.

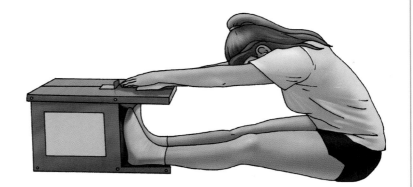

Sit and reach flexibility test results table (cm)

Rating	Male	Female
Super	>+27	>+30
Excellent	+17 to +27	+21 to +30
Good	+6 to +16	+11 to +20
Average	0 to +5	+1 to +10
Fair	–8 to –1	–7 to 0
Poor	–19 to –9	–14 to –8
Very poor	<–19	<–14

Another test for flexibility is the shoulder hypertension test.

Task 12

1 – Choose either muscular strength or flexibility and write down how you would recognize accomplishment in your chosen health-related exercise component.

2 – Choose a sport and give two examples of how your choice improves the skills and performance of the activity.

Skill-related fitness testing

Agility testing

Agility is the ability to change direction quickly and still keep the body under control. This component of skill-related fitness is needed in most games, gymnastics and skiing.

ILLINOIS AGILITY RUN TEST

Equipment needed

- Flat surface to set the course: approximately 15m x 8m
- Eight cones
- Stopwatch
- Recorder
- Recording sheet
- Pen

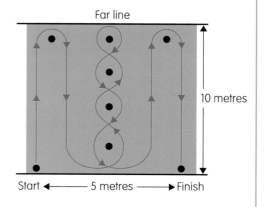

Far line

10 metres

Start ◄—— 5 metres ——► Finish

How it works

1. The performer begins by lying face down on the floor at the starting point.
2. On the whistle, the performer jumps to their feet and makes their way around the course to the finish.
3. A stopwatch is used to time how long it takes to reach the finish.

Illinois Agility Run test results table for 16 year olds					
Gender	Excellent	Above average	Average	Below average	Poor
Male	<15.9 secs	15.9–16.7 secs	16.8–17.6 secs	17.7–18.8 secs	>18.8 secs
Female	<17.5 secs	17.5–18.6 secs	18.7–22.4 secs	22.5–23.4 secs	>23.4 secs

Balance

Balance is the ability to keep the body stable whether still, moving or in different shapes by keeping the centre of gravity over the base.

STANDING STORK TEST

Equipment needed

- Any warm and dry space
- Stopwatch
- Recorder
- Recording sheet
- Pen

How it works

1. The performer stands upright on both feet in a comfortable position with their hands placed on their hips.
2. One leg is lifted and the toes of that foot are placed on the knee of the other leg.
3. When directed to do so the performer raises the heel of their standing foot and stands on their toes.
4. At the same time the stopwatch is started.
5. The performer balances for as long as possible without putting their heel on the ground or moving the other foot away from the knee.
6. A record is made of how long the balance was held.
7. The test is repeated using the other leg.

Standing stork test results table for 15 to 16 year olds

Poor	Below average	Average	Above average	Excellent
<11 secs	11–25 secs	26–39 secs	40–49 secs	>50 secs

Task 13

1 – Choose either agility or balance and write down how you would recognize accomplishment in your choice of skill-related fitness component.

2 – Choose a sport and give two examples of how your choice of skill-related fitness component improves the skills and performance of the activity.

For example: agility in netball
1. Wing Attack changing direction to dodge marker.
2. Goal Defence changing direction, turning and moving to recover shot off the netball post's ring.

Coordination

The ability to use two or more body parts together. It can also be defined as the ability to carry out a series of movements smoothly and efficiently.

THREE BALL JUGGLE There are several different juggling tests used to test your coordination. This activity could be done in pairs, to time how long it takes everyone to learn how to juggle. The results of the class can be used to devise a rating scale.

Equipment needed

- Three juggling balls
- Record sheet
- Pen
- Assistant
- Stopwatch

How it works

1. Hold two juggling balls in the dominant hand and one juggling ball in the weaker hand.
2. Throw one juggling ball from the dominant hand to the weaker hand.
3. When this first ball reaches its highest point, throw the ball from the weaker hand to the dominant hand so the second ball passes underneath the first ball.
4. Catch the first ball in the less dominant hand.
5. One ball should now be in each hand with one in the air.
6. Throw the next ball from the dominant hand and catch the airborne ball.
7. Keep repeating these instructions.
8. The recorder should record the number of repetitions.

Task 14

1 – Write down which test you would use to recognize coordination accomplishment.

2 – Choose a sport and give two examples of how coordination improves the skills and performance of the activity.

3 – Work together in a small group: one person conducts the test, the rest take the test.

4 – Collate your results and create a bar chart.

Power/explosive strength testing

Explosive leg strength is vital to athletes and games players needing to jump, whether it is for distance or height. The Sergeant Jump test and the standing broad jump test measure leg strength.

SERGEANT JUMP TEST

Equipment needed

- Indoor area
- Measuring tape
- Chalk
- Recorder
- Recording sheet
- Pen

How it works

1. The performer stands sideways to a wall.
2. While standing with feet flat, the performer reaches up with their arm nearest to the wall.
3. The height where the stretched fingers reach is measured.
4. Standing slightly away from the wall (for safety), the performer jumps vertically, as high as possible, using arms and legs for maximum height.
5. They touch the wall at the highest point possible (by chalking the fingers first a clear mark is left to measure).
6. The distance between the two measures is recorded.
7. The performer has three attempts.

Sergeant Jump test results table		
Rating	**Male (cm)**	**Female (cm)**
Excellent	>70	>60
Very good	61–70	51–60
Above average	51–60	41–50
Average	41–50	31–40
Below average	31–40	21–30
Poor	21–30	11–20
Very poor	<21	<11

Standing Board Jump

Equipment needed

- Long jump pit
- Tape measure
- Record sheet
- Pen
- Assistant recorder
- Teacher/coach measurers

How it works

1. The athlete positions themselves at the end of the sandpit.
2. The athlete should stand with both feet together and with feet up to the edge.
3. They then crouch, lean forward, swing their arms for momentum to jump as far horizontally into the sandpit as possible.
4. They land with both feet into the sand.
5. The start of the jump must be from a static position.
6. A measurement should be taken from the edge of the sandpit to the nearest point of contact into the sand.

Standing board jump results table for 15 to 16 year old athletes					
	Excellent	**Above average**	**Average**	**Below average**	**Poor**
Male	>2.01m	2.00–1.86m	1.85–1.76m	1.75–1.65m	<1.65m
Female	>1.66m	1.65–1.56m	1.55–1.46m	1.45–1.35m	<1.35cm

Source: Brianmac

Reaction time

The time it takes for a performer to react to a stimulus is a simple reaction time. When a performer is presented with two stimuli, each requiring a different response, this is choice reaction time. The ruler drop test measures simple reaction time.

RULER DROP TEST

Equipment needed

- One 1m ruler
- Recording sheet
- An assistant
- Pen

How it works

1. The assistant holds the ruler, with arm outstretched.
2. The ruler is between the outstretched thumb and finger of the assistant's dominant hand.
3. The performer's thumb is level with the '0' on the ruler.
4. The assistant instructs the performer to catch the ruler between the thumb and finger as soon as the ruler is released.
5. The assistant records the distance between the bottom of the ruler and the top of the performer's thumb at the point of the catch.

Ruler drop test table of results: national norms for 16 to 19 year olds	
Excellent	<7.5cm
Above average	7.5–15.9cm
Average	15.9–20.4cm
Below average	20.4–28cm
Poor	>28cm

Task 15

1 – Choose either power or reaction time.

2 – Write down how you would recognize accomplishment in your choice of skill-related fitness component.

3 – Choose a sport and give two examples of how your choice improves the skills and performance of the activity.

For example: Reaction time – football
1. Attacker in the six-yard box reacting to the keeper spilling the ball and moving quickly to kick the ball to score.
2. Keeper moving and diving quickly to save a power shot struck in the 18-yard box.

Speed

Speed is the fastest rate at which a person can complete a task or cover a distance. Most sports rely on a performer to move the whole body at speed, so tests for this type of speed are appropriate.

30-METRE SPRINT

Equipment needed

- Flat, even running surface
- 30m tape measure
- Two cones
- Stopwatch
- Recording sheet
- Pen

How it works

1. A 30m straight is measured out.
2. Performer sets off as quickly as possible from a standing start.
3. At the same time the stopwatch starts.
4. Performer sprints to the finishing line as quickly as possible.
5. As performer crosses finishing point the stopwatch is stopped.
6. Time recorded to 100th/sec.

30-metre sprint national norms for 16 to 19 year olds (measured in seconds)

	Male	Female
Excellent	<4.1	<4.6
Above average	4.3–4.1	4.7–4.6
Average	4.5–4.4	4.9–4.8
Below average	4.7–4.6	5.1–4.10
Poor	>4.7	>5.1

Task 16

1 – Choose either speed or strength and write down how you would recognize accomplishment in your choice.

2 – Choose a sport and give two examples of how your choice improves the skills and performance of the activity.

6 — Heart rate and exercise

Heart rate changes according to the level of activity undertaken. When at rest, the rate slows as there are few working muscles demanding the need for oxygen. The average resting heart rate is 72 beats per minute. When exercise takes place and increases, the heart rate increases too. There are three stages when the heart rate indicates the level of exercise and fitness:

1. Resting
2. Working
3. Recovery.

The recovery rate is the time it takes for the heart to return to its resting state after exercise. The time it takes to return to the resting state can indicate the level of fitness of the performer – the quicker the recovery, the fitter the performer.

Active challenge

1 – Be prepared to do some physical exercise!

2 – In a group, follow these instructions:

- Sit or lay down for three minutes.
- After that time, take your resting heart rate.
- After a warm-up exercise go all-out for one minute – it could be step-ups using a bench.
- After the minute, stop and take your pulse immediately.
- Record this heart rate reading – this is your working heart rate.

- Remain inactive by sitting or laying still.
- Wait a minute.
- Take your pulse again and record it – this is the recovery rate.
- Continue to take your pulse every 30 seconds and record it until it matches your resting pulse rate. The time taken for your pulse to return to the resting pulse rate is your recovery rate.

3 – Plot your readings on a graph.

4 – Compare your results with others in the group and discuss why they differ.

Resting
Active
REcovery

The initial letters make the word RARE – this can help you learn the different rates.

Target zones and training thresholds

Keeping the pulse rate between 60 and 80 per cent of the maximum heart rate works the body in the target zone and trains the aerobic system. When the pulse rate reaches above 80 per cent of the maximum heart rate, the body is working in the training zone and training the anaerobic system.

Working above 60 per cent of the maximum heart rate will have beneficial effects to fitness. When working aerobically, in the target zone, fat will be burned. Athletes training continuously, just below the anaerobic threshold, will build up their lactic acid tolerance, allowing the body to continue exercising while coping with greater levels of lactic acid without muscular pain or fatigue.

A graph showing pulse rate changes in a 16 year old working just below the anaerobic threshold.

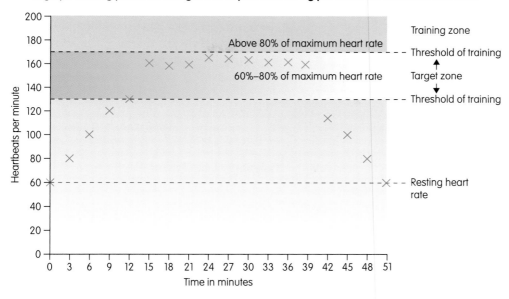

Key term

PEP – **Personal Exercise Programme**

Summary

For tests to be useful to the coach and the performer they should focus on the muscle groups and energy systems used in the activity for which the athlete is training. Each test should be carried out in the same way each time so that the results are reliable and can be compared to previous tests and recognized norms. The tester should be aware of the many variables that can affect the test results and measurements. Every attempt should be made to reconstruct the same conditions as for previous tests so the results are a true reflection of the development of the performer's fitness.

Exam questions

Multiple-choice questions

1. (a) Which of the following describes circuit training?

   ☐ A This method of training involves times of work followed by times of rest

   ☐ B A series of exercises, completed for a certain amount of time, after one another

   ☐ C Exercising, often running, varying time, distance and effort

   ☐ D Involves shifting weight to increase the strength of muscles, using a programme of repetitions and sets

   (1)

   (b) Which of the following describes interval training?

   ☐ A This method of training involves times of work followed by times of rest

   ☐ B A series of exercises, completed for a certain amount of time, after one another

   ☐ C Exercising, often running, varying time, distance and effort

   ☐ D Involves shifting weight to increase the strength of muscles, using a programme of repetitions and sets

   (1)

   (c) Which method would a sprinter most likely use to improve performance?

   ☐ A Weight training

   ☐ B Cross training

   ☐ C Interval training

   ☐ D Continuous training

   (1)

   (d) Which method of training is a triathlete most likely to use?

   ☐ A Cross training

   ☐ B Weight training

   ☐ C Circuit training

   ☐ D Fartlek training

   (1)

   (e) Fartlek training depends on varying:

   ☐ A The people in the training session

   ☐ B The sports played

   ☐ C The weights lifted

   ☐ D The time, distance and effort in the session

   (1)

2. Which of the following best describes the components of an exercise session?

   ☐ A Sprinting, competition, cool-down

   ☐ B Warm-up, main activity, competition

   ☐ C Main activity, competition, cool-down

   ☐ D Warm-up, main activity, cool-down

   (1)

3. Which of the following best describes the considerations to the individual when devising a personal exercise programme?

   ☐ A Resting heart rate, VO_2 maximum, preferred exercise, frequency

   ☐ B Body composition, resting heart rate, VO_2 maximum, preferred exercise

   ☐ C VO_2 maximum, preferred exercise, height, body composition

   ☐ D Motivation, VO_2 maximum, preferred exercise, frequency

   (1)

4. The following questions are related to the graph below.

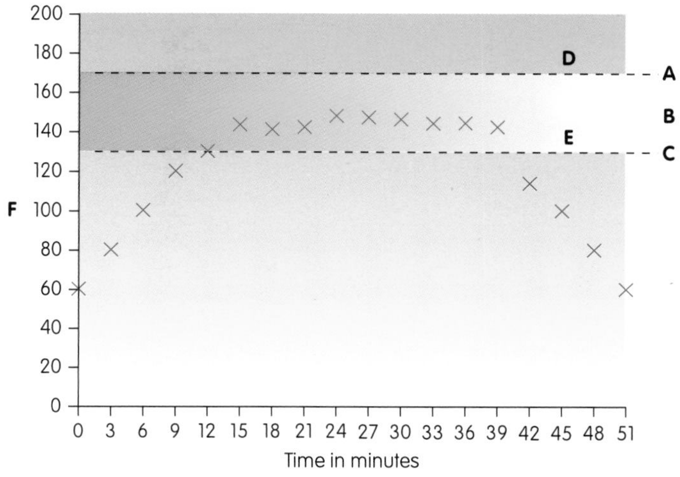

Time in minutes

(a) Which of the labels fits at A?

☐ A Training zone

☐ B Target zone

☐ C Threshold of training

☐ D 60–80% of heart rate

(1)

(b) Which of the labels fits at C?

☐ A Training zone

☐ B Target zone

☐ C Threshold of training

☐ D 60–80% of heart rate

(1)

5. Which training method does the recorded heartbeat indicate?

☐ A Interval training

☐ B Continuous training

☐ C Circuit training

☐ D Fartlek training

(1)

6. If the resting heart rate of the athlete is 60 bpm how long did it take to return to that rate after the exercise?

☐ A 10 minutes

☐ B 5 minutes

☐ C 24 minutes

☐ D 12 minutes

(1)

Short-answer questions

7. What is the average heart rate of an adult?

(1)

8. Which kind of respiration is used when lifting maximum weights?

(1)

9. What does the Harvard Step Test measure?

(1)

10. What test would you choose to test an athlete's flexibility?

(1)

Longer-answer questions

11. Interval training is used in training sessions and can be adapted to many activities. Devise an interval training session lasting 30 minutes for an activity of your choice.

(4)

12. Why would a performer use cross training in their training programme?

(4)

13. What test would be best suited to an outfield games player and why?

(3)

1.1 ~ Healthy, active lifestyles

1.1.5 Your personal health and well-being

What you will learn about in this topic:

1 — Diet, work and rest
2 — Requirements of a balanced diet
3 — Timing dietary intake with performance

1 — Diet, work and rest

Exercise, diet, work and rest influence a person's health and well-being, with each aspect linking together. Exercise prepares the body so it is physically capable of completing tasks without becoming exhausted. In order to exercise, the body needs to be fuelled by food. A good diet will see that the correct amount of calorie intake provides the body with enough energy to complete tasks. Work and rest create a mental and physical balance for the individual, providing times which are demanding and times when the body systems can recover and adapt to the demands made of it. The correct balance of these aspects enables the body to function at its optimum level.

The food you eat fuels your body just like petrol fuels a car. As the human body is more complex than a car engine, there are different types of food to keep the various parts of the body functioning properly. Food does the following:

- provides energy
- helps our bodies grow
- repairs injured tissue
- contributes to good general health.

There is a link between diet, work and rest. A correctly **balanced diet** should allow enough energy to be released for the successful completion of daily work and exercise. After work, regular times set aside for rest enable the body's natural healing process to take place. At rest, the mind has a chance to relax and reduce stress levels, and the body has the opportunity to repair and restore tissue that may have been damaged during the day. The balance of diet, work and rest reduces the risk of health problems such as:

- heart disease
- stroke
- high blood pressure
- high cholesterol.
- stress

Individual energy requirements

There are many factors that change the energy requirements of people. The more exercise a person undertakes, the more fuel is required. At different stages of life, greater or lesser levels of energy are needed; for instance, teenagers need more than adults. Women, on average, need less energy than men as they have a smaller build. As people get older their pace of life slows down and their energy requirements reduce. Even same age, same gender people rarely have the same energy needs owing to variations in their lifestyles and build.

Some of these factors are out of our control, but what does dramatically change our energy requirements and is in our control is the amount of activity we undertake.

Below is an approximate calculation of the daily intake requirements for people of different ages:

- **15 year-old boys** 11,500 kJ (2700 kcal approx.)
- **15 year-old girls** 8800 kJ (2100 kcal approx.)
- **Adult men** 10,500 kJ (2500 kcal approx.)
- **Adult women** 8400 kJ (2000 kcal approx.)
- **Older men** 8800 kJ (2100 kcal approx.)
- **Older women** 8000 kJ (1900 kcal approx.)

Active challenge

Discuss with a partner four different reasons why people have different energy requirements.

How energy is calculated

The body needs energy all of the time, even when sleeping. This is because the body is still functioning – the heart is beating, blood is circulating, the body is breathing. This lowest form of energy requirement is called the **basal metabolic rate** (**BMR**).

Each sport then has a different energy requirement depending on:

- length of activity
- intensity of activity
- level of opponent (easy game/lower level opponent).

Each food type has an energy value, which can be calculated in two ways:

Different exercises and the intensity at which they are performed use varied amounts of energy.

- Joules are calculated by a moving force – energy needed when one kilogram is moved by one metre by a force of one **Newton**.
- Calories are calculated by a rise in temperature – amount of energy needed to raise the temperature of one gram of water by 1°C.

The main ways we understand the above calculations are as kilojoules (kJ) and kilocalories (kcal). This is because diets and nutritional information on food packaging deal in large quantities and so the equation is multiplied by 1000 to make the figures more manageable. A food with a low kilojoule or kilocalorie value will have to be eaten in a larger quantity than one with a high value to do the same job.

Energy per hour needed for different activities			
Activity	Approx. energy (kJ)	Activity	Approx. energy (kJ)
Weight lifting	676	Cycling	1806
Mowing the lawn	1016	Swimming	1357
Housework	790	Circuit training	1806
Walking	903	Tennis	1579
Ice skating	376	Water aerobics	903
Gardening	1016	Running	2033

2 — Requirements of a balanced diet

It is important to have a balanced diet consisting of all of the types of food listed in the following table. Eating the correct quantities and combinations of food will keep the body's systems functioning properly, keep hair and skin in good condition and reduce the chances of obesity if combined with exercise. In general, a balanced diet is important, but by changing the amounts of each nutrient eaten, a diet can be adapted to have a specific result for a sportsperson training for a particular event.

Food type	About the food	Aid to the sportsperson
1. Carbohydrates (sugars and starch) 	• Consists of: fruit, cakes, beer, sweets, granulated sugar, bread, pasta, rice and potatoes. • Stored in the liver and muscles as glycogen. Converts to glucose and used as energy for muscles of the body, brain and other organs. • Excess converted and stored as fat. • Should provide over 47 per cent of daily energy requirements and if training hard this should rise to 65 to 70 per cent.	• Provides a ready source of energy when the muscles require it. • Carbohydrates in the highly processed form of sugars provide us with energy but no other nutrients, so it is better to eat more starches. • Excess carbohydrates are stored in the body as glycogen and, on demand, release energy slowly – athletes in long-distance events can take advantage of this.
2. Protein 	• Consists of: meat, fish, pulses (chick-peas, lentils and beans), nuts, eggs and poultry. • Builds body muscle, repairs tissue, enzymes and hormones. • Proteins are broken down in the body as amino acids; 21 types are needed for our bodies to work properly. • Our bodies can produce 13 types (non-essential amino acids) but the other eight (essential amino acids) come from pr otein foods. • Excess is converted and stored as fat.	• Builds muscle and repairs tissue within the body. • Essential after an injury to heal quickly. • Sportspeople who need large muscle size will take in extra proteins for this effect.
3. Fats 	• Consists of: milk, cheese, butter, oils, chocolate, fatty meats, soya beans and corn. • Provider of energy. • Recommended daily intake is 30 per cent of a combination of saturated, polyunsaturated and monounsaturated fatty acids. • Can be stored in the body.	• Increase size and weight of body. • Important for performers who benefit from having extra bulk, shot-putters for instance. • Unnecessary weight can inhibit performance and lead to high cholesterol levels. • Fats are a form of stored energy, released slowly when there is a lack of carbohydrates.

Food type	About the food	Aid to the sportsperson
4. Vitamins 	• Sources include fruit (vitamin C), liver and carrots (vitamin A), whole grains and nuts (vitamin B1) and vegetable oil (vitamin E). • Help with the general health of vision, skin condition, forming of red blood cells and blood clotting, and the good condition of bones and teeth. • There are 13 vitamins in all.	• The general health of athletes is important if they are to perform well. When training hard, vitamins from the B group are used more and so need to be replenished. This can be done by eating more of that food type or using supplements.
5. Minerals 	• Sources include milk, saltwater fish (iodine), red meat, liver, green vegetables (iron), cheese and cereals (calcium). • Calcium helps growth of bones, iron helps the making of red blood cells and the way oxygen is carried in the body by the haemoglobin. • The more a person exercises the greater the intake needed, provided by a varied diet or supplements. • Excessive amounts of the mineral salt can lead to high blood pressure.	• Increases efficiency of carrying oxygen to the working muscles of the body. • Iodine aids normal growth, essential for the athlete to help energy production. • Iron helps produce red blood cells and so carry more oxygen round the body, helping to prevent fatigue. • Calcium helps blood to clot, aiding recovery from injury, and strengthens bones and muscles.
6. Fibre 	• Consists of: leaves, seed cases, cereals and whole grains. • Fibre, or roughage, helps digestion but contains no nutrients. • There are two types: insoluble – this adds bulk to our food helping it to keep moving through the digestive system and so preventing constipation, and soluble – helps to reduce cholesterol, keeping the heart healthy.	• Less cholesterol in the body makes the heart more efficient, which is important for transporting blood to the working muscles. • By keeping the digestive system functioning regularly the body retains less waste.
7. Water 	• Consists of: fluids and food. • Two-thirds of the body is made up of water. • We need regular intakes to replenish what is lost in urine, sweat and condensation as we breathe.	• Water allows the blood to flow more easily around the body. This is extremely important when exercising, as the body demands more oxygen, nutrients, heat control and waste removal. • In endurance events, or when exercising in hot weather, water is lost quickly and can lead to dehydration and heatstroke if not replenished. • However, recent cases have shown drinking excess water during exercise can be fatal so care should be taken in this matter – if in doubt seek medical advice.

The seven types of food are divided up into the following:

- macro nutrients
- micro nutrients
- water
- fibre.

Macro nutrients include carbohydrates, fats and protein. They are present in our diets in large amounts, making up the bulk of the dietary intake.

Micro nutrients include vitamins and minerals. They are found in very small amounts in our diet. They do not provide energy but are essential to enable the cells of our body to function correctly.

Water is in all foods in bulk. Water is essential to the body, keeping temperature under control and the body hydrated.

Fibre keeps the digestive system active and helps lower cholesterol.

Task 1

Answer the following questions on nutrients.

1 – What is the major role in the human diet of:
   a. Carbohydrates   **b.** Protein   **c.** Fats   **d.** Vitamins

2 – Give three examples of foods that are good sources of:
   a. Vitamins   **b.** Carbohydrates   **c.** Protein

3 – What two types of carbohydrates are there and in what form are they stored in the body?

4 – How does a sportsperson use the following:
   a. Carbohydrates   **b.** Protein   **c.** Water   **d.** Fats

3 — Timing dietary intake with performance

What an athlete eats leading up to an event can greatly affect performance. Their diet should be carefully monitored. What and how much is eaten should be carefully noted and the timing of the intake should be carefully planned.

Redistribution of blood during exercise

Muscles need oxygen to work and the way oxygen reaches the working muscles is via lungs, alveoli and capillaries as it diffuses into the blood stream. The blood therefore plays a role as the carrier of oxygen to these working muscles, so, during exercise, the role of blood becomes vital to the body's well-being.

When exercising, the body needs more oxygen at the site of the working muscles. The distribution of blood around the body changes according to the demand, allowing the working parts to be supplied with the necessary amounts of oxygen. This redistribution of the cardiac output is called 'blood shunting'. Blood flow reduces to systems not in use. The digestive system, for instance, receives less oxygen during exercise, as its needs are negligible under such circumstances.

Special diets for sport

An increase in demands on the body from exercise means an increase in energy requirements. This should result in a change of diet to compensate for the new demand. The general diet for an athlete is high in carbohydrates, low in fat, with a high fluid intake, including **energy drinks** and/or water. This provides energy and keeps the fluid levels balanced.

Diets can be organized around an exercise programme. This will involve timing when meals are taken, the content of the meal depending on the activity and the quantity of food to be eaten. A top-class athlete acquires knowledge of how to use the different types of food to their best advantage. Each sportsperson's diet will vary due to individual differences of build, demands of the sport, position played in the team and any injury incurred.

Diet plays an important part in an athlete's performance. It is seen to be so important that many sportspeople are guided by specialist dieticians and follow strict eating habits. The dietician will play their part in the performer's success just as the coach does. There are crucial times when a sportsperson can adapt their diet to help performance.

By adapting their diet over the following periods the athlete can get the best results:

- the week before the event
- the day of the event
- during the event
- after the event.

Carbohydrate loading
Traditionally, **carbohydrate loading** is linked with long-distance events but other competitors can benefit too. Swimmers can use this diet effectively for their event. Carbohydrates are important to an athlete, as they are easy to digest and provide an instant source of energy. By eating more carbohydrates, a store of glycogen is built up in the body. In competition this store will reduce levels of fatigue and so help to maintain a standard of performance.

Carbohydrate loading can be useful for long-distance athletes.

High-protein diet
This diet requires the intake of a large amount of protein. Weightlifters and athletes needing a loss of weight over a fairly short period of weeks can adopt this diet. High-protein diets can also be used in a rehabilitation programme after injury for the repair of damaged tissue. A bodybuilder or a rugby player will use this type of diet to burn fat and increase muscle size. Taking creatine supplements (a form of protein) increases the effect. A rugby league player can eat as many as six meals a day taking in mainly protein, some carbohydrates, but little or no fat. Throughout the day, they are encouraged to drink plenty of fluids and eat fruit as well as the prescribed meals. The protein will build up the muscle, carbohydrates will provide energy and fluids will keep the body hydrated.

Eating a high-protein diet has the effect of reducing the storage of fat in the body. Some performers, who need to lose weight quite quickly, can use this type of diet. However, there is now evidence of long-term problems with this type of diet. For example, when a bodybuilder takes in a high level of animal proteins this raises the cholesterol levels in the body, leading to the possibility of heart disease, diabetes, stroke and cancer. The performer using a high-protein diet to control their weight can develop kidney damage in the long term.

Water

Water is essential, especially to athletes when the balance in their body is changing due to the extra stresses put on them through the demands of the event. Strenuous exercise will raise the temperature of the body and cause sweating. The loss of water and salt in this way must be replaced to stop dehydration.

Dehydration will especially occur in hot conditions and in long-distance events. If a sportsperson becomes dehydrated it will make them weak and disorientated.

Taking in water is essential for the body to function correctly.

Diet and hydration before, during and after exercise for a long-distance athlete

Pre-event
The week before an event a runner's training routine and diet change. Due to the excesses of previous training, carbohydrates are low in the body while proteins are high. This combination is not appropriate for a long-distance athlete. So, four or five days before the race, many more carbohydrates are eaten in order to build up these energy stores for the event.

The training programme is now tapered so fewer miles are covered, allowing energy levels to build up and the speed of the shorter runs increases, preparing for a burst of speed during the race. By taking in extra carbohydrates and fewer fats, together with reducing the intensity of the training programme, the body is able to store these nutrients, as glycogen, for use in the race.

The usefulness of carbohydrates is so widely recognized by the long-distance athlete that 'pasta parties' are organized for the athletes two days before the London Marathon. Eating foods such as noodles, rice, potatoes and even beans on toast will have a similar effect.

Day of event

On the day of the event athletes will choose, from preference and experience, either a large meal three to four hours before the race, or a lighter one up to two hours before the race. This is the final chance, before the competition, to make sure that carbohydrates are stocked up and fluid levels are high.

During the event

The prolonged, moderate to hard intensity of a long-distance race reduces the amount of water in the body. Low water levels reduce performance and prevent correct circulation and temperature control. Regular water intake is essential to the athlete to prevent dehydration. Energy drinks help the body to work hard for longer by using the carbohydrates in them.

Taking fluids during an endurance event is essential.

After the event

An athlete must continue to drink fluids and energy drinks to replace the fluids and carbohydrates lost. High-energy food can be eaten immediately after the race. Depending on the training programme following the event, a sensible meal including various carbohydrates is usual.

1. Week before competition – complex carbohydrates to build glycogen stores.

2. Three or four days before competition – small snacks every two to three hours – high carbohydrates plus smaller portion of protein.

3. Morning of competition – eat high complex carbohydrate, low fat, protein and fibre.

4. Pre-competition – carbohydrates in solid or liquid form (as glycogen is only stored for 12 hours) helps with energy in the latter stages of long-distance events.

5. Just before competition – eat a small amount (50g) of fast absorbing carbohydrates to keep blood-sugar levels high.

6. During competition – for long-distance events take in carbohydrate drinks – in tournaments eat carbohydrates between matches.

7. After competition – drink fluids to rehydrate the body and eat small amounts of carbohydrates (2g per kg of body weight) to replenish glycogen stores and speed up recovery time.

Task 2

Make a ten-point list about carbohydrate loading and the procedure for food and fluid intake for a long-distance event. Include ideas on the week before, day of, during and after the event.

Key terms

Balanced diet – a diet that contains an optimal ratio of nutrients

Basal metabolic rate (BMR) – the level at which energy is used without exercise

Newton – a unit of force

Energy drinks – fluids containing carbohydrates

Carbohydrate loading – building up carbohydrates in the body to use in endurance events

Summary

For general health, a balance of all seven nutrients in the daily diet is important. Different types of food provide these nutrients, helping the body to function properly. It is important to eat a variety of foods within a day so that all the body systems can function properly. In general, there needs to be a balance of all seven nutrients for everyday healthy living.

Each food has a different energy value. A person who strikes the correct balance between food intake and energy output according to activity levels will maintain a constant weight. The performer pursuing high-energy activities will have to increase the amount of food eaten to cope with the energy demand. When athletes understand the different qualities of food, they can use food to their best advantage. Once the requirements of the sport have been identified, the sportsperson can choose a special diet containing foods to help their performance. For example, a weightlifter needs to increase muscle size and strength so a high-protein diet is appropriate. Whereas a long-distance athlete needs a slow release of energy lasting the whole of the race, therefore a high carbohydrate-loading diet suits them.

Combining training with eating certain foods in definite quantities can help an athlete to become more effective in their event. The following changes may then occur:

- change to their natural shape (changing the fat ratio and muscle size)
- improve their energy levels
- reduce their recovery periods.

Exam questions

Multiple-choice questions

1. (a) Which of the following does not describe a function of food?

    ☐ A Provides energy

    ☐ B Increases fast twitch muscle fibres

    ☐ C Repairs injured tissue

    ☐ D Contributes to general healthy growth

    (1)

   (b) Which of the following are examples of carbohydrates?

    ☐ A Pasta, beer, bread, meat

    ☐ B Rice, cheese, fruit, milk

    ☐ C Pasta, rice, potatoes, bread

    ☐ D Bread, milk, cheese, beans

    (1)

   (c) Which combination of food would best help tissue repair?

    ☐ A Fish, nuts, eggs, poultry

    ☐ B Fish, lentils, bread, eggs

    ☐ C Beans, eggs, butter, fruit

    ☐ D Eggs, cereals, liver, nuts

    (1)

   (d) Which of the following best describes carbohydrate loading?

    ☐ A Eating foods that allow a store of glycogen to build up in the body

    ☐ B Eating foods that are high in bulk to fill you up

    ☐ C Eating foods that give a balance of all nutrients

    ☐ D Eating foods that will reduce weight and build muscle

    (1)

   (e) Sportspeople will use a high-protein diet for different reasons. Which of the following is not one of them?

    ☐ A To help with weight loss

    ☐ B To burn fat and increase muscle size

    ☐ C To store energy

    ☐ D As an aid to rehabilitation after injury

    (1)

   (f) Macro units are important to the body. Which of the following best describes their importance?

    ☐ A Provides energy, stores energy, repairs tissue

    ☐ B Repairs tissue, helps general health, increases oxygen carrying efficiency

    ☐ C Repairs tissue, helps digestion, stores energy

    ☐ D Stores energy, helps blood flow, helps digestion

    (1)

Short-answer questions

2. Which nutrient provides instant energy?

   (1)

Longer-answer questions

3. A balanced diet helps a person in many ways in everyday life. State four functions of eating a good balance of food.

   (4)

4. There are seven constituents of a balanced diet: vitamins and water are two, list the other five.

   (5)

5. The following question is about endurance events and diet.

   (a) Name the recognized special diet helping endurance athletes optimize success.

   (b) At what stages, in relation to an endurance competition, should a performer fine-tune their diet for optimum performance and recovery?

   (2)

1.2 ～ Your healthy, active body

1.2.1a Physical activity and your healthy mind and body: Your body and its effects on participation and performance

What you will learn about in this topic:

1 — Different weights
2 — Why optimum weight varies
3 — Body types

1 — Different weights

There is clear link between the amount of calories taken in, the amount of exercise undertaken and weight levels. If there are more calories consumed than exercise taken then an increase of weight can be expected.

By regularly exercising:

- the appetite can be reduced, decreasing calorie intake
- the basal metabolic rate (BMR) increases (this uses fat up even at rest)
- the body uses stored fat faster when extra energy is needed during exercise
- weight may increase because muscle weighs more than fat.

If a person eats more but does not increase the amount of exercise they do, then the extra food will be stored in the body as glycogen and fat.

The effects of under- and overeating

Weight gain: if the calorie intake exceeds the energy expended, then weight is gained.

Maintaining weight: if calorie intake is balanced with energy used, weight is maintained.

Weight loss: if more energy is expended and less calories are taken in, then the result is weight loss.

Weight problems affecting performance

Every athlete has an **optimum weight** at which they perform at their best. This depends on the correct balance of height, gender, bone structure and muscle girth (measurement around the flexed muscle).

Some athletes can keep to their optimum weight easily, whilst others constantly have to check what they eat. Some sports, such as boxing and horse racing, demand a certain weight restriction; so for the boxer and the jockey, diets and quick weight loss are sometimes vital for them to compete. It is the fluids in the body that are lost when an athlete needs to make a weight category in a short period of time. The consequences of losing weight quickly can be that the body becomes dehydrated and the level of performance is reduced, making the competitor less effective. Some athletes will appear to be overweight; their large muscle girth will give a reading that is misleading. If a sportsperson is overweight it can have a bad effect on their performance as well as a poor effect on their health.

The demands of some sports for an athlete to be the optimum weight are essential for the greatest success. The effect of having too much fat can restrict the flexibility of the joints and so the athlete cannot move appropriately to execute the correct technique. Carrying too much weight will decrease the speed of movement, slowing a player down in a game. A performer will tire quickly because of the extra effort needed to carry more weight. In some sports, such as archery and bowls, where speed is not a necessity, then being overweight is not a problem. It may even make the person more stable and so help accuracy.

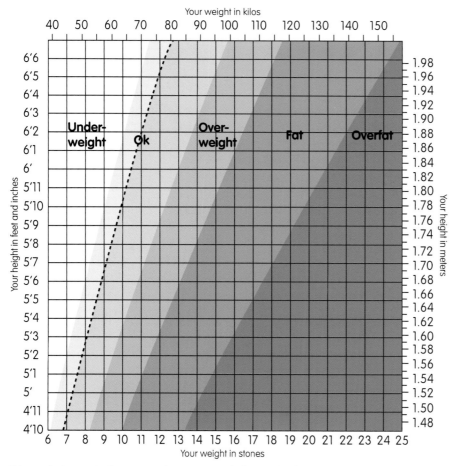

This graph shows whether you are the correct weight for your height.

Degrees of being overweight

An **overweight** person can be said to be heavier than the average person of that gender, height and build. The extra weight, however, is not necessarily a threat to the person's health (sometimes a lot of it is muscle).

Overweight.

Being **overfat** can have a direct effect on a person's health. In this category a person will have a high level of fat in comparison with their total body composition. Having this amount of fat can lead to obesity-related disease: problems may include high blood pressure, strokes, cancer and heart attacks.

Overfat.

When a person reaches the stage of being **obese**, they are abnormally fat (more than 20 per cent over the standard weight for their height). At this stage the health risks become more dangerous and can include diabetes, high blood pressure, heart disease, osteoarthritis and early mortality.

Obese.

Being overweight is a problem of the twenty-first century. Many nations now record more than 20 per cent of their population as clinically obese and well over half the population as overweight. This trend has increased throughout the world as fast food chains reach various areas. In the USA, 66 per cent of the population is overweight, giving America the nickname 'the fat capital of the world'.

Underweight

To be classed as **underweight** a person has to be ten per cent under their optimal weight. Some athletes are naturally underweight, others succumb to pressures to be a certain weight to be the best they can be at their chosen sport. When people are unnaturally small, there are consequences:

- women have irregular periods
- some people suffer osteoporosis in later life
- low food intake leads to malnutrition and greater risk of injuries
- insufficient vitamins and minerals are taken in to maintain a healthy body
- lack of eating leads to an energy drain, affecting performance.

How to minimize the risks of weight loss
The risks can be minimized by making weight loss realistic and gradual. Any weight loss should be planned, carefully monitored and related to the optimal weight of the individual. Consulting specialist dieticians will keep the weight loss safe. Losing weight should be attempted at the beginning of the season or out of season, as high-energy requirements will increase as the training builds up and competition arises.

Possible dietary problems

Athletes may put pressure on themselves in an attempt to reach and maintain a low body weight that is ideal for their sport, but unnatural for themselves. In some cases this may lead to an eating disorder such as anorexia nervosa. An **anorexic** person does not eat because they see themselves as fat. Their obsessive state of mind forces them to severely reduce their intake of food. This condition leads to excessive weight loss.

Anorexia can lead to bouts of depression and many severe medical problems, including kidney and liver damage, and even death.

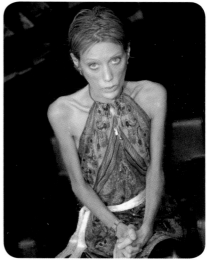

Anorexic.

Task 1

1 – Choose five different types of sportsperson.

2 – Write a sentence on what they may say about their diet and how it affects them.

Include ideas on: energy needs of the activity, weight problems and how training changes natural food preferences.

2 — Why optimum weight varies

Calculating body mass index (BMI) is a general way of working out whether a person is the right weight for their height. It does not, however, take into consideration a person's muscle mass, proportion of fat and frame size, which all have a bearing on a healthy body weight.

Usually, the higher the BMI, the higher the percentage of body fat – BMI is therefore a general indicator of how fat someone is. Sportspeople with a high percentage of lean body mass will have a higher than average BMI because muscle weighs more than fat. So the BMI is not always the best indicator of health for these people.

- Underweight = below 18.5 BMI
- A healthy body = 18.5–25 BMI
- Overweight = 25–30 BMI
- Obese = 30–35 BMI
- Morbidly obese = 40 BMI and over

To calculate body mass use the following formula:

$$BMI = \frac{\text{weight (kg)}}{\text{height (m)} \times \text{height (m)}}$$

For example:
A person's weight is 80kg and their height is 1.7m.

Multiply the height by itself: $1.7 \times 1.7 = 2.89$
Divide the weight into this figure: $80 \div 2.89 = 27.7$

Therefore, this person's BMI is 27.7 meaning they are in the overweight category.

Task 2

1 – Calculate your own body mass index.

2 – Write down your calculations.

Factors affecting optimum weight

Optimum weight is the most favourable weight for a person. Many factors have a bearing on the optimum weight of a person:

Height – the taller a person the greater the optimum weight as the percentage of bone that makes up the body weight becomes larger.

Gender – men and women have different percentages of fat in their bodies. Men have 20 per cent of total body weight in fat; women have 30 per cent of total body weight in fat. Their frames may also be different – increasing or decreasing the amount of bone making up the body.

Bone structure – the frame of a person may have a bearing; for instance, a person with a broad frame will vary in weight to a person with a narrow frame. Studies have shown that if a child follows a physically active early life more layers of bone will form along the shaft of long bone, increasing the density and weight.

Muscle girth – people who have a higher than average muscle mass will be heavier (muscle weighs more than fat) and so will have an optimum weight higher than the healthy range. This is not harmful unless a person is overfat as well.

Expected weight and optimum weight may affect participation by:

Influencing the sport taken part in

How effectively skills are performed

The speed of movement over a distance

The speed of performing skills

How quickly **fatigue** sets in

The strength to perform skills

Performers know the best weight they perform at and so variation leads to change in success rates

The needs of the sport – weight varies with teammates as the position played may require a certain weight

Flexibility may be hindered by carrying extra weight

Task 3

1 – Choose a sport and consider how a change in weight could affect the level of performance.

2 – Write out your views.

Think of the following to help you start: performing skills, maintaining level of performance, being competitive.

Key terms

Optimum weight – ideal weight for a person, giving them the best chance of success in an activity

Overweight – having weight in excess of normal (not harmful unless accompanied by over fatness)

Overfat – a way of saying you have more body fat than you should have (more body fat than is recommended for your gender and height)

Obese – a term used to describe people who are very over fat (more than 20 per cent over the standard weight for their height); this condition can lead to many health problems

Underweight – weighing less than is normal, healthy or required

Anorexic – a prolonged weight loss eating disorder due to obsessive control of food intake

Fatigue – the body's inability to complete a task

3 — Body types

There are many differences in people's physical shape and size. The following are the main factors creating the individual shape of a person:

- height
- weight
- muscle girth
- bone size
- body fat

Depending on the combination of these different factors, a person may be influenced to participate in a certain sport or even to play in a particular position within a team due to the suitability of their shape and size.

Somatotypes

Somatotyping is a method of identifying people by their body shape. WJ Sheldon devised this method in 1940 when he originally adapted his findings to criminology. Professor Tanner studied sportspeople from the 1960 Olympic Games and applied Sheldon's ideas to sport. There are three extreme categories of body type; each type is determined by the amount of fat, muscle and bone making up the body.

The three **somatotypes** are:

- **Endomorph:** tendency to put on fat, soft roundness of shape, short tapering limbs, small bones, wide hips.
- **Mesomorph:** high proportion of muscle, bone, large trunk, heavy chest, broad shoulders and narrow hips.
- **Ectomorph:** lean, fragile, delicate body, small bones, narrow at shoulders and hips.

Each somatotype has a one to seven score, one is low and seven is high. Each person is measured to find their personal mark. Measuring a person to find their somatotype involves measuring their body fat, bone, muscle and weight, with each measurement compared to a score chart. A non-sportsperson may have the following combination: four, three, three (four = medium endomorphy, three = low mesomorphy, three = low ectomorphy).

Sport attracts extremes

There are very few people with the extreme examples of each somatotype. Most people have a combination of all three. However, sportspeople have more mesomorphic (muscle) and ectomorphic (thinness) than endomorphic (fatness) characteristics and a top-class sport will attract the best extremes of body type suitable to that game. Basketball, for instance, will attract players who are all very tall and thin with sinewy muscles, falling into the ectomorph/mesomorph categories.

  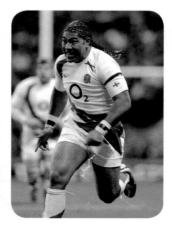 

Each sport is different and suits people of a certain somatotype.

Task 4

1 – Put the following into the correct somatotype category:

a. basketball player   **d.** gymnast   **f.** marathon runner
b. hockey player   **e.** swimmer   **g.** shot-putter
c. rugby player forward

2 – For each of the photos on page 130, write a sentence on how they might describe themselves.

> You may need to do some research to find out about the sports mentioned. Use your judgement to decide the somatotype by using the photographs on page 130 to help your decisions.

Measuring the body

When working out a person's body type, their age, gender, height, weight, size of bones, amount of fat on the body and size of muscle are all taken into consideration.

Measuring somatotype is used to find the shape category of a person using size, composition and build. Knowing their somatotype can steer people into a sport to which they are naturally suited or show areas of the body that need to change in order to reach maximum success rate in an activity.

Fat ratio of the body

The fat layer is just below the top layer of skin on the body. Fat is a good insulator and can be of benefit in activities in cold climatic conditions. The amount of fat people have on the body varies with age and gender. Babies and women have thicker layers than men. Both sexes can increase their fat ratio as they get older. Men increase the amount around their middle; women the amount on their thighs and buttocks.

Measuring fat

A **skin-fold calliper** is an instrument used to calculate a person's body fat percentage by measuring the thickness of a fold of skin with its underlying layer of fat.

Measuring bones

Measuring bones gives the size of bones in relationship to the muscle and fat levels of the body. The places to measure are the elbow and knee joints.

For the elbow:

- Flex the biceps until the joint is at right angles.
- Use a skin-fold calliper to measure across the elbow at the widest point. This is a condyle measurement of the humerus.

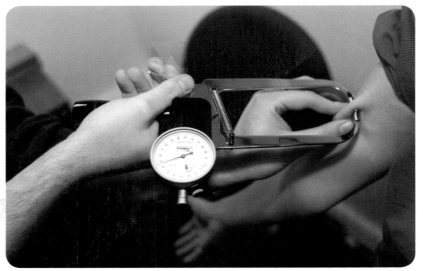

A skin-fold calliper.

Active challenge

Using the same method as described on page 131, write how you would take the condyle measurement of the femur.

Measuring muscles

A measurement is taken, in centimetres, of a muscle while it is flexed and at its widest point. The muscles measured are the biceps (upper front arm) and gastrocnemius (back lower leg, commonly known as the calf muscle).

Taking a biceps girth reading:

- Hold the humerus horizontally.
- Flex the biceps so arm is at right angles.
- Take measurement around widest part in centimetres.

Taking a gastrocnemius girth reading:

- Stand with feet slightly apart.
- Flex gastrocnemius by standing on toes.
- Take measurement around widest part in centimetres.

Active challenge

Measure your partner's flexed biceps.

Key terms

Somatotype – classification of body type

Endomorph – a somatotype, individuals with wide hips and narrow shoulders characterized by fatness

Mesomorph – a somatotype, individuals with wide shoulders and narrow hips, characterized by muscularity

Ectomorph – a somatotype, individuals with narrow shoulders and narrow hips, characterized by thinness

Skin-fold calliper – a device that measures the thickness of a fold of skin with its underlying layer of fat

Summary

Somatotype is the shape and body composition of an individual. The tissue ratio can be changed by adapting the type of diet consumed and exercise undertaken. However, extreme diets can badly affect the health of an individual. Certain somatotypes are better suited to some sports than others; shape may encourage a person to make a natural choice to take part in a particular activity.

Exam questions

Multiple-choice questions

1. Which of the following is not a direct danger of being overweight?

    ☐ **A** High blood pressure

    ☐ **B** Being run over by a car

    ☐ **C** Diabetes

    ☐ **D** Stroke

    (1)

2. There are factors that have a bearing on a person's optimum weight. Which of the following best describes these factors?

    ☐ **A** Bone structure, skill levels, height, gender

    ☐ **B** Muscle girth, age, ability, energy levels

    ☐ **C** Gender, flexibility, bone structure, height

    ☐ **D** Height, bone structure, gender, muscle girth

    (1)

3. Which of the following sports suit an ectomorphic somatotype?

    ☐ **A** Horse racing, hockey, marathon running, volleyball

    ☐ **B** Basketball, horse racing, marathon running, volleyball

    ☐ **C** Marathon running, judo, volleyball, basketball

    ☐ **D** Volleyball, diving, basketball, horse racing

    (1)

4. Which of the following sports suit a mesomorphic somatotype?

    ☐ **A** Hockey, volleyball, football (outfield), sprinting

    ☐ **B** Gymnastics, basketball, cricket (wicket keeper), diving

    ☐ **C** Marathon running, netball (goal keeper), judo, gymnastics

    ☐ **D** Hockey, judo, diving, gymnastics

    (1)

Short-answer questions

5. What term relating to weight does the following definition describe?

    'Having weight in excess of normal (not harmful unless accompanied by overfatness).'

    (1)

Longer-answer questions

6. Describe the effects of under- and overeating on a person's weight.

    (4)

7. What possible risks to a person's health could there be if a person reached the stage of being obese?

    (3)

8. When a person is lower than ten per cent of their optimum weight they are classed as underweight. What are the risks to both men and women's health by being underweight?

    (3)

9. Anorexia nervosa is an eating disorder. What are the mental and physical effects this disorder can have on the sufferer?

    (3)

10. How does a person's weight affect their participation in sport?

    (6)

1.2 ～ Your healthy, active body

1.2.1b Physical activity and your healthy mind and body: substances and the sportsperson

What you will learn in this topic:

1 — Effects of smoking and alcohol on the performer
2 — Different categories of drug
3 — Risks associated with participation in physical activities

1 — Effects of smoking and alcohol on the performer

Consuming alcohol and smoking are considered recreational activities but they both have harmful side effects.

Cigarettes are legal but are becoming less socially acceptable. Since 2007, smoking has been banned in virtually all enclosed public spaces (such as pubs and bars) and in workplaces. It has been recognized that smoking can contribute to long-term illness (such as coronary heart disease).

When a person smokes, they take harmful chemicals into their body. The worst substance is tar, which collects in the lungs and is believed to be directly related to cancer. Tobacco contains nicotine, which is not a banned **drug** but it has an addictive quality. Nicotine affects the body by stimulating the brain to release noradrenaline, which is usually released in times of stress.

Smoking raises the pulse rate and so makes the heart work faster for no reason. The smoker's blood vessels contract, raising the blood pressure and causing a sensation of cold. Smoke contains carbon monoxide and when this enters the blood stream it reduces the red blood cells' ability to transport oxygen. As a result, fitness levels are reduced.

Stephen Harmison and Andrew Flintoff celebrate winning the Ashes.

In endurance activities, where the good condition of the cardiorespiratory systems is required, smoking can be a major hindrance as it can affect the necessary blood flow around the body.

Alcohol is a socially acceptable drug but is banned in most sports as it has an unfair or detrimental effect on the performer. It can act as a sedative, slowing reactions and impairing judgement. It is dangerous if combined with a sport relying on judgement at speed, such as motor racing.

Depending on the individual, the immediate effects of alcohol can be that they become more talkative as the alcohol chemicals reach the brain and affect thinking. Their heart rate can speed up and a sensation of warmth is felt due to the alcohol making the small blood vessels expand, meaning more blood flows nearer to the surface of the skin. Drinking within government guidelines reduces the risk to health as too much alcohol can have detrimental effects on health, including:

- a greater feeling of anxiety
- slower breathing and heartbeat, which affects the effectiveness of blood circulation – this could lead to a stroke
- judgement can be impaired, which is dangerous if driving operating machinery
- can cause osteporosis

- impotence – can destroy sperm producing cells
- loss of consciousness
- vomiting
- increased weight or gain due to alcohol having a high calorie content
- liver disease

The following sports ban certain levels of alcohol in competition:

- aeronautics (0.20 grams per litre)
- archery (0.10g/L)
- automobile (0.10g/L)
- bowls (0.10g/L)
- karate (0.10g/L)

- modern pentathlon (0.10g/L) for disciplines involving shooting
- motorcycling (0.10g/L)
- powerboating (0.30g/L)

Active challenge

Look on the Internet and find out more about alcohol bans in sport. Start with the 'g/L' figures above and the full names of the governing bodies' (for example WKF = World Karate Federation).

2 — Different categories of drug

The rewards for winning can be great in sport. So much so that some athletes are tempted to cheat in order to win. This undermines the integrity of the sport and so the governing bodies of different sports have clear drug-testing policies to try to keep their sport 'clean'.

Each sport has its own list of banned substances, which are published to make it clear to performers and their coaches what cannot be taken during training and competition. The effects of taking **performance-enhancing drugs** are wide and varied; some help to hide pain, such as methadone (a narcotic analgesic), others develop the body artificially, such as anabolic steroids.

Task 1

Give your opinion on why different sports have different lists of banned substances.

The governing bodies work to try to keep a good name for sports and look after the interests of the athletes. The International Olympic Committee (IOC) medical commission works to: 'Protect the health of athletes ... ensure respect for both medical and sport ethics ... enforce equality for all competing athletes.'

The IOC produces a guide to classes of prohibited substances and methods of doping. The different classes are divided by substances used, methods applied and drugs that can be prescribed but used to enhance performance.

Classes of drugs subject to restriction include:

- alcohol
- cannabinoids
- local anaesthetics.

Performance-enhancing drugs that are prohibited substances include:

- stimulants
- narcotic analgesics
- anabolic steroids
- diuretics
- peptide hormones (including erythropoietin (EPO))
- beta-blockers

Prohibited methods include:

- blood doping
- pharmacological, chemical and physical manipulation.

Stimulants

- **Stimulants** are the second most commonly used drugs.
- Examples of the drug include: amphetamines, ephedrine, cocaine, caffeine.
- Effects: reduce feelings of tiredness so a person can train for longer, stimulate the central nervous system (CNS) and make people more alert.
- Side effects: user is irritable, unable to sleep, has high blood pressure, irregular or faster heartbeat.
- Some stimulants, such as amphetamines, are addictive.

Stimulants improve reaction time.

Narcotic analgesics

- Examples of **narcotic analgesics** include: heroin, methadone, pethidine, morphine, codeine.
- Effects: reduce the sensation of the CNS (Central Nervous System). They help pain relief, so athletes come back from injury sooner.

- Side effects: loss of concentration, loss of balance, loss of coordination making sport dangerous. Using these drugs can make an injury worse and may cause a long-term problem related to the first injury.
- Usually injected into the blood stream.
- They are addictive.

Anabolic steroids

- **Anabolic steroids** are the most commonly used drugs in sport – they mimic testosterone, a male hormone.
- Examples of the drug include: testosterone, nandrolone, stanozolol, boldenone, clenbuterol.
- Effects: increase muscle mass and develop bone growth, increase strength, allow the athlete to train harder. Have a quick effect so there is a rapid improvement. Increase aggression, so seen as good for competitive contact sports. Prevent muscle wastage and are an aid to rehabilitation.
- Side effects: they have the greatest effect on women – deepen voice, increase facial hair, users have irregular periods and can become infertile. Men grow breasts, can become impotent and develop kidney problems. Men and women experience mood swings, anxiety, aggression, high blood pressure, heart attacks, strokes and their faces can swell up. Increased risk of muscle injury and liver disease.
- Injected into the blood stream.
- Recent research indicates long-term users show signs of addiction.

Dwain Chambers suffered a two-year ban for taking anabolic steroids.

Diuretics

- Examples of **diuretics** include: furosemide, triamterene, chlortalidone. Mannitol is prohibited if intravenously injected.
- Effects: speeds up work of kidneys by producing more urine. Reduces fluid retention, which causes rapid weight loss; used in sports where there are weight categories. Sportspeople use diuretics to 'make the weight'.
- Side effects: dehydration and possibly dizziness, muscle cramps, headaches, nausea, fatigue. Kidney illness can develop.

Diuretics can be used as a **masking agent**. These are drugs taken to hide the presence of another drug. Some masking agents do not appear on the list of banned substances for particular sports, so their presence is legal. The masking agent hides the presence of a banned substance, which would otherwise disqualify the performer. Diuretics mask the presence of anabolic steroids.

Peptide hormones

- Examples of **peptide hormones** include: Human Growth Hormone (HGH) and **erythropoietin** (**EPO**) – a synthetic substance that copies natural hormones of the body.

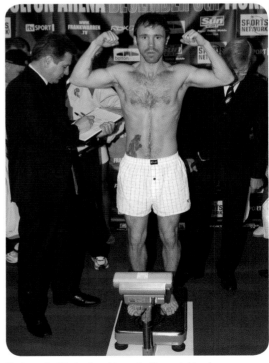
Graham Earl trains hard to make the weight, whereas some athletes are tempted to use drugs.

- Effects: HGH develops muscle, makes the body use fat and helps reduce tiredness. Recovery from injury and training is quicker, increases red blood cells and so helps the endurance athlete. EPO is a synthetic hormone that copies the natural hormones of the body. It stimulates the bone marrow to produce more red blood cells, improving oxygen uptake.
- Side effects: EPO thickens the blood-inhibiting circulation, which can lead to a heart attack or stroke and HGH acts like anabolic steroids. The side effects of HGH include irregular heart beat, increased risk of diabetes, increased cholesterol in blood, impotence and joint and facial deformities.

Beta-blockers

- Examples of **beta-blockers** include: atenolol, nodolol. Some beta-blockers are available on prescription to treat angina and have a similar effect to alcohol. Their use in sport is subject to certain restrictions. They are completely banned in some sports involving a steady hand and a calm nerve such as archery, curling and snooker.
- Effects: users maintain a slow heart rate and low blood pressure, used as a relaxant, useful in tense situations. They also have the effect of steadying the hand, important to competitors in target sports. The calming effect can also help in high-risk sports where speed is involved.
- Side effects: reduce the heart rate so much that there is a danger that the heart may stop.

Beta-blockers are banned in snooker as a steady hand is required. Here, Allister Carter bridges to make a shot.

Active challenge

1 – Look on the Internet and find the named types of beta-blockers that are included in the banned list.

2 – Now study all the information on banned substances and in a small group test each other's knowledge.

Task 2

Set out the information on banned substances in table form using the following headings:

- Type of drug
- Drugs in this category
- Which athletes may use it?
- Effect on the athlete
- Side effects/dangers

Key terms

Drug – substance (other than food) that has a physiological effect when taken into the body

Performance-enhancing drug – substance that artificially enhances personal characteristics and performance

Stimulants – drugs that have an effect on the central nervous system, such as an increased mental and/or physical alertness

Narcotic analgesics – drugs that can be used to reduce the feeling of pain

Anabolic steroids – drugs that mimic the male hormone testosterone and promote bone and muscle growth

Diuretics – drugs that elevate the rate of urine excretion

Masking agent – a legal substance for a sport, hiding the presence of an illegal one

Peptide hormones – drugs that cause the production of other hormones

Erythropoietin (EPO) – a type of peptide hormone that increases the red blood cell count

Beta-blockers – drugs that are used to control heart rate and that have a calming and relaxing effect

3 — Risks associated with participation in physical activities

All players have a responsibility to prepare well for their chosen event. By listening to their coach and completing their **training programme**, they learn the rules and **techniques** of the activity. From experience, they build up an understanding of the risks and hazards of the chosen sport and can learn to avoid them in the competition. The rules help to keep the play safe and prevent unfair play.

Warming-up

Warming-up before an event is vital to train the mind and prepare the body and so reduce the risk of injury. Warm-ups in the winter may have to be extended and extra clothes worn to get the body in the correct condition for competition because of the colder temperatures.

Aims of a warm-up are to gradually increase:

- stress on body systems
- heart rate
- temperature
- muscular contractions
- movement of the joints
- concentration of the mind on the activity
- experience of the skills involved in the activity
- speed of execution of the skills involved.

Cooling-down

Allowing the body to cool-down after the main activity will return it to its resting state by slowing the heart down and giving muscles a chance to relax. Gentle stretching will stop the build-up of lactic acid in muscles so will prevent immediate cramp, aching and soreness the next day (DOMS – delayed onset muscle soreness).

Checking equipment and facilities

All facilities and equipment should be regularly checked for their condition and suitability for use. Such maintenance and upkeep is the duty of the owners or custodians of the equipment. In private clubs the owners employ staff to maintain standards. In publicly run facilities the local council look after the equipment. Before a match the officials are responsible for the playing area and checking the field of play, whilst the organizers of events follow guidelines to ensure the safety of the performers and spectators.

Reducing the risk in specific activities

There are certain safety requirements a club must fulfil. These are to do with the safety of the sports area and safety of the spectators. People watching the event should be managed properly and be able to watch the match without intimidation from other supporters. The St John Ambulance Brigade attend large venues to deal with any first aid requirements.

There are strict guidelines to do with venue exits, making sure the spectators are able to leave the venue safely. The players should also be able to play their game without fear of the crowd invading the pitch. In top-class events, stewards and police play a part in ensuring the players' safety.

The club is also responsible for the state of the playing surface. The ground should have the correct netting and corner flags. The surface should be level and safe, not slippery, and should be free from litter, sharp or protruding objects, and so on. The playing surface condition may change due to the weather, so guidelines are pre-stated so officials are able to make the most appropriate decision.

Potential safety hazards.

Task 3

1 – Study the illustration on page 140. There are 12 hazards shown.

2 – Record each hazard and the injury each one could cause.

> It will help to think about personal presentation.

Using the correct equipment for the type of user is important for safety. Having equipment that is too big or too heavy could lead to risk of injury. The equipment should suit the size, age and experience of the user.

Invasion, striking and racket games
The size of the equipment should relate to the age and experience of the performer. Using full-size footballs for under elevens, for example, will not match the strength and skill of the players.

There are many modified games, which resemble the full game but have been adopted for a younger age group. These games have lighter equipment, smaller playing areas, smaller team numbers and simple rules.

Gymnastics
Whether training or competing, the landing areas should be safe and stable. Competition landing areas are 120–200mm thick and have safety mats around them to a depth of 22–60mm. The landing after a vault, for instance, needs to be technically correct for a good overall mark and also for the safety of the performer. A two-footed landing on the toes, cushioning the force of landing, reduces the risk of a jarring injury to the back. The safety requirements for landing areas are set out by the governing body, the Federation International of Gymnastics (FIG).

The supports for the asymmetric bars and fixings are specialized and fitted by professionals. This ensures they can withstand the forces put on them by gymnasts during practice and competition.

A teacher should check equipment in school before a lesson starts. The correct technique should be taught for lifting and lowering vaulting boxes so back injuries are avoided.

Short handled rackets are used for younger players.

A hall set out for a gymnastic training session.

Each piece of equipment must be set out so that it does not interfere with any other piece.

Trampolining
When using a trampoline, the setting out and putting away of the equipment should follow strict guidelines and always be supervised. The weight, size and tension of the trampoline are potentially dangerous.

Moving and setting out of a trampoline requires well-trained teamwork. Each person should know their role and be able to carry it out at the correct time, at the correct pace and in the correct way. An awareness and understanding of the energy and resistance the springs contain should help to reinforce how important everyone's role is.

It can take a team of six people to set out a trampoline safely. In general the procedure is as follows:

- Move to the site and align squarely to the space and on a level surface.
- Remove the wheels and store them safely.
- Lever over the ends.

- Engage the braces.
- Check the braces and safety cushions are in place.
- Arrange the mats around the trampoline.

A note of caution: Remember to keep elbows out of the way whilst the trampoline levers over.

SPOTTING IN TRAMPOLINING Trampolining is a potentially dangerous activity. It is important that not only is the equipment in good order, but also the **spotters** are fully trained and their skills are routinely refreshed each session.

Their training could involve:

- Positioning around the trampoline – at least one spotter at the ends and two at the sides.
- Hand position whilst watching – on top of the protective cushion.
- Where to look whilst watching – at the upper part of the performer.
- An understanding of the weight distribution of the performer – the top is the heaviest part.
- Hand position if the performer travels in their direction – contact wrist and upper arm.
- Easing performer back to the trampoline centre – hold wrist and upper arm and gently push back onto trampoline.

Spotters need to be trained so they know to concentrate and be confident that they can do their job when required. More spotters are used in schools than shown here.

Dance

The surface the dance is performed on should always be safe and non-slippery. It should be smooth with no splinters. Costumes reflecting the dance and adding drama to the performance should be fitted to each performer securely and allow free movement during the event.

Athletics

All surfaces to run on, throw from and jump off should be flat and free from obstacles and protruding objects.

The throwing cage protects people at the event from a miss-throw. Robert Harting prepares to throw.

Throwing events, such as the discus and hammer, require netting or a cage around the throwing area. These should be maintained regularly to prevent equipment escaping through gaps in the fencing. The throwing area should be clearly marked and marshalled. As the competition begins, warnings should be sounded to alert other judges, marshals and competitors that the throw is about to commence.

In jumping events, guidelines for the size, depth and composition of the landing areas are regulated by the governing body. Mats should have a continuous covering over them to keep them together. Throughout the high jump and pole vault competition a check should be kept on the correct placement of the landing area in relation to the bar.

Some equipment is dangerous, the javelin being an obvious example. There are special carry cages and trolleys for transporting awkward equipment. In schools, how to move and use such equipment, especially javelins and shot-putt, should be reinforced in every lesson.

Equipment, such as javelins, needs to be stored correctly for safety reasons. Carolina Kluft selects a javelin.

Swimming

The safety awareness needed when swimming in open water compared to a pool is very different. Hazards can be caused by the environment, equipment and the activity undertaken.

In open water the following considerations can include:

- Tidal influence: Is the tide phase suitable for swimming? Are the lifeguard's flags out? Does the user know what they mean? Will the user keep to the instructions?
- Temperature: The temperature of the water needs to be monitored. Does the swimmer need a wet suit?
- Depth: Will it be appropriate to the standard of the swimmer?
- Hazards under the water: Is there unseen debris under the surface?
- Condition of the water: Is the water quality acceptable?
- Who else is using the water: Speedboats, jet-skis? Could they prevent a danger to swimmer?

In the swimming pool all safety information and equipment should be clearly on display at the poolside. Any change of depth in the pool should be clearly marked on the pool edge and visible on the wall too. The surface around the pool should be non-slip and clean to prevent injury and infection.

NO running

NO fighting

NO bombing

NO young children unsupervised

Swimming pool safety information.

Although it may be seen as unglamorous, the swimming cap is a safety aid in a variety of ways. It keeps hair out of the eyes, giving a clear view of the direction for the swimmer, and it keeps hair out of the swimmer's mouth, allowing clear, unhindered breathing. Keeping the hair in a cap also helps prevent loose hair entering and blocking the swimming pool filters.

Although a verruca can be painful, a person can still swim. However, they must take care when changing so they do not infect the floor and should wear a verruca sock when swimming to prevent it spreading. Gels are also an effective way of treating verrucas as they are easy to apply and are waterproof.

Wearing goggles allows the swimmer to see underwater when their face is submerged. This allows turns to be made safely. Goggles also protect the eyes from the chemicals in the water.

Active challenge

With a partner, choose a sport. Think of as many risks as possible related to that sport. Use examples from television, personal experience and incidents told to you.

Outdoor and adventurous activities

Outdoor and adventurous activities include mountaineering, climbing, caving, canoeing, mountain biking and sailing. Some considerations for mountaineering and general leadership in difficult surroundings will be included in this section.

The clothing taken on any adventurous activity should suit every kind of weather possibility. The clothing mountaineers take on an expedition should be appropriate for any extreme conditions that they might face. These clothes range from undergarments to the outer layers. Boots should be comfortable and sturdy, with a good grip. An activity may begin in warm and sunny weather but, as the day goes on, the weather may change. As the altitude rises the temperature drops on hills and mountains. Experienced mountaineers will be well equipped for this.

In addition to a compass and map a mountaineer may also carry the following:

Personal safety kit:

- extra warm clothing
- extra gloves
- food and water
- bivvy bag (waterproof bag large enough for two people to shelter from the elements)
- whistle for distress call (a mobile phone would help but there are some areas where a signal cannot be picked up)
- torch

Personal first aid kit:

- two crepe bandages: one ankle, one knee-size tubular bandage for sprains
- army knife with scissors
- sterile wipes for dirty wounds
- various sized plasters
- 12 pack of swabs for compression
- one roll of tape for holding the swabs in place
- safety pins

The ability to use a map and compass properly needs specialist training and much practice. If walking over a long distance and in hostile terrain then it is important to be able to navigate. A route plan should be worked out before the party sets off to include escape points at certain parts of the route there is an accident or the weather deteriorates in case. When visibility is zero, owing to mist coming down, it is possible, as long as you know your position, to navigate with a map and compass alone.

The safety equipment should suit all possible conditions of the day. This equipment may be bulky to carry, but it can be shared between members of the group. Often it will not be used but it is there should it be needed. If mountaineering or walking in conditions where snow and ice may be present, specialized equipment is essential for safety, such as crampons and ice axes. Training and experience are necessary so that they can be used properly.

Regular checks on the condition of the equipment should be made. Ropes do not last forever; they have a life determined by the number of hours used. After this time they cannot be relied on to do their job and so should not be used for climbing again.

Wearing the correct gear and carrying appropriate safety apparatus protects the performer from extreme elements and hazardous situations.

EXTERNAL FORCES   Before setting out on any expedition a detailed weather report should be studied. The Met Office can supply this for the British Isles. The weather at sea or in the mountains can change rapidly, so preparations should be made accordingly. By obtaining the weather report, predictions can be made as to whether it is viable to go out in the first place or what possible weather changes may occur during the day. If the elements are too much to handle, then it is sensible to turn back or take a safer route home. In mountainous areas the weather can bring wind, mist, rain, snow, heat, sun and storms all in the same day. The key is to prepare for the worst.

EXPERIENCE OF THE LEADER AND THE GROUP A major factor in the safety of the party is the experience, knowledge and ability of the leaders. They should plan the route, taking into account the ability of each member of the group. They should have expertize in the use of a map and compass, carry safety equipment and know the safety procedures.

Environmental conditions
- Does the sailor or canoeist know the tides and currents?
- Wind may blow the party off course. Rain may dampen morale. Is the group equipped for snow?
- In mist, would they still know where they were going?
- In a storm, would they know what to do?
- Are they prepared for the heat?

Degree of difficulty of the activity
- Is the group able to complete the route?
- Has the group got the correct equipment for the route?
- Will safety be compromised because of the difficulty of the activity?
- Is the route too difficult for the conditions?
- Are group members strong enough to canoe the distance?
- Has everyone got enough and the right kind of protection for the climb?

Planning the activity
- Is the plan accurate?
- Are there any escape routes?
- Does the route include rests?
- Is it suitable for all members of the group?
- Will it stretch the abilities of the group too far?
- Have the route and planned times of return been left with a reliable source so the alarm can be raised if the group are not back on time?

Factors affecting the safety of an outdoor activity

Experience of the party
- Are they fit enough? Have they got the correct equipment?
- Have they enough experience for the degree of difficulty they may face?
- Have they the skills to finish the expedition?
- Do they know what is expected of them?

Experience of the leaders
- Do they know the area?
- Have they planned the route?
- Are they experienced in safety procedures?
- Can they use the safety equipment they have?
- Can they motivate the group?
- Will they set the speed to the pace of the slowest member?

Condition of the equipment
- Is the rope too old?
- Is there a record of the equipment's use?
- Is the compass still reliable?
- Is someone taking the correct map?
- Has the torch got good batteries?
- Is the equipment in good order?

Leaders should be able to assess the group, encourage the weaker members and adapt the pace to suit the whole party. Their ability to make correct decisions under pressure to suit a situation can help ensure the safety of the party. For long expeditions, leaders should have the personal ability to keep the morale of the group high, even in difficult and demanding conditions.

Task 4

1 – Compile a list of five outdoor and adventurous activities.

2 – Name two specialized pieces of equipment required for each activity.

3 – Write two sentences about the job of the safety equipment.

> Use the photographs in this section to help you as well as reference books and the Internet.

Task 5

1 – Choose an outdoor and adventurous activity.

2 – Complete a risk assessment for that activity and include any steps taken to reduce any risk.

Environmental conditions

Changes in the environment may cause extra risks. In hotter weather, dehydration is an issue. Good weather may encourage people to train more frequently and overuse injury may occur. Working in the winter will change the way a training session is conducted. The daylight is gone quicker, so the timing of training may change or be moved indoors. New safety considerations must also be taken into account, as working surfaces may become wet and icy, making them slippery to train on. Athletes should be aware of the need to change their footwear to combat the conditions or the session should be moved indoors.

In the winter, the standard and condition of facilities may drop. For example, maintenance of throwing cages may not be scheduled out of season. Landing areas may not be kept or dug over properly. For athletes training for throwing events, especially shot and discus, wet weather makes the equipment slippery and hard to control.

Personal readiness

With any game, competitive activity or adventurous pursuit, there are potential dangers. Participants should be prepared properly for the event and trained for skill, strength and tactics. Coaching, training and experience build up knowledge and an awareness of the sport and its rules, making the game safer to play. Some dangers are easier to spot than others. In body contact sports, the risk of injury is plain to see. In racket sports there are dangers too. In squash, for example, the confined area could lead to collisions with the opposition and a squash ball just fits in the eye socket!

A person's PAR-Q (Physical Activity Readiness Questionnaire) will assess an individual's physical condition to check their suitability and readiness for exercise. Any problems highlighted can be discussed with a doctor.

Coaching and training

Coaching is essential at all levels of sport. The coach is responsible for giving the performer an understanding of the game. The skills learnt will be within the laws of the game and prepare the player for competition. The correct techniques are learnt, not only for success, but also to prevent risk: this is especially important for tackles and lifts.

Training improves the body so it is strong enough to deal with the stresses of the event. This reduces the possibility of fatigue, which often leads to injury. Coaching trains the performer to complete skills in a technically correct way. Body alignment is important in take-offs and landings, especially in activities such as gymnastics, trampolining and volleyball, to reduce the risk to the bones and tissues of the body. Knowledge and experience of how to control the equipment for the activity comes about through training. A hockey stick used without training can become a danger to all on the pitch, not just the opposition.

Using the correct techniques can reduce the risk of injury.

Correct clothing

The clothing for team events not only gives a feeling of unity to the group but it can also play its part in safety. Each sport has a unique type of clothing, which has developed due to the nature of the game. It may allow protective guards underneath or be close fitting so it does not catch on equipment. Importantly, it provides free movement so the full range of skills can be performed in each sport.

Clothing should:

- be in good order
- not flap in the opposition's face and hinder their performance
- not catch on equipment and be a danger and hinder performance
- ensure the performer can keep a clear view ahead
- allow free movement to perform the skills of the game
- fit appropriately.

Sports equipment and clothing should be checked regularly. Repairs should be made so that there is nothing to act as a hindrance or danger to anyone. The correct design of equipment should be used for the job. Specialized equipment should always be worn properly. Loose straps and poorly fitting helmets can be a danger.

Footwear to fit the event

Footwear is a specialized part of sports gear; each sport has its own design. Some sports have several different technical designs to suit a variety of conditions. The correct footwear helps in many ways: it gives support, protection, grip, greatest or least amount of movement and is an aid to performance and streamlining.

The condition of studded footwear should be smooth so that studs do not cut into another player. Checking studs is the job of a referee at the beginning of the game and linesmen can be seen checking the studs of football substitutes. There are specific rules set out in certain sports in which some footwear may be seen as dangerous. It is therefore essential to keep footwear in good order.

Sport A

Sport B

Sport C

Sport D

Task 6

1 – Study the footwear photos A to D. Notice that each sport has a different kind of footwear.

2 – Say which sport is shown in each picture.

3 – Give a reason why the footwear has been developed in that way for each sport.

> Look at the differences in the sole, strapping and material.

Protect and be safe

Each activity needs its own protective equipment. Each item of protection guards against a different kind of injury. These injuries could take the form of: impact of another player, the playing surface, the ball, external conditions, forces put on the body by lifting or friction caused by repeating the skills of the event.

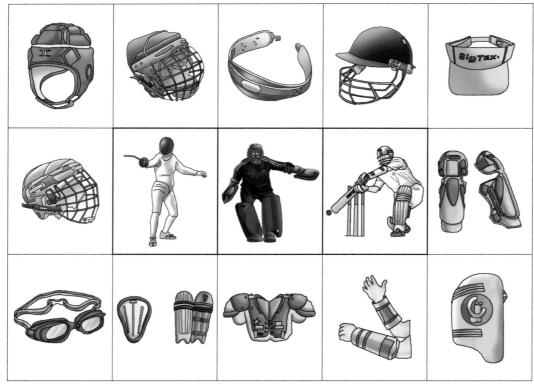

Protective clothing and equipment.

Task 7

Choose a type of sportsperson and list the items they would need to dress for safety.

> Use the pictures on page 148 to help you with this task.

Active challenge

With a partner, discuss and decide on as many items of protection in as many sports as possible. Now link each item of protection with an incident that could happen in a game.

> Hint: work down from head to toe!

Jewellery

Before a team game begins, players are checked for any jewellery they may be wearing. This may seem petty, but each type of jewellery has its own hazards. Sometimes players put a plaster over earrings so they are not as dangerous. In games where physical contact regularly occurs, it is essential that there is no jewellery to mark the wearer or the opposition.

- Rings – if fingers are jarred or a ball knocks the end of the finger (called 'stumped finger') and the finger swells, a ring could get stuck and cut into the flesh. Also rings could get caught and cut the performer or an opponent.
- Necklaces – if caught and pulled could cause a scar around the neck.
- Earrings – if caught could injure the wearer or an opponent.

Personal presentation

Fingernails need to be clipped to prevent catching and scarring, especially in games such as netball and basketball in which reaching for the ball around head height is common.

Hair should be tidy and not in the performer's eyes so players can see where they are going and so it does not flick into another player's eyes.

If glasses are worn they should be made of plastic so if they break they do not shatter and injure someone.

Clothing worn for sport should be kept in good order. Ripped or frayed clothing can catch and be a danger.

Having tidy hair and short fingernails reduces the risk of injury. Here, the England women's football team display their impeccable personal presentation.

All footballers need to keep their hair tied back in order to see properly and not hinder the opposition.

Attitude and etiquette

Etiquette is the unwritten code of behaviour a player stands by when competing. Each sport has its own code of behaviour. A general example of this is shaking hands before and after a game. In tennis, new balls are used after the first seven games and every nine games after that. It is not a rule, but it is also good etiquette for the player about to serve to show the ball to the opposition by raising it in the air.

A player showing a bad attitude may throw or kick the ball away in anger after a decision by the referee. The referee can punish this demonstration of bad sportsmanship in an attempt to discourage other players from such behaviour.

Tennis players shake hands after a match.

Task 8

1 – Read the table of part sentences below.

2 – Link the beginnings of sentences with the endings.

3 – When the sentences are complete, write them in your workbook.

Beginning of the sentence	Ending of the sentence
1. Players are checked for…	a. …which spread in moist areas like swimming baths.
2. If a ball jars a finger,…	b. …so the rules of netball state they should be short.
3. Long fingernails can catch and scar,…	c. …a player, wearing a ring, could cut their flesh.
4. Keeping a sports kit washed…	d. …is good etiquette.
5. Having sweaty and dirty feet…	e. …can stop athlete's foot.
6. Keeping feet clean and dry between the toes…	f. …jewellery before a game.
7. Verrucas are viral warts,…	g. …players keep to for the good of the sport.
8. Verrucas can be treated quickly by being removed,…	h. …stops the spread of bacteria.
9. Etiquette is an unwritten code of behaviour…	i. …or over time with gel.
10. Shaking hands at the beginning and end of a match…	j. …causes athlete's foot.

Balanced competition

In most sports there are rules that keep similar age groups together and that separate the sexes at certain ages. This is an attempt to make the competition even and safe by keeping the experience and strength of the players at a similar level. Different factors are taken into account to ensure a **balanced competition**. These include:

- Grading: reaching a particular standard and competing against those in the same category.
- Skill level: being skilful enough to play in a certain team irrespective of age.
- Weight: can be an advantage so particular categories are formed for fairness.
- Age: with age comes maturity and personal development, some sports have sophisticated strategies; grouping young people in ages can make for fairer competition.
- Gender: younger children of both sexes can compete against each other. When boys develop physically, same-sex competition becomes dangerous.

An even match ensures a good competition such as between Sarah Stevenson and Noha Abd Rado in the 2008 Olympics.

Active challenge

With a partner, think of activities that have different groups for competitions. Can you think of an activity that divides groups by both weight and age? Look on the Internet to help you.

Adherence to rules

Each game has its own set of rules or laws. These rules are connected to the type of equipment and competition involved. They are designed to make the event safer and fairer. Its set of rules helps to give the game its own individual style.

Yellow card: first warning in football for foul play.

The governing bodies of the sports make the rules. The players play to the rules. The referee, umpire or judge makes sure the rules are kept. Within the rules are a series of stages of discipline; often the player is given one warning to stop any bad play. If the foul play continues, a player will be asked to leave the game. In 2008 the 'Respect' campaign began in football. As part of the initiative players were encouraged to readily accept decisions made by the referees and not attempt to influence them by arguing. In rugby there is less questioning of decisions. The referee is at liberty to award a ten-yard penalty for such behaviour. As the game is based on working hard to gain territory such a penalty can hit the team hard so players show more control. This ten-yard rule shows how rules support referees in their jobs.

In football, red card offences lead to disciplinary hearings where the Football Association (FA) may take further action. It is in the player's best interests to obey the rules. Players may lose their competitive edge if the thought of another yellow card, and therefore a sending off, is a possibility.

A second yellow (or violent act) earns a red card. Deco is ordered off the pitch.

Officials make sure that there is safe and fair play. When the whistle blows, the game should stop immediately to prevent any further infringements and dangerous play. The referee is impartial and makes decisions according to the rules.

Referees make decisions on the spur of the moment and from where they are standing. In professional games, these verdicts are made under the extreme pressure of hundreds of fans who have their own viewpoints on the referee's decisions! Increasingly in some sports, such as rugby and tennis, the use of video playback is used to help the referee make the correct call.

In rugby and ice hockey, players are sent by the referee to 'cool down' in the sin bin.

Players have a responsibility to follow the instructions of the officials and to carry on with the game as soon as possible. The flow of the game needs to be maintained and by getting on with the game quickly a surprise attack can begin. This can be especially successful if the other team is still concentrating on the incident.

Task 9

1 — Write down four different responsibilities of a referee.

2 — Choose four games or activities. For each one write down a rule that attempts to prevent injury.

> Think of how the referee deals with rules, players and safety.

Umpires use hand signals so that everyone can clearly see the decision made.

Key terms

Training programme – a well-planned programme which uses scientific principles to improve performance, skill, game ability and motor and physical fitness

Technique – way in which a skill is performed

Spotters – trained and alert people surrounding the trampoline prepared to prevent the performer coming off dangerously

Etiquette – unwritten and unofficial codes of practice followed in an activity

Balanced competition – grouping based on size, age or experience for an even match

Summary

Taking drugs has an effect on the body and mind of a person. Some of these effects are useless to the sportsperson. However, research has shown that some drugs have a beneficial effect on performance. By taking some drugs the health of the performer can be seriously endangered. Regulations and procedures are put in place by the governing bodies of each sport to help and guide the performer to make an ethical choice. Some sportspeople are tempted to break the rules of the governing bodies as they see only the rewards of their drug abuse. The sporting authorities want athletes to be safe, sport to have a good name and competition to remain fair.

With most activities there are risks involved. Training and coaching help players to be aware of the risks of the activity. Warming-up gradually prepares the body for increased intensity and strain, reducing the likelihood of injury.

Most sports have a correct code of dress. It is important that kit fits the participant appropriately and is in good condition. All people taking part in an activity should be familiar with the relevant protective equipment. It is important that everyone understands that it should be worn in practice and competition, fit correctly and be kept in good order.

Competition is why many people take part in physical activity. A sport may be so popular that it attracts a wide range of ages and abilities. To make the competition safe, fair and enjoyable, different categories exist ensuring all compete at the appropriate level. The rules are designed to allow the game to continue in a fair and safe way.

Exam questions

Multiple-choice questions

1. (a) Which of the following best describe the effects of stimulants?

    ☐ **A** Increase muscle mass, develop bone growth, increase strength, allow athlete to train harder, increase aggression, aid rehabilitation

    ☐ **B** Allow athlete to train harder, relieve pain, hide pain of an injury, reduce the sensations of the central nervous system

    ☐ **C** Increase muscle mass, hide pain of an injury, increase strength, aid rehabilitation

    ☐ **D** Reduce the sensation of the central nervous system, increase aggression, relieve pain

    (1)

    (b) Which of the following best describe the effects of peptide hormones?

    ☐ **A** Develop muscle, relieve pain, reduce tiredness, increase red blood cells helping the endurance athlete

    ☐ **B** Make use of body fat, speed recovery from injury, aid rehabilitation, develop bone growth

    ☐ **C** Reduce tiredness, speed recovery from injury, make use of body fat, reduce the sensation of the central nervous system

    ☐ **D** Develop muscle, make use of body fat, reduce tiredness, speed recovery from injury, increase red blood cells helping the endurance athlete

    (1)

    (c) Which of the following best describe the effects of narcotic analgesics?

    ☐ **A** Relieve pain, reduce the sensation of the central nervous system, develop bone, increase muscle mass

    ☐ **B** Hide pain of an injury, increase strength, reduce tiredness, allow athlete to work harder

    ☐ **C** Relieve pain, hide pain of an injury, reduce the sensations of the central nervous system

    ☐ **D** Reduce the sensations of the central nervous system, increase aggression, relieve pain, make use of body fat

    (1)

2. Which of the following sportspeople would be most tempted to use beta-blockers?

    ☐ **A** Darts player, diver, footballer, hockey player

    ☐ **B** Snooker player, skier, volleyball player, fencer

    ☐ **C** Darts player, snooker player, golfer, archer

    ☐ **D** Archer, bowler, rugby player, netball player

    (1)

3. A warm-up benefits the performer by:

    ☐ **A** Increasing temperature gradually, gives an opportunity to see the opposition, gradually increases movement at joints, gradually increases the heart rate

    ☐ **B** Concentrates the mind, gradually increases movement at joints, gradually increases the heart rate, allows you to meet up with your friends

    ☐ **C** Gradually increases movement at joints, gradually increases the heart rate, a chance to take it easy, concentrates the mind

    ☐ **D** Increasing temperature gradually, concentrates the mind, gradually increases movement at joints, gradually increases the heart rate

    (1)

4. Which of the following contains safety considerations for long jump?

☐ **A** Sand is clear of stones, take-off board in good condition, the results are recorded correctly, run up clear and level

☐ **B** Take-off board in good condition, run up clear and level, the competitors jump in the correct order, sand is clear of stones

☐ **C** Sand dug over, sand is clear of stones, take-off board in good condition, run up clear and level

☐ **D** Sand dug over, sand is clear of stones, take-off board in good condition, throwing cage is in good order

(1)

5. Personal readiness for sporting requires the participant to:

☐ **A** Be familiar with tactics, have the correct skills, have the ability to apply the rule to the game, have the most up-to-date kit

☐ **B** Understand their role in the activity, be familiar with tactics, have the correct skills, have the ability to apply the rule to the game

☐ **C** Have the ability to apply the rule to the game, understand role in the activity, be familiar with tactics, be popular in the team

☐ **D** Have the correct skills, provide the equipment, be familiar with tactics, have the ability to apply the rule to the game

(1)

6. Which of the following questions could be asked in a Physical Activity Readiness Questionnaire? Has your doctor ever said that you suffer from…

☐ **A** Chest pains, dizziness, over competitiveness, bone or joint problems?

☐ **B** Dizziness, chest pains, high blood pressure, not understanding the tactics?

☐ **C** High blood pressure, dizziness, inability to work in a team, bone or joint problems?

☐ **D** Chest pains, dizziness, high blood pressure, bone or joint problems?

(1)

Short-answer questions

7. (a) What effects on performance would a sportsperson expect if they were tempted to use stimulants?

(1)

(b) Which sportspeople could be tempted to use stimulants?

(3)

8. Why would a performer use beta-blockers?

(1)

Longer-answer questions

9. Having a balanced competition makes the activity safe and fair. What factors would be considered when making an activity have balanced competition and why?

(3)

10. What responsibilities do referees have in relation to keeping play within the boundaries of the rules?

(3)

11. (a) Describe the mesomorphic body type.

(4)

(b) Select a sport a mesomorph type would suit.

(1)

12. Describe the effects of alcohol on health and performance.

(4)

1.2 ～ Your healthy, active body

1.2.2 A healthy, active lifestyle and your cardiovascular system

What you will learn about in this topic:

1 — Parts and function of the circulatory system
2 — How the cardiovascular system works
3 — A healthy and active lifestyle and the cardiovascular system

1 — Parts and function of the circulatory system

The **circulatory system** involves the heart, blood vessels, blood, the **pulmonary circuit** and the **systemic circuit**. It is known as the cardiovascular system – cardio meaning heart and vascular relating to blood vessels.

The function of the circulatory system is to:

- Transport oxygen and nutrients to parts of the body and remove waste or toxic products such as salt, carbon dioxide and urea, water and heat, from the body. The body relies on these functions to stay alive. The balance of nutrients also keeps the body functioning properly.
- Control body temperature – the body is affected by changes of temperature, so keeping it in an acceptable range keeps the body functioning properly.
- Protect – antibodies in the blood fight disease and platelets help to clot the blood at the source of a cut and prevent other germs entering the body.
- **Superior vena cava** – carries deoxygenated blood from the body to the heart.
- Right atrium – upper chamber on the right of the heart receives deoxygenated blood from the vena cava and pumps it into the right ventricle.

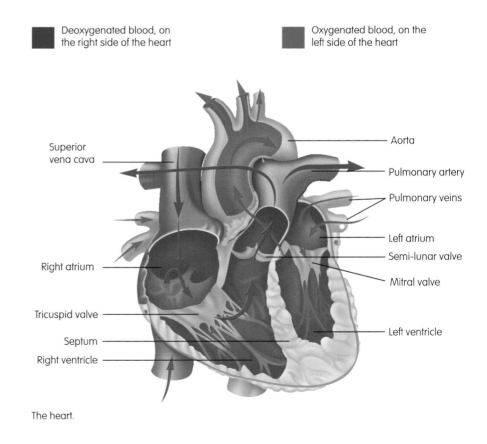

Deoxygenated blood, on the right side of the heart

Oxygenated blood, on the left side of the heart

Superior vena cava

Aorta

Pulmonary artery

Pulmonary veins

Left atrium

Semi-lunar valve

Right atrium

Mitral valve

Tricuspid valve

Left ventricle

Septum

Right ventricle

The heart.

- Tricuspid **valve** – valve between the right atrium and the right ventricle, which stops backflow of blood.
- Right ventricle – lower chamber on the right of the heart receives deoxygenated blood from the right atrium and pumps it into the left pulmonary artery.
- **Septum** – wall dividing the two sides of the heart.
- **Aorta** – carries oxygenated blood from the heart to the body.
- Pulmonary artery – carries deoxygenated blood from the heart to the lungs.
- Semi-lunar valve – prevents backflow of blood from the arteries into the ventricles.
- Left atrium – upper chamber of the heart receives oxygenated blood from the pulmonary veins and pumps it into the left ventricle.
- Pulmonary veins – carry oxygenated blood from the lungs to the heart.
- Mitral valve – lies between the left atrium and the left ventricle and prevents backflow of blood.
- Left ventricle – lower left chamber of the heart receives oxygenated blood from the left atrium and pumps it into the aorta.

Task 1

Learn the names of the different parts of the circulation system.

> Remember, the left side of the heart has the pulmonary vein bringing oxygenated blood back to the heart and the right side has the pulmonary artery taking deoxygenated blood away from the heart.

Key terms

Circulatory system – transports blood using the heart and blood vessels

Pulmonary circuit – transports blood from the heart to the lungs and back again

Systemic circuit – transports blood from the heart to the body and back to the heart again

Superior vena cava – blood vessel transporting deoxygenated blood back to the heart

Valve – openings allowing blood flow in one direction only, found in the heart and veins

Septum – wall of muscle dividing the left and right sides of the heart

Aorta – main blood vessel leaving the heart

A comparison of arteries, capillaries and veins

Arteries

Arteries carry blood away from the heart. Due to the closeness of some of them to the heart, they have a pulse and work under high pressure. The walls of arteries, therefore, need to be very thick and flexible.

Blood leaves the heart in the aorta, the longest artery in the body. Smaller arteries branch off the aorta, so that the oxygen gets to all parts of the body. In its transportation of blood, the aorta divides into smaller **arterioles** and then into even smaller capillaries. The outer layer of an artery is tough and fibrous. The inner lining (**endothelium**) is elastic. The diameter of the inner layer is controlled involuntarily. It automatically changes size according to the amount of blood flowing at any time.

Endothelium lining

Elastic fibres of involuntary muscle (not controlled consciously and thicker than in a vein)

Tough, non-elastic fibres (thicker than a vein)

An arteriole.

Capillaries

Arterioles lead in to the capillaries, which are grouped in clusters. Capillaries are the smallest of all the blood vessels with walls just one cell thick: they are thinner than strands of hair. At one end, they feed muscles, organs and body tissue with oxygen and nutrients. At the other, carbon dioxide and waste products pass through their walls to flow into veins for removal from the body. Blood enters the capillaries under pressure. Capillaries bring blood within reach of every cell. Because substances pass through the walls they are called 'semi-permeable'.

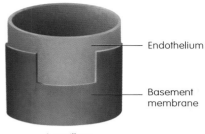

Endothelium

Basement membrane

A capillary.

Veins

Capillaries feed the veins. The walls of veins are thinner than arteries. Their function is to bring the deoxygenated blood back to the heart and they work at lower pressure. They have an inner layer (endothelium) and two tough outer fibrous layers. These are thinner than the arterial layers and less elastic. To help the veins get the blood back to the heart they have valves to stop the blood flowing backwards due, in part, to gravitational pull. Additionally, pulsating muscles, close to the veins, help to keep the blood moving. This action is called the 'skeletal pump'.

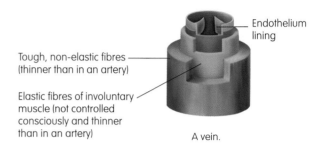

Endothelium lining

Tough, non-elastic fibres (thinner than in an artery)

Elastic fibres of involuntary muscle (not controlled consciously and thinner than in an artery)

A vein.

Valves in veins allow the blood to flow in one direction only.

Task 2

Make a table of information about the three types of blood vessel.

Look at the above sections on arteries, capillaries and veins. Think about the similarities and differences between them.

2 — How the cardiovascular system works

Heart rate

At rest, the heart has a chance to slow down, as it does not have to work so hard against gravity to circulate the blood. The **resting heart rate** is about 72 beats per minute, although this varies with gender and age (males and young adults usually have a lower heart rate). This is sufficient to supply the muscles with the necessary blood and nutrients. Every heartbeat pumps blood out of the heart; this is called the **stroke volume**. The total volume of blood pumped out of the heart, calculated over a minute, is called the **cardiac output**.

The heart rate increases when extra demands are made on the body. The rate depends on the type of activity. If it is easy, the pulse goes up a little; if the activity is more intense, then the pulse rises further.

Performers can regulate the intensity of their training if they know their **maximum heart rate**. Usually, the heart rate needs to be raised to at least 60 per cent of the maximum to improve cardiovascular fitness levels.

To work out the maximum heart or pulse rate the following formula is used:

220 – age = maximum heart rate

Stroke volume is the amount of blood pumped out of the heart with each beat. At rest, the heart pumps about 85ml of blood. During exercise this could increase to 130ml (nearly a quarter of a pint) depending on fitness levels. This is a lot of blood considering the heart is only the size of a clenched fist!

Cardiac output is the amount of blood ejected from the heart per minute. To work out the cardiac output multiply the stroke volume by the heart rate.

Heart rate (HR) × Stroke volume (SV) = Cardiac output (CO)

As the heart rate and stroke volume increase with exercise so does the cardiac output.

After exercise, the heart returns to its resting rate. The time it takes to do this is referred to as the **recovery rate**. A cool-down can help the body gradually return to the resting heart rate. This takes about five minutes depending on the fitness level and type of cool-down.

Task 3

Create a spider diagram showing the effects of exercise on the heart.

Key terms

Arterioles – blood vessels that are sub-divisions of arteries

Endothelium – internal space of the blood vessels; in arteries this changes according to the amount of blood to be transported

Resting heart rate – amount of heartbeats per minute when the body is at rest

Stroke volume – the volume of blood pumped out of the heart by each ventricle during one contraction

Cardiac output – the amount of blood pumped by the heart in one minute

Maximum heart rate – calculated as 220 minus age

Recovery rate – the time it takes for the heart to return to resting rate after exercise

Finding a pulse

There are several places in the body where the pulse is strong and easy to count. These places are where the arteries are easily located. The arteries take blood away from the heart and so work under high pressure: this is why they have a pulse. The pressure gets less by the time the blood reaches the veins and so the veins have no significant pulse.

The two most common places to take a pulse are at the wrist and at the throat. The inside of the wrist on the thumb side is the radial artery. In the throat, on either side of the larynx, is the carotid artery. Two other places where the pulse is strong are at the temple (the temporal pulse) and the groin (the femoral pulse).

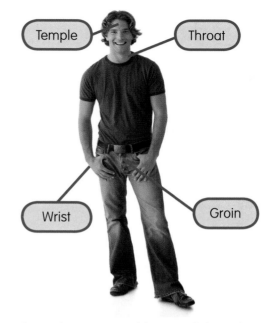

The temple, groin, wrist and throat are all places where the pulse is strong and can be found relatively easily.

The double circulatory system

The heart is the pump in a double circulatory system. The pulmonary circuit carries deoxygenated blood from the heart to the lungs. It is then oxygenated and is returned to the heart from the lungs.

The systemic circuit carries oxygenated blood from the heart to the rest of the body; the oxygen is used and so deoxygenated blood is taken back from the body to the heart.

The pulmonary circuit is a complete circuit that carries blood from the heart to the lungs and back. It moves deoxygenated blood from the right ventricle, via the pulmonary artery, to the lungs. In the lungs it picks up oxygen and thus becomes re-oxygenated. It leaves the lungs by the pulmonary vein and is taken to the left atrium of the heart.

The systemic circuit is also a complete circuit. It carries blood from the heart to all parts of the body and back to the heart. The oxygenated blood is pumped from the left atrium to the left ventricle and into the aorta. It travels around the body to be used by the working muscles. The blood, once used, is deoxygenated. It makes its way back to the right atrium of the heart via the superior vena cava to start the cycle over again.

When the heart beats or contracts it is called 'systole' or 'systolic phase' giving the systolic blood pressure. This action forces blood through the arteries around the body. When the heart relaxes, it fills up with blood returning from the veins. This is called the 'diastole' or 'diastolic phase' – giving the diastolic blood pressure.

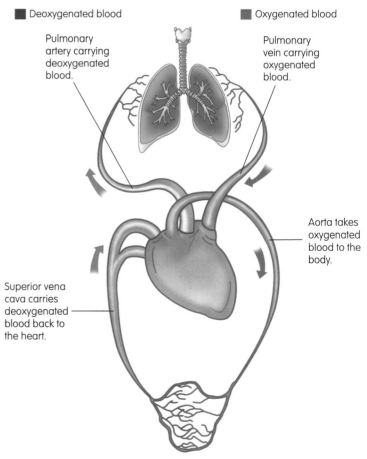

The double circulatory system.

Task 4

1 – Using the diagram on page 159, trace the pathway of blood: start at the heart, leading into the pulmonary artery.

2 – Draw a black and white diagram of the double circulatory system and colour in the systemic and pulmonary systems.

> You could number the parts so they remind you of the order.

Function of the blood

Red blood cells

Red blood cells (erythrocytes) are small but there are many of them. Two million are produced and destroyed in your body every second! Their main job is to carry oxygen, but they also transport nutrients and waste products, such as carbon dioxide and salt. They are produced in the bone marrow of long bones. During exercise the blood increases in thickness as water is removed as waste.

In these cells is **haemoglobin**. Oxygen chemically attaches itself to haemoglobin to make oxyhaemoglobin. It is in this way that oxygen is transported to the working muscles of the body and carbon dioxide is taken away to the lungs transported in solution in the plasma.

Human blood, showing red blood cells.

White blood cells

The job of the white blood cells (leukocytes) is to protect the body. There are five types of white blood cell. The main functions of leukocytes are to fight infection at its source, repair damaged tissue after an injury and destroy bacteria. When a cut or graze occurs, the white blood cells gather to stop bacteria entering the body. When a scab forms it is made up of dead leukocytes. There are fewer white than red blood cells in the body. The cells are produced in the marrow of long bones and lymph tissue of the body.

Platelets

These are small fragments of larger cells. They are in charge of clotting the blood. They clot at the skin's surface after a graze or cut. They do the same job internally, on small, damaged blood vessels. Clotting is important to stop blood loss from the body and stop internal bleeding.

Plasma

Plasma is straw-coloured and is 90 per cent water. It makes up 55 per cent of the volume of blood. It helps the blood flow more easily by the use of plasma proteins. The ten per cent of plasma that is not water contains a mixture of the following: salts, chlorine, amino acids, glucose, antibodies, **fibrinogen** (helps clotting), hormones and waste products, such as urea and carbon dioxide. During exercise hormones such as endorphins, cortisol, adrenalin and testosterone are produced and are transported in the plasma. Adrenalin can help a performer heighten their performance levels during competition.

Inactivated blood platelets are oval, whereas activated platelets develop extensions from the cell wall, as seen here.

Task 5

From your knowledge of the composition of blood, copy and complete each of the following sentences:

a. Red blood cells are called _____.

b. The main function of red blood cells is to _____.

c. Red blood cells contain haemoglobin; this helps the _____.

d. White blood cells protect the body by _____.

e. White blood cells are also called _____.

f. White blood cells are produced in _____.

g. The job of the platelets is _____.

h. Platelets are smaller parts of _____.

i. Plasma is 90 per cent water and makes up _____.

j. Plasma contains plasma proteins that help _____.

Key terms

Haemoglobin – found in red blood cells, transports oxygen to body tissue

Fibrinogen – a protein found in blood that helps clotting

Blood pressure

Blood pressure is the amount of force the blood applies on the sides of the blood vessels. It is used as an indicator of how fit the circulatory system is. Blood pressure is affected by exercise. The immediate effect of exercise raises blood pressure but over time, exercise can lower blood pressure, reducing the risks of circulatory problems.

A sphygmomanometer is the instrument that measures blood pressure. The reading is given in units of millimetres of mercury (mmHg). One reading is the systolic pressure; the other is the diastolic pressure. On average, the systolic pressure for an adult will range between 100 and 140mmHg and the diastolic between 60 and 90mmHg.

When exercise begins, the blood pressure increases. This increases the blood flow, meeting the demand for oxygen by the working muscles.

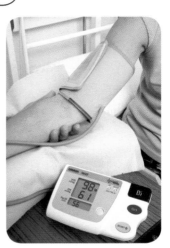

The differing pressures of the cuff around the arm give the systolic and diastolic blood pressures.

The sphygmomanometer aims to check how well the heart (pump) and the blood vessels (pipes) are working. The higher the numbers on the reading, the harder the heart is having to work due to the restrictions in the blood vessels. The harder the heart has to work, the sooner it could wear out.

The procedure for taking blood pressure is as follows:

- The cuff is wrapped around the arm and pumped up.
- The pressure of the cuff stops the blood supply. This is heard by listening through a stethoscope.
- The cuff is released so the blood starts to flow again. At this point a reading is taken showing the maximum output of pressure of the heart, which equals the systolic pressure reading.
- The cuff continues to release until there is no sound of heart beat in the stethoscope. Another reading is taken showing the pressure when the heart is relaxed, which equals the diastolic pressure reading.

Blood pressure is at its greatest when the blood is forced into the arteries by the contraction of the left ventricle. This reading gives the systolic pressure. Blood enters the ventricle from the atrium and then the left ventricle relaxes. When the arteries relax, the pressure reduces, thus giving the diastolic pressure reading.

A blood pressure reading is shown in the following way:

$$\frac{\textbf{systolic pressure}}{\textbf{diastolic pressure}}$$

The range of blood pressure can be between 100 over 60 and 140 over 90 for an average person. For younger children the average is about 120 over 80.

When the heart beats, it makes two sounds. One is made when the cuspid valves close, forcing the blood into the arteries from the ventricles; the other is the sound of the semi-lunar valves closing, the blood having been forced down into the ventricle.

What affects blood pressure?

There are many circumstances affecting blood pressure. Exercise will make the systolic pressure rise, whereas it will drop during sleep. Age has an effect: if you are young, blood pressure is low and the older a person becomes the higher it will be. Weight also has an effect: the more overweight you are, the higher your blood pressure. Children's blood pressure will vary according to their age, gender and height.

Older arteries are less elastic, which means they cannot expand to move the greater amounts of blood needing to be moved. This is called hardening of the arteries. A man will usually have a higher reading than a woman. If a person is tired, stressed or even at a different altitude, their blood pressure will change.

Smoking raises the pulse rate and so makes the heart work faster for no reason. The smoker's blood vessels contract, raising the blood pressure and causing a sensation of cold. Smoke contains carbon monoxide so when this enters the blood stream it reduces the red blood cells' ability to transport oxygen. As a result, fitness levels are reduced. In activities where the good condition of the cardiovascular system is required, smoking is a major hindrance as it can affect the necessary blood flow around the body.

Drinking alcohol over time also raises blood pressure although it is not currently known how. One theory is that chemicals in alcohol causes blood vessels to tighten and close. Excessive alcohol consumption affects all drinkers but with particularly adverse effects in men over 50. Drinking alcohol can cause 'blood-sludging'. The red blood cells clump together and cause the small blood vessels to clog up; this starves the tissue of oxygen and causes the cells to die. This happens in the brain and on the skin, recognizable by red blotchy patches on the face. Alcohol affects the blood by causing anaemia, lowering the red and white blood cell count and the bone marrow, weakening the bone structure.

How blood pressure can be reduced
There are several ways to control blood pressure:

- Keep within the guidelines of body weight recommendations.
- Do not smoke, as it makes the blood pressure rise and reduces the efficiency of the heart and blood vessels.
- Avoid too much alcohol.
- Eat less salt.
- Avoid stresses and worrying situations.
- Exercise regularly, as it will relieve stress, keep the body systems working properly and help to keep your blood pressure within normal boundaries.

Immediate effects of exercise on circulatory system

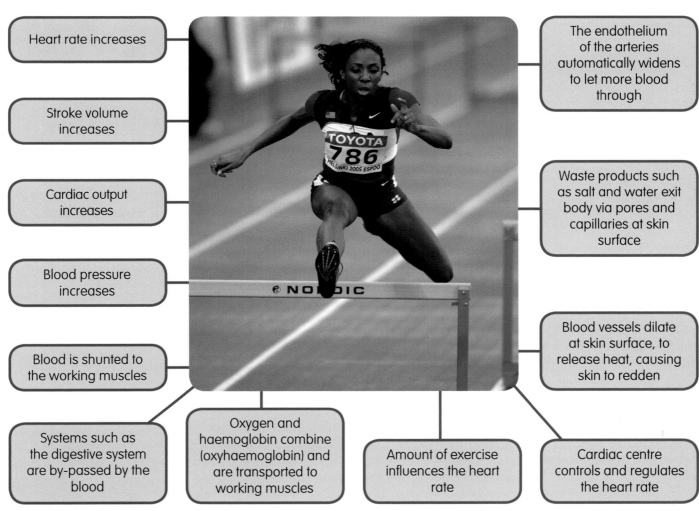

Heart rate increases

Stroke volume increases

Cardiac output increases

Blood pressure increases

Blood is shunted to the working muscles

The endothelium of the arteries automatically widens to let more blood through

Waste products such as salt and water exit body via pores and capillaries at skin surface

Blood vessels dilate at skin surface, to release heat, causing skin to redden

Systems such as the digestive system are by-passed by the blood

Oxygen and haemoglobin combine (oxyhaemoglobin) and are transported to working muscles

Amount of exercise influences the heart rate

Cardiac centre controls and regulates the heart rate

Task 6

1 – List six ways that blood pressure can be controlled.

2 – Where is it easy to count the pulse?

3 – Why is it that arteries work under high pressure?

4 – Which pressure is the greater, systolic or diastolic?

5 – What actions make the sounds of the heartbeat?

6 – What should an average person's blood pressure be?

7 – Give four factors that affect blood pressure.

Active challenge

1 – Find your carotid pulse at your neck (press your first two fingers to the side of your throat).

2 – Record your resting pulse.

3 – Now jump on the spot for one minute.

4 – Take your pulse again. How has it changed?

5 – Are you showing any other immediate effects of exercise?

6 – Record your results.

3 — A healthy and active lifestyle and the cardiovascular system

Diet

Diet can have a bearing on blood pressure and cholesterol. A diet which is low in fat, salt and sugar, but high in fruit and vegetables, can reduce the risk of high blood pressure. Different types of cholesterol are found in food:

- Low density lipoprotein (LDL) is mainly made up of fat and small amounts of protein. Too much LDL can cause deposits to build up in the arteries. This makes blood flow more difficult and can be linked to cardiovascular disease. LDL can be referred to as 'bad cholesterol'.
- High density lipoprotein (HDL) is mainly made up of protein and small amounts of fat. This can help reduce the amount of cholesterol building up in the arteries. HDL can be referred to as 'good cholesterol'.

Eating a regular, balanced diet can help support a healthy, active body. By eating a varied diet the body will have a chance to take in all the different nutrients and vitamins required to keep it healthy and free from long-term illness. Eating particular foods can help keep the body in good condition and reduce the risk of health problems:

- To lower cholesterol levels – reduce intake of animal fats and salt and increase intake of fibre, fruit and vegetables.
- To help regulate blood pressure – reduce salt and increase omega 3 essential fatty acids (which helps to keep blood from clotting).

Active challenge

Create an example of a main meal that would provide the essential variety of nutrients for a healthy diet.

To help, you can use the information in the diet topic on page 114 or use the Internet.

Water intake

The body is approximately 67 per cent water (that is, two-thirds). Maintaining this percentage is important, as a drop of only two percent will cause feelings of fatigue. Drinking water regularly (one to two litres daily, although this can vary according to the exercise levels undertaken) can be an aid to a healthy body. Kidneys can be kept in good order and the chances of cancer of the bladder and heart attacks can be reduced.

Water:

- lubricates the joints
- helps with digestion
- flushes toxins out of the body

- keeps the eyes healthy and lubricated
- helps to keep the skin healthy.

It is essential to take in water before, during and after exercise in order to keep hydrated.

Dehydration
If the body loses its normal percentage of water then dehydration can occur. When this happens the balance of chemicals in the body is changed. The result can be disorientation, irrational behaviour, coma and, in extreme cases, even death can occur.

Effects of regular exercise and training on the circulatory system

Endurance training, commonly known as aerobic training, helps strengthen the heart. This type of training is progressive, over time. With training the general size of the heart gets bigger, the walls become thicker, stronger and more robust. The resting stroke volume increases and so does the cardiac output.

Whilst everything else is increasing, the heart rate does the opposite. A useful indicator of good fitness is the resting heart rate. The slower it is per minute, the more efficient the heart is. It can pump the required amount of blood with fewer beats. Therefore, the slower the resting heartbeat, the fitter the person. With good aerobic fitness, a person will usually be able to keep working efficiently without tiring or losing skill.

Long-term benefits of exercise on the circulatory system

Stronger heart – lasts longer and is more efficient

Lower resting rate – transports sufficient blood with fewer beats

Lower active heart rate – less stress on heart

Increased VO₂ max (the maximum amount of oxygen used in a minute per kilogram of body weight)

Can cope with increased stress more effectively

Can deliver oxygen to the working muscles more effectively

Can recover from the stress of exercise quicker

Can reduce risk of heart and coronary artery disease

Increases size of heart

Task 7

1 – Taking regular exercise affects the body in many ways. Using the two headings 'Immediate effects of exercise' and 'Long-term effects of exercise', make lists of the different changes that happen to the body.

2 – Make a visual presentation of your findings.

Rest and work

When the object is to improve fitness by training hard the performer often forgets the need for rest. These times of relaxation are essential if the maximum is to be gained from the training. To improve, the body needs to be exposed to increased stresses in the training programme, but then the body needs time to adapt to these stresses and recover. Days of light training and days of complete rest are important to incorporate into the training programme.

Rest is essential if injury is to be avoided. Rest allows the body to adapt to the training, muscle tissues to repair and the body to build up the correct balance of chemicals again. Training affects the immune system and so to keep healthy, rest time is needed to build this back up and avoid illness.

Summary

The contents of blood keep the body alive. The circulation of blood to different parts of the body is vital. Oxygen, nutrients and hormones give the tissues of the body what they need to work. Waste products such as salt, heat, water, carbon dioxide and urea are all removed from the body so it is not poisoned.

When a person exercises, the circulatory system needs to work faster as there is greater demand by the muscles for oxygen. With regular exercise, the body can be trained to make these adjustments quickly and efficiently.

Exam questions

Multiple-choice questions

1. (a) Which of the following best describe the function of the circulatory system?

    ☐ **A** Protects the body by transporting white blood cells to the site of infection, helps with breathing, is an indicator of fitness

    ☐ **B** Transports blood around the body, helps control body temperature, protects the body by transporting white blood cells to the site of infection

    ☐ **C** Helps control body temperature, works via the central nervous system, is an indicator of fitness, controls movement

    ☐ **D** Shunts blood to working muscles, helps with breathing, controls the intake of oxygen

    (1)

    (b) Which of the following best describes veins?

    ☐ **A** Work at lower pressure than other blood vessels, have semi-permeable walls

    ☐ **B** Have valves, work under high pressure, transport oxygenated blood

    ☐ **C** Have thin walls, have valves, work at lower pressure than other blood vessels, transport deoxygenated blood

    ☐ **D** Transport deoxygenated blood, divide into arterioles, have walls one cell thick

    (1)

    (c) Which of the following best describe the pulmonary circuit?

    ☐ **A** Heart – pulmonary arteries – lungs – pulmonary vein – heart

    ☐ **B** Heart – aorta – lungs – pulmonary vein – heart

    ☐ **C** Heart – pulmonary arteries – capillaries – lungs – pulmonary vein – heart

    ☐ **D** Heart – pulmonary arteries – lungs – vena cava – heart

    (1)

    (d) Which of the following best describes the effects of exercise on blood flow?

    ☐ **A** Blood shunted to working muscles, stroke volume increases, heart rate remains constant, cardiac output increases

    ☐ **B** Heart beats harder, blood shunted to working muscles, stroke volume increases, blood changes colour

    ☐ **C** Blood shunted to working muscles, cardiac output decreases, heart rate increases, plasma is reduced

    ☐ **D** Heart rate increases, heart beats harder, blood shunted to working muscles, cardiac output increases

    (1)

Short-answer questions

2. What is the term that describes the amount of blood ejected from the heart in one minute?

    (1)

3. Blood is the transportation system of the body. Which type of blood cell is responsible for carrying oxygen around the body?

    (1)

Longer-answer questions

4. What are the immediate effects of exercise on the circulatory system?

    (4)

5. What are the effects of regular exercise and training on the circulatory system?

    (3)

6. What are the long-term benefits of exercise on the circulatory system?

    (3)

1.2 ～ Your healthy, active body

1.2.3 A healthy, active lifestyle and your respiratory system

What you will learn about in this topic:

1 — Parts and functions of the respiratory system
2 — How the respiratory system works
3 — A healthy, active lifestyle and the respiratory system

1 — Parts and functions of the respiratory system

The function of the respiratory system is to help get oxygen into the body and carbon dioxide and waste products out of the body. This happens through the act of breathing. Breathing in (inhalation) gets the oxygen in, so it can be used by the body to release energy. Breathing out (exhalation) removes the carbon dioxide so it does not build up and poison the body.

The parts of the respiratory system are:

- air passages
- lungs
- **diaphragm**.

Air passages

The air passages are a series of linking tubes. They create the pathway for the air to get to the lungs. Air can enter the body through the mouth or the nose. Air entering the body through the nose, rather than the mouth, has distinct advantages:

- It is warmed, making it a similar temperature to the internal organs.
- There are hairs and mucus in the nose, which filter the air, stopping the larger particles of dust and pollen getting into the lungs. The absence of particles allows the **alveoli** to work well.
- The nose moistens the air so it can be absorbed by the alveoli more easily.

Role of the lungs

The lungs are positioned inside the chest cavity. The ribs form a cage, protecting them. The right lung is bigger than the left lung because it has three cavities and the left only has two.

The action of breathing means that the lungs are constantly moving in and out.

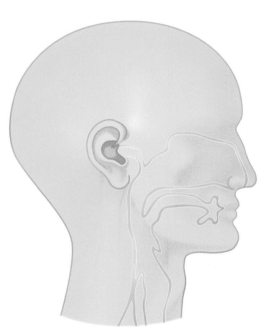

The air passages of the nose and throat are outlined in orange.

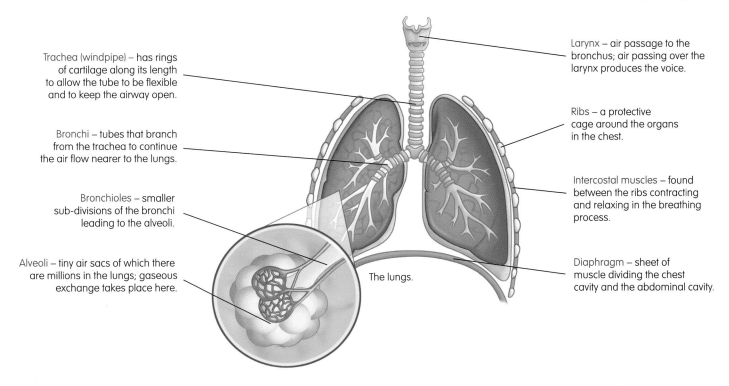

Trachea (windpipe) – has rings of cartilage along its length to allow the tube to be flexible and to keep the airway open.

Bronchi – tubes that branch from the trachea to continue the air flow nearer to the lungs.

Bronchioles – smaller sub-divisions of the bronchi leading to the alveoli.

Alveoli – tiny air sacs of which there are millions in the lungs; gaseous exchange takes place here.

Larynx – air passage to the bronchus; air passing over the larynx produces the voice.

Ribs – a protective cage around the organs in the chest.

Intercostal muscles – found between the ribs contracting and relaxing in the breathing process.

Diaphragm – sheet of muscle dividing the chest cavity and the abdominal cavity.

The lungs.

To protect the lungs from any friction, due to movement, the pleural membrane forms a complete lining around them. The pleural membrane is smooth and has a moist, slimy mucus.

From the nose or mouth, air enters the trachea and moves towards the lungs. It divides into two branches called the bronchi. These sub-divide into smaller tubes called bronchioles. At the end of these are alveoli. These are air sacs with many mini blood vessels called capillaries running from them.

The millions of alveoli allow gases to exchange inside them. Here is a simplified version of what happens:

- Oxygen from the air breathed in enters the circulatory system to be used by the working muscles.
- Carbon dioxide, which is toxic or harmful to the system, transfers from the used blood, out of the circulatory system, back into the alveoli, to be breathed out, along with oxygen, water and nitrogen.
- The capillaries, covering the surface of the alveoli, link the respiratory system with the circulatory system.

The exchange of gases is vital for our survival. With training, this exchange becomes more efficient as more alveoli are prepared to make the swap between oxygen (in) and carbon dioxide (out). Regular exercise conditions the lungs to excrete more of the poisonous carbon dioxide from the body. If too much carbon dioxide remained in the body, it would be fatal.

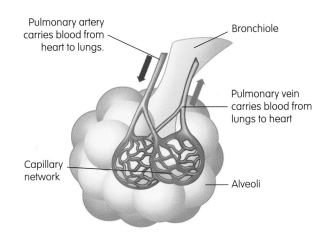

Pulmonary artery carries blood from heart to lungs.

Bronchiole

Pulmonary vein carries blood from lungs to heart

Capillary network

Alveoli

The bronchiole and alveoli.

Task 1

In your own words, write a description of the following parts of the body linked with the respiratory system: trachea, bronchi, bronchioles, lungs, alveoli, diaphragm, intercostal muscles and ribs.

Task 2

Write four sentences on key points about the lungs. Use the following words as headings:

- Position
- Protection
- Exchange of gases
- Effects of training

2 — How the respiratory system works

The mechanism of breathing

Lungs are not muscles. Lungs cannot move of their own accord, nor are they controlled by the central nervous system. So, how do they move when we breathe in and out? The key to breathing is the diaphragm and the intercostal muscles between the ribs.

When we breathe in – **inspiration** – the following happens:

- the diaphragm pulls down
- the intercostal muscles contract
- air pressure is reduced
- air is sucked through the tubes into the lungs
- our chest expands.

When we breathe out – **expiration** – the opposite happens:

- the diaphragm relaxes into its dome position
- the intercostal muscles relax
- our chest becomes smaller
- pressure increases on our lungs
- air is forced out.

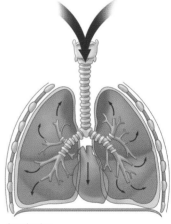

Inspiration.

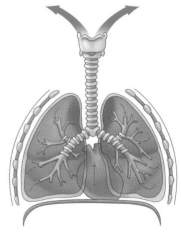

Expiration.

Task 3

In your own words, describe the action of breathing.

Use the following words to help you: nose, mouth, trachea, lungs, ribs, intercostal muscles and diaphragm.

Key terms

Diaphragm – muscle that divides the chest cavity from the abdominal cavity

Alveoli – air sacs where gaseous exchange takes place

Inspiration – breathing in, inhalation

Expiration – breathing out, exhalation

Respiration and exercise

The body converts fuel (usually glucose) to energy and releases it into the body through aerobic and anaerobic respiration. The systems automatically kick in depending on the type and intensity of the exercise performed.

Aerobic exercise

Energy released in aerobic activity needs a sufficient supply of oxygen to the tissues. With enough oxygen present the activity can go on for long periods, as long as the difficulty or intensity does not become too great. This aerobic fitness allows us to keep going at a moderate level. The aerobic system is used in moderate to hard continuous activities that usually take place over a period of more than 60 seconds. The oxygen is breathed in and diffused into the circulatory system. In this type of activity, breathing becomes more regular and deeper. The muscles need oxygen to contract and in aerobic respiration this oxygen enters the body by the breathing process.

The formula for aerobic respiration is:

Aerobic = extra oxygen

glucose + oxygen ⟶ carbon dioxide + water + energy

Anaerobic fitness

When energy is produced anaerobically no oxygen is used in its initial release. Some sports wholly use anaerobic respiration. These are activities where there is a need for a single maximum burst of energy. Athletic field events are good examples of anaerobic exercise. In throwing and jumping events the actions used are explosive. They use one all-out burst of maximum effort to complete the event. The time it takes to complete the attempt is very short, so the energy is produced from the supplies already in the body.

Long-distance runners, such as Dan Robinson, need aerobic respiration.

The demand of the muscles for oxygen is so great that the cardiovascular system does not have time to supply the demand. In anaerobic respiration the energy is provided, not by oxygen, but by adenosine triphosphate (ATP) and creatine phosphate (CP).

ATP and CP can only supply energy for a short time. If the demand for energy continues for over a minute then this releases energy by breaking down carbohydrates. This is called the **lactic acid** system. The side effect of the body using this system is that a build-up of lactic acid could occur in the muscles, which can lead to fatigue. The fitter the athlete, the higher the work rate achieved before the need to supplement the energy by the carbohydrates being broken down to lactic acid.

Athletic field events use anaerobic respiration; Jessica Ennis demonstrates this in the Women's Heptathlon.

The formula for anaerobic respiration is:

$$\text{glucose} \longrightarrow \text{energy} + \text{lactic acid}$$

Anaerobic = no oxygen

As the oxygen debt is repaid, the lactic acid converts into carbon dioxide and water.

You can tell when a player has just used their anaerobic system from their breathing pattern. After working very hard in the activity their breath may be shallow and gasping. This is an indication that there is an **oxygen debt**, a state in which the body needs more oxygen than it can supply.

This type of energy provision can only carry on for 45 to 60 seconds. After this, the lactic acid in the muscles becomes too high and prevents muscular contraction. The anaerobic system stops. The body then cannot keep running at its fastest speed or keep lifting heavy weights.

In all games, a combination of aerobic and anaerobic respiration is required. A player, while moving and positioning themselves correctly on the pitch according to the play, is using aerobic respiration. This is aerobic because the intensity of the exercise is moderate and will continue throughout the game. When the player takes a shot, for example, one maximal contraction is used. For this action, the anaerobic system comes into operation.

Sports such as badminton require both aerobic and anaerobic respiration as demonstrated by Gail Emms and Nathan Robertson.

Badminton players, for example, use both types of respiration, due to the need for a maximal effort whenever they strike the ball during a rally, whereas footballers use anaerobic respiration more.

Task 4

Study the comments below on the changes in respiration for an athlete in a sprint race. Put them into the order in which the athlete would experience them.

a. The oxygen debt is repaid.
b. The athlete breathes quickly and respires aerobically.
c. The athlete's muscles ache.
d. The lactic acid system begins to provide energy.
e. The athlete begins anaerobic respiration in their muscles.
f. The athlete breathes slowly and respires aerobically.

> Aerobic = extra oxygen
> Anaerobic = no oxygen

How exercise affects breathing

During exercise there is an increased breathing rate and increased depth of breathing, resulting in more breaths being taken per minute and more air inspired per breath. This is due to the greater need for more oxygen to supply the working muscles during exercise. As a result, more waste products need to be removed from the body. The rate of breathing rises according to the new workload intensity. The rate of breathing can increase up to 50 breaths per minute during extreme exercise. As a result, the amount of oxygen a person needs to take in increases. There is a limit to the increase for each person, called the VO_2 maximum. During exercise, the vital capacity will increase because of the demand for a greater intake of air. Both the **residual volume** and the **tidal volume** increase, but only slightly.

More efficient oxygen and carbon dioxide diffusion

During exercise the demand for oxygen increases. As the muscles use the oxygen they produce carbon dioxide. Carbon dioxide is a poison and needs to be quickly removed from the body. Therefore, there needs to be an exchange or diffusion of gases.

Diffusion can be said to be a movement of gases from an area where there is a high amount to an area where there is a low amount. The greater the difference in concentration of gases, the greater the rate of diffusion.

Undertaking an exercise programme that demands more oxygen by the working muscles will also require the increased removal of carbon dioxide from the body. This removal takes place in the alveoli via the capillaries. Increased fitness also increases the number of capillaries and so improves the diffusion of the gases when exercising; breathing in through the nose moistens and warms the air. This prepares the air, making it more conducive for the gaseous exchange. An efficient gaseous exchange allows the muscles to work for longer periods.

Improved delivery of oxygen to working muscles

As a person becomes fitter, the body's ability to breathe in more air for longer periods of time develops. This increases the amount of oxygen entering the body for use by the working muscles. A fit person also begins to increase the quantity and quality of their blood: more red blood cells are formed as a result. These provide more opportunity for oxyhaemoglobin to be delivered to the working muscles, allowing the person to work harder for longer.

Active challenge

1 – Count the number of breaths you make at rest for one minute.

2 – Perform maximum exercise, such as step-ups, for one minute and then count the number of breaths for one minute.

3 – Time how long it takes breathing to return to rest.

Composition of inspired and expired air

At rest, on average, a person breathes about 15 times a minute. This rate adequately supplies the body systems with enough oxygen to keep them working and the subsequent removal of harmful substances under normal circumstances.

We can feel our chest expand and fall as we breathe in and out. What we are not aware of is the change in the air going into and out of our body. The air we breathe in is different from the air that we breathe out. The parts that make up inhaled and exhaled air are called its 'composition'.

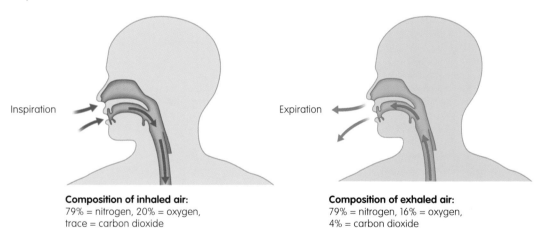

Inspiration

Composition of inhaled air:
79% = nitrogen, 20% = oxygen, trace = carbon dioxide

Expiration

Composition of exhaled air:
79% = nitrogen, 16% = oxygen, 4% = carbon dioxide

Task 5

Make a table showing the composition of inhaled and exhaled air.

The lungs, at different stages of breathing, have varying amounts of air in them. Tidal volume is the amount of air breathed into and out of the body during normal breathing. During exercise, the volume is forced to change. Therefore, it is called **forced breathing**. **Vital capacity** is the largest amount or volume of air that can be exhaled (breathed out) after the largest possible inhalation (breathed in). Residual volume is the amount of air that, even after as much air as possible has been exhaled, is left in the lungs.

Active challenge

Exhaled air has more moisture in it. This is because water is a waste product. Some water is removed from your body as you breathe out. Moisture in exhaled air is demonstrated by the mirror test.

Hold a mirror just below your lip and exhale. What do you see?

When you are exercising, how else is water removed from the body?

Key terms

Lactic acid – chemical built up in the muscles during anaerobic exercise

Oxygen debt – the amount of oxygen consumed during recovery above that which would have ordinarily been consumed in the same time at rest (this results in a shortfall in the oxygen available)

Residual volume – the amount of air left in the lungs after a maximal exhalation

Tidal volume – amount of air breathed in or out during normal breathing

Forced breathing – breathing during exercise when requirements increase

Vital capacity – amount of air that can be breathed out, after a deep breath in

Respiration and circulation link

There has to be a link between the respiratory and circulatory systems. The oxygen has to go from the respiratory system to the circulatory system and back to the respiratory system again. It follows this order:

- The oxygen breathed in goes through the mouth or nose, down the trachea, into the lungs and into the alveoli (air sacs).
- The oxygen passes through the alveoli walls into the red blood cells, via the capillaries.
- The oxygen joins with haemoglobin to make oxyhaemoglobin.
- The oxyhaemoglobin is used by the working body and is transported by the circulatory system to cells needing to release energy.
- Carbon dioxide is produced as a waste product.
- The carbon dioxide is converted into a gas and passes back through the alveoli walls, via the capillaries into the blood plasma.
- Blood takes the carbon dioxide back to the capillaries in the lungs.
- The carbon dioxide passes through the capillary and alveoli walls into the alveoli.
- The carbon dioxide is then exhaled from the body.

3 — A healthy, active lifestyle and the respiratory system

The respiratory system is the way oxygen is transported to the working muscles and so needs to be kept in good order. A healthy and active lifestyle can improve the effectiveness of the system. But, diet, exercise, recreational drugs and rest all have a bearing on respiration.

Respiration and diet

In order for respiration to take place the body needs to take in food. On average, 1200 calories need to be consumed for the body to keep functioning, but more if a greater amount of exercise is to be undertaken. Respiration comes about from the release of energy from the food we eat. When food is taken in it is stored in the body as glucose and then used to release energy through respiration.

Respiration and recreational drugs

Smoking

The lungs have a large surface area. The lungs contain alveoli and they have very thin walls so that the oxygen can enter the blood quickly and the carbon dioxide can leave the blood quickly. It is the large surface area and thin walls that allow the respiratory system to be efficient. A person who smokes affects the size and condition of these organs. Emphysema can be a result of smoking: it affects the lungs by reducing the amount of alveoli and the surface area. This results in the poor exchange of gases, leaving the person breathless after the slightest exercise.

Alcohol

Alcohol has many adverse effects on the body including effects on respiration, breathing and blood pressure.

The effects of alcohol depend on age, weight, fitness and drinking experience. Excessive, long-term alcohol drinking leads to poor respiration. It causes a fall in blood pressure and sometimes even alcohol poisoning (the result of excessive drinking, which affects the body's systems resulting in sickness, irregular breathing, seizures and unconsciousness). Alcohol slows breathing; it can go down to eight breaths per minute. It also causes breathing to be irregular with up to ten seconds between breaths.

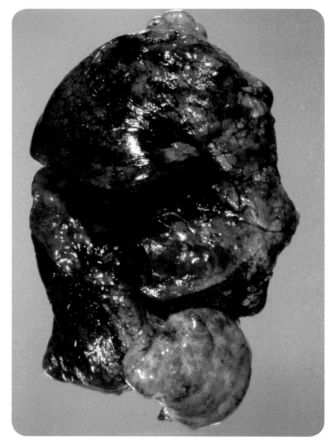

The right lung of a person with emphysema.

Respiration and exercise

The immediate and short-term effects of exercise on the respiratory system:

Oxygen inhaled regularly for aerobic respiration; tidal volume increases.

Air exhaled to stop the build-up of carbon dioxide.

Breathing rate increases and becomes deeper and more regular = aerobic respiration.

After short bursts of all-out effort, breathing is shallow and gasping, attempting to repay the oxygen debt = anaerobic respiration.

Gaseous exchange in alveoli – with training the gaseous exchange becomes more efficient as more alveoli are prepared to take on the exchange of oxygen and carbon dioxide.

Waste water is released from the body as sweat on the surface of the skin.

Release of energy: glycogen is stored in muscles and the liver and is released as glucose to allow the muscles to work.

As the intensity of the exercise becomes less, the demand for oxygen to fuel the muscles reduces. Breathing becomes less deep as a result.

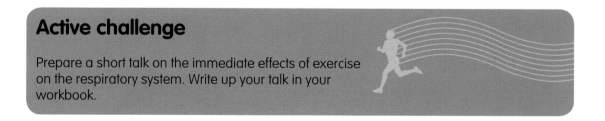

Active challenge

Prepare a short talk on the immediate effects of exercise on the respiratory system. Write up your talk in your workbook.

The long-term effects of exercise on the respiratory system

Correct training prepares the body in many ways. Regular long-term exercise enables the diaphragm and intercostal muscles to become stronger and work to allow more air into the lungs, increasing lung volume. Endurance training makes the exchange of gases in the alveoli more efficient. The muscles are able to work at a moderate to hard level for longer without tiring. The effect this has on the body is to increase the vital capacity of the lungs – the maximum amount of air that can be forcibly exhaled after breathing in as much as possible. This means that more air is exhaled and so more carbon dioxide can leave the body in one breath and more air can be breathed in, getting more oxygen to the working muscles, allowing the body to function well in physically demanding situations. During exercise the vital capacity shows a slight decrease and the residual volume shows a slight increase: lung capacity is made up of the vital capacity and the residual volume. Interval training over short distances at fast speeds results in an oxygen debt. By continuing this training new capillaries are formed, the heart muscle is strengthened and the delivery of oxygen is improved, which stops the build up of lactic acid. The overall effect is called an oxygen debt tolerance, which the performer develops through this type of training.

Key terms

Release of energy – amount and type of energy release used at different stages in different kinds of an activity.

Summary

A fit and healthy respiratory system is vital. It fuels the muscles and takes away poisonous carbon dioxide from the body. Aerobic and anaerobic systems are used at different times depending on the types of stress put on the body. The respiratory and circulatory systems are linked. The key is the link between the alveoli of the respiratory system and the capillaries of the circulatory system. With training, these systems can be improved.

Exam questions

Multiple-choice questions

1. **(a)** Parts of the respiratory system include:

   ☐ **A** Lungs, heart, kidneys, trachea

   ☐ **B** Mouth, alveoli, pancreas, lungs

   ☐ **C** Nose, bronchi, diaphragm, pelvis

   ☐ **D** Alveoli, bronchi, diaphragm, trachea

   (1)

   (b) Which of the following gives the correct order of inspiration?

   ☐ **A** Intercostal muscles contract, diaphragm pulls down, air pressure reduced, air sucked into lungs, chest expands

   ☐ **B** Air sucked into lungs, chest expands, diaphragm pulls down, intercostal muscles contract, air pressure reduced

   ☐ **C** Diaphragm pulls down, intercostal muscles contract, air pressure reduced, air sucked into lungs, chest expands

   ☐ **D** Air pressure reduced, intercostal muscles contract, air sucked into lungs, chest expands, diaphragm pulls down

   (1)

   (c) Which of the following gives the correct effects of exercise on breathing?

   ☐ **A** Tidal volume increases, increased carbon dioxide exhaled, breaths per minute increases

   ☐ **B** Tidal volume decreases, increased carbon dioxide inhaled, residual volume increases

   ☐ **C** Vital capacity increases, residual volume increases, tidal volume decreases

   ☐ **D** Breaths per minute increases, residual volume stays the same, tidal volume decreases

   (1)

Short-answer questions

2. How much do the carbon dioxide levels change from inhaled to exhaled air?

   (1)

3. Where do the branches of the bronchi (the bronchioles) lead to?

   (1)

4. What is the formula for anaerobic exercise?

   (1)

5. What kind of respiration do the following athletes use?

   (a) Marathon runner

   (b) Squash player

   (2)

Longer-answer questions

6. Aerobic respiration is one way energy is released.

   (a) Explain what aerobic respiration is.

   (b) Which athletes utilize this form of respiration?

   (c) Give the equation for this form of respiration.

   (3)

7. Explain the composition of inspired and expired air.

   (4)

8. What are the immediate effects of exercise on the respiratory system?

   (6)

9. What change happens to an athlete's breathing due to anaerobic respiration and why?

   (2)

10. As a performer increases their fitness levels, what effect does this have on the delivery of oxygen?

    (3)

1.2 ~ Your healthy, active body

1.2.4 A healthy, active lifestyle and your muscular system

What you will learn in this topic:

1 — The make-up of the muscular system
2 — How the muscular system works
3 — A healthy, active lifestyle and the muscular system

1 — The make-up of the muscular system

The following diagram gives the name, location and description of muscles:

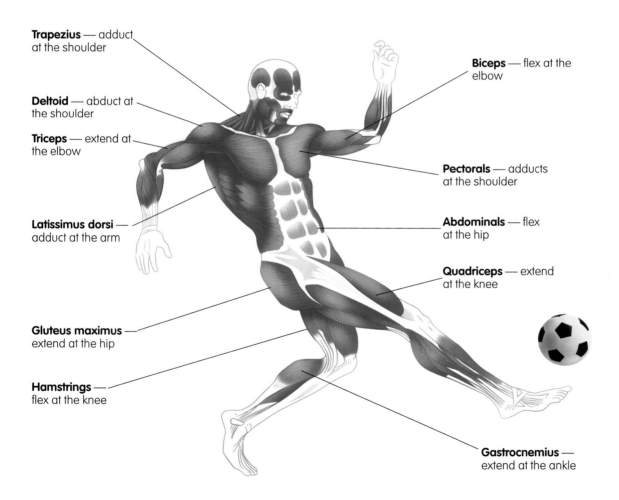

Trapezius — adduct at the shoulder

Deltoid — abduct at the shoulder

Triceps — extend at the elbow

Latissimus dorsi — adduct at the arm

Gluteus maximus — extend at the hip

Hamstrings — flex at the knee

Biceps — flex at the elbow

Pectorals — adducts at the shoulder

Abdominals — flex at the hip

Quadriceps — extend at the knee

Gastrocnemius — extend at the ankle

Task 1

Learn the names of the muscles of the body. Start by trying to memorize the muscles of the upper body. When you feel confident remembering these, go on to the muscles of the lower body.

> Link the muscles with a bone you already know, this may help you to remember them.

Active challenge

Work with a partner and take turns testing each other on names of muscles. Point to a muscle in your body and see if your partner can tell you its name. There are 11 types of muscle to remember.

Task 2

Link each of the muscles listed below with a sporting action and example. Use the examples of movement from the muscle diagram and the following photographs to help you.

- biceps
- triceps
- deltoid
- pectorals
- trapezius
- abdominals
- gluteus maximus
- latissimus dorsi
- quadriceps
- hamstrings
- gastrocnemius

> For example: abdominals – raise the knee so flexing at the hips – used prior to take-off in the high jump.

As the leg is driven back is the leg flexed or extended?

Are the arms adducting or abducting in the reach phase of the row?

Is the right leg flexed or extended?

Is the arm adducting or abducting when the ball is brought into the body?

Classification of muscles

Voluntary muscles, also known as skeletal or striated muscles, are the most common muscle type in the body. These muscles attach to the skeleton and provide a person's shape. We can consciously control these muscles and dictate their movement. Their movement happens like this:

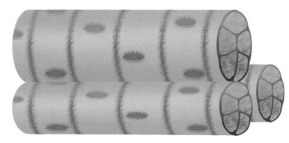

Voluntary muscle.

- A defender sees an attacker moving into a space.
- A message goes through the defender's nervous system to the brain.
- A decision is made through experience and training as to which muscles will be used in order to mark the opposition.
- The brain sends messages to the appropriate muscles.
- The action takes place.

All of this happens in a fraction of a second (it takes 0.33 seconds to respond to a stimulus) and demonstrates why an attacker has a slight advantage over a defender. The defender can compensate for this by learning to read the game and prepare for the most likely course of action by the attacker.

Involuntary muscles, also known as smooth muscles, are not controlled; they work automatically. They carry on functioning throughout life. They are found in the intestines, blood vessels and urinary organs.

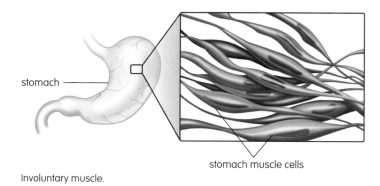

stomach

stomach muscle cells

Involuntary muscle.

Cardiac muscle is a type of involuntary muscle, as it is not controlled consciously but works automatically. It is special because it is found only in the heart and it never rests during life.

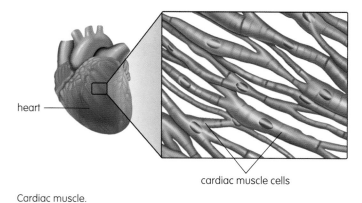

heart

cardiac muscle cells

Cardiac muscle.

Task 3

Using the headings voluntary, involuntary and cardiac, put the following words in the correct groups:

• automatic	• striated	• involuntary	• never rests
• controlled	• intestines	• heart	• automatic
• most common	• smooth	• blood vessels	• consciously

Key terms

Voluntary muscles – skeletal muscles attached to the skeleton, can be made to work consciously

Involuntary muscles – work automatically, controlled by the involuntary nervous system

Cardiac muscle – only found in the heart, and never tires

Types of muscle and their importance in health and fitness

Functioning cardiac muscle is vital to life, controlling the internal transportation system of the body. Although it works automatically, the quality of the muscle ensures its adaptability to increasing, stressful demands. Like cardiac muscle, involuntary muscle also works automatically. Their good condition aids the general functioning of the body, including:

• digestion
• excretion
• circulation.

Voluntary muscle has many functions. It is located around the bones of the body and serves to protect the bones. The condition of the muscle keeps the body upright and assists movement in everyday, sporting and dangerous situations. Good muscle tone and posture aids general health.

Muscle tone is voluntary muscles' readiness to work and be in a prepared state to react. Each muscle has slight tension, waiting to be used. A person's muscles never completely rest; the nearest they come to resting is when a person is asleep. Muscles' state of slight contraction helps with **posture**. The abdominals' toned state helps keep in place the internal organs of that area.

Posture relates to the way the body is supported by the muscles, whether standing, sitting or moving. In some activities where the look of the performer is important to the result, such as gymnastics, diving and dance, good posture is vital; it increases the marks awarded to the performer and enhances the performance. When muscles are trained, their tone increases and this can help posture.

Bad posture.

There are several advantages of having good posture:

- When breathing, there is more room for the lungs to expand and operate; round shoulders make it hard to breathe properly.
- The heart needs to be given enough space to function properly and beat without hindrance.
- The digestive system works well if it has the space to do its job properly.
- Bone alignment prevents strain and injury – poor posture can strain the bones, tendons and ligaments, such as, fallen arches in the foot.
- There is more energy available when the body is in alignment, as the muscles do not have to work so hard to keep the body stable. (Like carrying a ladder, if it is vertical it is easy to carry, if it is at an angle more energy is required to carry it.)
- Maintaining good posture can help the shape of a person. In turn, self-esteem is increased if a person feels good about the way they look. A person standing or sitting well can give a good impression to others.

Good posture.

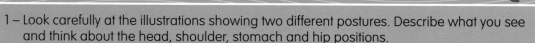

Task 4

1 – Look carefully at the illustrations showing two different postures. Describe what you see and think about the head, shoulder, stomach and hip positions.

2 – Complete a spider diagram including the information on good muscle tone and posture.

Fast and slow twitch muscle fibres

There are two different types of fibre in muscles. There are **fast twitch muscle fibres** and **slow twitch muscle fibres**. Each type is better suited to different activities. Every person has a natural combination of both in their body. This amount cannot be changed, although with the correct training improvements can be made to the efficiency of each type. Games and racket sport players will have a fairly even distribution but some will have a higher percentage of fast twitch muscle fibres.

Fast twitch muscle fibres
When the nervous system decides an event requires short bursts of energy, the fast twitch muscle fibres are used. These are for the more explosive activities, which need quick reactions. They contract fast and produce a powerful action. They have only limited oxygen supply and so tire quickly. Under a microscope they are white in colour. They are best used for speed events, throwing and jumping.

Slow twitch muscle fibres
The nervous system can detect when an event is slow and prolonged and will activate the slow twitch muscle fibres. These are more suited to endurance activities. They can contract many times and stay efficient over long periods. They have a very good oxygen supply, which gives them their energy. Under a microscope they are red in colour. They are suited to events that take a long time to complete, such as long-distance running, cycling and swimming.

Explosive events like the discus, performed here by Shelley Drew, rely on fast twitch muscle fibres.

Slow twitch muscle fibres are needed in long-distance events, as demonstrated by Olympic gold medallist Nicole Cook.

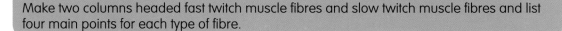

Task 5

Make two columns headed fast twitch muscle fibres and slow twitch muscle fibres and list four main points for each type of fibre.

Active challenge

In pairs, take turns in naming a sport. Your partner should say whether it needs fast or slow twitch muscle fibres for greatest success.

Key terms

Muscle tone – muscles' state of slight tension and readiness to work

Posture – the way the muscles hold the body when still or in motion

Fast twitch muscle fibres – muscle fibres used in events requiring quick reactions and power

Slow twitch muscle fibres – muscle fibres required in endurance events

Summary

The body uses three types of muscle. Some can be controlled consciously; others work automatically. The greatest amount of muscle is voluntary muscle, which makes up about 40 per cent of the body.

Muscles contract in two different ways. When sudden bursts of energy are needed, fast twitch muscle fibres are used. When moderate effort over a long period is required, then slow twitch muscle fibres come into operation. When you are awake your muscles are in a constant state of readiness to work: this is called muscle tone. This tone helps to maintain good posture. Holding your body, whilst standing, in as straight a line as possible helps internal systems work without hindrance.

2 — How the muscular system works

Antagonistic pairs of muscles

As muscles can only pull they have to work in pairs. The muscles are attached to the bone at fixed points where there is movement. Understanding the relationship of muscle to bone is important when looking at movement.

Muscles' relation to bone

Voluntary muscle is attached to the bone by tendons. The muscle, at the point where it moves, is called the **insertion** and, at the point where it is fixed, is called the **origin**. When the arm flexes at the elbow the movement is at the elbow, so the fixed point – the origin – in this example is the shoulder.

The origin for the triceps and biceps is at the shoulder.

Flexing at the elbow.

The insertions are the triceps and biceps at the elbow.

The insertion is at the elbow and the origin is at the shoulder.

Task 6

1 – Copy the illustration of an arm on page 186 showing the muscles.

2 – Label all the parts clearly.

3 – Add in the origin and insertion of the muscle in another colour.

How muscles work in pairs

The body is moved by muscle groups, not by individual muscles. Muscles work in pairs. As muscles can only pull, they need to work in partnership so movement can occur. The pulling muscle is called the **prime mover** (agonist). When a muscle pulls, it contracts or becomes shorter. The muscle relaxing is the **antagonist**. When a muscle relaxes it lengthens.

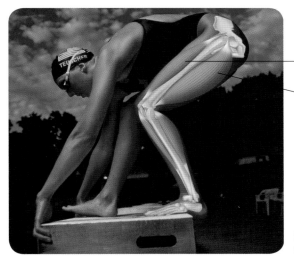

Quadriceps are relaxed.

Hamstrings contract.

Muscles work in pairs. Here, the quadriceps and hamstrings are working.

Task 7

In your own words, describe how muscles work in pairs.

Isotonic and isometric muscle contraction

Isotonic muscular contractions
Isotonic contraction occurs whenever there is movement of the body. The ends of the muscles move closer to make the action. This is the most frequently used type of contraction in games play. As a muscle contracts (shortens and fattens), it causes concentric movement. When it relaxes to its first shape, it is an eccentric movement (lengthens and flattens). The eccentric action is the more efficient of the two types.

An easy way to remember the difference between concentric and eccentric is to think about using the stairs at home. When walking up stairs, it is a concentric contraction, as the muscles are shortening to step up. When walking down stairs, it is an eccentric contraction, as the leg has to lengthen and stretch to the next step down.

Working the muscles isotonically improves dynamic (moving) strength. This is especially good for games players. It develops the cardiovascular and cardiorespiratory systems and increases power and endurance. As isotonic muscular contractions come about through movement, there may be a greater possibility of injury than with isometric muscular contractions.

Isotonic muscular contraction takes place whenever there is movement.

Isometric muscular contractions

Isometric contraction takes place when the muscle length stays the same. It is used for stabilizing parts of the body and holding the body steady so that movement can take place elsewhere. Isometric muscular contraction improves static strength. It is easy to perform and needs little or no equipment. However, it does not develop power or muscular endurance. The cardiovascular and cardiorespiratory systems are not improved. Few sports require this type of contraction alone.

Isometric muscular contraction takes place whenever the body is held still.

Task 8

Choose four sporting examples for each type of contraction.

Key terms

Insertion – the point where a tendon attaches a muscle to bone where there is movement

Origin – the end of a muscle that is attached to a fixed bone

Prime mover – contracting muscle, causing movement

Antagonist – relaxing muscle, allowing movement

Isotonic contraction – muscle contraction that results in limb movement

Isometric contraction – muscle contraction that results in increased tension, but the length does not alter; for example, when pressing against a stationary object

Summary

For movement to take place, the muscles work as antagonistic pairs. There are many pairs of muscles in the body but the ones to concentrate on are the biceps and triceps, and the quadriceps and hamstrings. When exercising for a particular activity, working the muscles in the correct way (either isotonic or isometric) to benefit performance is crucial.

3 — A healthy, active lifestyle and the muscular system

A healthy and active lifestyle can affect the condition and performance of muscle. Diet, drugs and exercise all cause the muscle to adapt and develop.

Diet

Diet can play a major part in the condition of muscle. For example, an athlete may adapt their diet after injury by taking in more protein to:

- repair tissue
- build body cells
- build muscle mass.

There are different types of protein. Eating both animal and vegetable proteins will provide the full balance required for healthy living. The total intake of protein should be around 15 per cent of daily food. An egg is the only food that has the complete balance of nutrients required. The recommended daily intake of protein is one gram of protein per kilogram of body weight for an adult. For a performer aiming to build body mass then the daily intake of protein rises to two grams per kilogram of body weight. Therefore a person who weighs 80kg and is not aiming to build body mass, should consume 80g of protein a day, and divide the protein intake between vegetable and protein on a 40g–40g split.

Performance-enhancing drugs

Taking performance-enhancing drugs can have a massive impact on the size and condition of a performer's muscles. Although useful to the athlete, they are usually illegal and can have detrimental side effects.

Anabolic steroids – build muscle tissue so speed up training recovery, enabling more frequent training.

Blood doping – increases red blood cells. After altitude training more red blood cells are produced. The blood is then removed and frozen. The body makes more red blood cells to replace those removed. Before competition, the blood is thawed and reinjected. With more red blood cells more oxygen can be carried to working muscles. Endurance athletes benefit from this.

Narcotic analgesics – these are painkillers. An athlete can train and compete even when injured, but can cause further harm to the injured area without realizing.

Peptide hormones – encourage muscle growth, increase red blood cell production and improve the transportation of oxygen to working muscles. They delay fatigue so athletes can run harder for longer.

Exercise and physical activity

Maximal muscular contractions can continue for up to eight seconds until the lactic acid system takes over. Muscle contractions take place at a sub-maximal intensity and can be maintained for up to five minutes. After this time the lactic acid hinders the muscular function and fatigue sets in.

Immediate effects of exercise on the muscles:

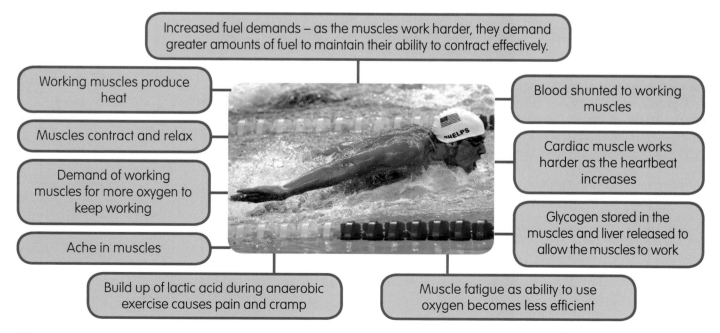

Increased fuel demands – as the muscles work harder, they demand greater amounts of fuel to maintain their ability to contract effectively.

Working muscles produce heat

Muscles contract and relax

Demand of working muscles for more oxygen to keep working

Ache in muscles

Blood shunted to working muscles

Cardiac muscle works harder as the heartbeat increases

Glycogen stored in the muscles and liver released to allow the muscles to work

Build up of lactic acid during anaerobic exercise causes pain and cramp

Muscle fatigue as ability to use oxygen becomes less efficient

The type of exercise affects the muscles in different ways. Exercising for muscular strength will have a completely different effect on the muscle than exercising for muscular endurance.

Muscle strength

Strength can be defined as a maximum weight lifted or moved in one try. By repeating strength exercises the size of the muscle increases. A person who would take advantage of an increase in muscle size would be a rugby player in the scrum or any activity where bulk is an advantage. The strength of tendons, ligaments and bone will increase too. The strength of the muscles around a joint will make that joint more stable. Weight training is a method used to improve muscular strength. To do this an athlete would lift heavy weights for a few repetitions.

A weightlifter, like Matthias Steiner, winner of the men's +150 kg at the Beijing Olympics, concentrates on developing muscular strength in training.

When muscles are overworked, they cannot contract, fatigue sets in and the muscles cannot work any more. When the muscles work intensely for over one minute the energy is released by breaking down carbohydrates; the side effect of this is the build up of lactic acid in the working muscles. Cramp can automatically result, due to the presence of the lactic acid, a mild poison, affecting the muscles. Massage and gentle moving of the affected part can help to relieve the pain.

When a muscles increase in size, this is called **hypertrophy**. If training stops, due to inactivity or injury, then muscles lose their size; the muscle is said to **atrophy**. After injury or inactivity, muscles will lose their strength and size. Treatments for muscle atrophy can include applying moist heat to the area, taking whirlpool baths and using a resistive exercise programme.

Increasing the strength around a damaged area such as a joint is important to **rehabilitate** a player. This will give strength to the damaged area and make it less likely to be injured again. A rehabilitation programme, specific to the performer, will be designed according to their needs. Some serious injuries need rehabilitation over many months. Part of the programme would start with moving light weights many times. Gradually, the amount of stress on the injured area is increased; this is achieved by increasing the amount of weight to be moved.

Muscle endurance

Endurance is the ability to keep working over a long period without tiring. People who take part in events that take a long time to complete need muscular endurance. These events include long-distance running, cycling and swimming. To improve muscular endurance an athlete could lift light weights many times.

A top-class long-distance runner like Liz Yelling has sinewy muscles that can keep working over long periods.

When training for a specific activity the body should be prepared so that it can perform the skills needed throughout the event without losing effectiveness. The muscles are able to perform the tasks properly due to a regular repetitive training pattern. Regular exercise improves fitness. Activities that increase the heart rate above 60 per cent of its maximum, for 20 minutes, three to five times a week, will generally make a person fitter.

The result of regular exercise and training is to repeat actions needed in the game so that when they are called for, they can be applied to the game. This will train the muscles to repeat actions at the appropriate speed and position.

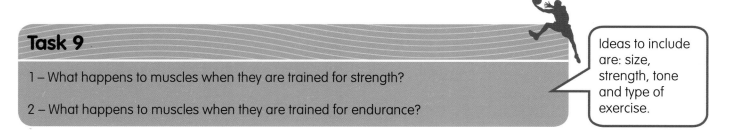

Task 9

1 – What happens to muscles when they are trained for strength?

2 – What happens to muscles when they are trained for endurance?

Ideas to include are: size, strength, tone and type of exercise.

Muscles and injury

When exercising, there is always a risk of injury. Muscle **strains** can often occur when training or in competition. This common injury should be dealt with quickly to prevent the problem becoming worse or medical advice may be needed. **RICE** (see page 217) is the recommended treatment for strains.

STRAIN – Soft tissue injury.

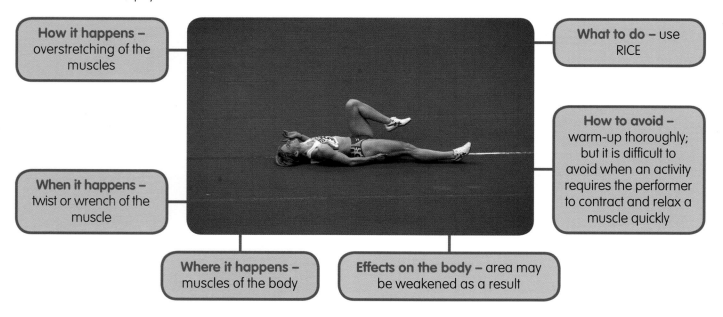

How it happens – overstretching of the muscles

What to do – use RICE

When it happens – twist or wrench of the muscle

How to avoid – warm-up thoroughly; but it is difficult to avoid when an activity requires the performer to contract and relax a muscle quickly

Where it happens – muscles of the body

Effects on the body – area may be weakened as a result

Sprains can often occur during training, exercise or competition. Treatment should be made quickly and medical advice should be sought if there is a suspicion of a fracture. RICE is the recommended treatment for a sprain.

SPRAIN – Soft tissue injury.

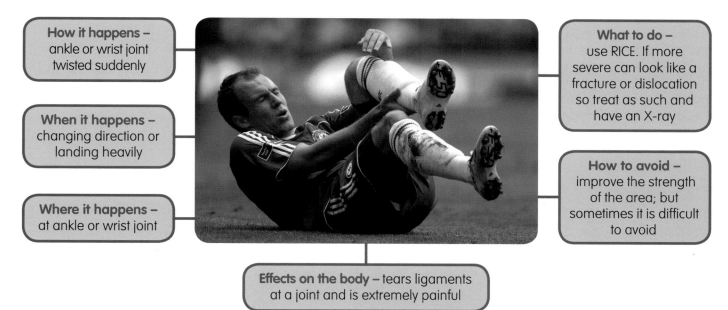

How it happens – ankle or wrist joint twisted suddenly

When it happens – changing direction or landing heavily

Where it happens – at ankle or wrist joint

What to do – use RICE. If more severe can look like a fracture or dislocation so treat as such and have an X-ray

How to avoid – improve the strength of the area; but sometimes it is difficult to avoid

Effects on the body – tears ligaments at a joint and is extremely painful

TENNIS ELBOW – Overuse injury.

Tennis elbow is where the outer part of the elbow becomes sore: even gripping the hand or movement of the wrist results in pain. It occurs as a result of overuse of the elbow due to repetitive actions such as hitting a ball. RICE is the recommended treatment.

How it happens – too much use of the tendons

How to avoid – choose the correct-sized equipment; moderate the amount of play

What to do – use RICE or seek medical advice

When it happens – playing tennis; playing with a racket with the wrong-sized handle

Where it happens – at elbow joint

Effects on the body – inflamed elbow joint

GOLFER'S ELBOW   Golfer's elbow is similar to tennis elbow. Anyone can suffer from the ailment, but is so-called due to the fact that golfers are frequent sufferers. It is a repetitive strain injury and can result in muscle, ligament and tendon inflammation. Playing sport without adaquate rest or using the wrong sized equipment can cause this injury. People regularly using weight machines or even working with a computer can suffer from the problem.

Rest and work

Achieving the right balance between work and rest is the key to successful training. If rest times are not long enough then the muscles will not be able to contract to the necessary degree and will suffer damage. In order to complete a successful workout the tiredness and fatigue of the muscle should have disappeared prior to the session; if not, the muscles are too tired and there is possibility of injury. It can take up to 48 hours for recovery to take place – as far as the muscles are concerned this is time for renewal, giving the body time to adapt to the stresses of the training session, and repair. Taking too much recovery time wastes the effort made in the previous session.

Key terms

Hypertrophy – when muscle increases in size because of exercise

Atrophy – when muscle loses its size because of lack of exercise

Rehabilitate – recovery from injury

RICE – Rest, Ice, Compression, Elevation (a method of treating injuries see page 217)

Strain – pulled muscle as a result of overstretching

Summary

Diets that include proteins will help the performer by repairing and building muscle tissue.

Different drugs have varied effects on muscle including building tissue, killing pain, increasing oxygen supply to the muscle and increasing muscle growth. Anabolic steroids and muscle building and recovery, but are illegal and can have detrimental side effects.

Training can make muscles stronger. Training and practice, if conducted properly, help the body to remember how to complete tasks well. After training for strength, the muscles will hypertrophy. Strength coupled with speed will give the power required to complete explosive events when the fast twitch muscle fibres are used.

Exercising for endurance will help an athlete perform long-distance events. This kind of exercise requires moderate effort and takes a long time to complete. Slow twitch muscle fibres are used in long-distance events.

Rest and work should strike a balance if the maximum benefit is to be gained from the training.

Exam questions

Multiple-choice questions

1. **(a)** Which of the following best describes cardiac muscle?

   ☐ **A** Tissue surrounding the bone aiding protection

   ☐ **B** Controlled voluntarily responding to different stimuli

   ☐ **C** Involuntary muscle found in the intestines, blood vessels and urinary organs

   ☐ **D** Involuntary, working automatically and never tiring

   (1)

   (b) Which of the following muscles contract to extend the leg at the knee?

   ☐ **A** Quadriceps

   ☐ **B** Hamstrings

   ☐ **C** Gastrocnemius

   ☐ **D** Gluteus maximus

   (1)

   (c) Which antagonistic pair of muscles work to bend the arm at the elbow?

   ☐ **A** Biceps and pectorals

   ☐ **B** Trapezius and deltoids

   ☐ **C** Triceps and biceps

   ☐ **D** Gastrocnemius and hamstrings

   (1)

2. Which of the following describes an action that is linked with isotonic muscular contraction?

   ☐ **A** Dribbling the ball and making a lay up shot

   ☐ **B** Holding space blocking the pathway of the attacker

   ☐ **C** Keeping stable in a rugby scrum

   ☐ **D** Remaining in a handstand for three seconds

   (1)

3. Which of the following does not describe an immediate effect of exercise?

   ☐ **A** Blood shunts to the working muscles

   ☐ **B** Heart becomes larger and stronger

   ☐ **C** Muscles contract and relax

   ☐ **D** Muscles can tire as the ability to use the oxygen becomes less efficient

   (1)

Short-answer questions

4. When rugby players hold their position in a scrum which type of muscular contraction is being used?

   (1)

5. Which type of muscle fibres are used in long-distance events?

   (1)

Longer-answer questions

6. Exercising over a long period of time affects the muscles in different ways. Describe three of these long-term effects.

   (3)

7. Describe the cause and effect of a muscle strain.

   (3)

1.2 ～ Your healthy, active body

1.2.5 A healthy, active lifestyle and your skeletal system

What you will learn about in this topic:

1 — The make-up of the skeletal system
2 — How the skeletal system works
3 — A healthy, active lifestyle and the skeletal system

1 — The make-up of the skeletal system

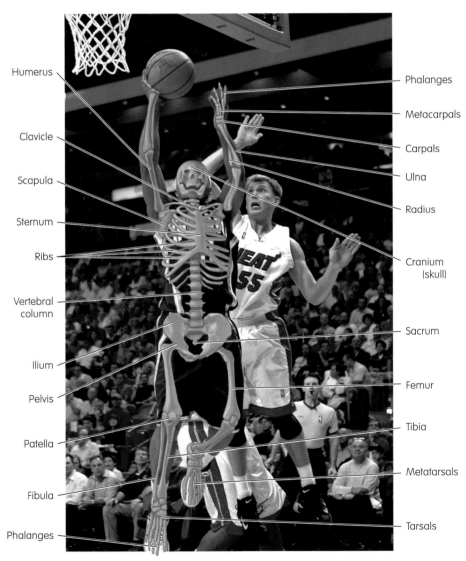

Humerus
Clavicle
Scapula
Sternum
Ribs
Vertebral column
Ilium
Pelvis
Patella
Fibula
Phalanges

Phalanges
Metacarpals
Carpals
Ulna
Radius
Cranium (skull)
Sacrum
Femur
Tibia
Metatarsals
Tarsals

The skeletal system.

Task 1

1 – Learn the names of the bones in the body.

2 – Start by trying to memorize the bones of the upper body.

3 – When you feel confident go on to the bones of the lower body.

> Remember **u**lna is **u**nderneath the radius and the **t**ibia is on **t**op of the fibula. The phalanges are both fingers and toes!

Active challenge

Take turns in testing a partner. Point to a bone in your body and see if your partner can tell you its name. Use the image on page 196 only when you need to.

The vertebrae

The vertebrae are irregular bones. There are 33 of these bones making the vertebral column. They are placed in five groups according to where they are along the vertebral column.

All the vertebrae fit together neatly to protect the spinal cord. This is an important job because damage to the cord can paralyse. In between the vertebrae there are cartilage discs. These help stop damage, wear and tear, and grinding down of the vertebrae through constant movement.

The definition of a joint

A **joint** is the place where two or more bones meet. There does not have to be movement there. The **fused** bones of the cranium are as much a joint as the meeting of the humerus and ulna at the elbow. The joints where there is movement are more significant to the actions of the sportsperson.

Some joints allow a large range of movement, such as the hip joint. Other joints, such as the joint at the knee, give much more restricted movement. This is due to the size and arrangement of the bones. Although there are elements common to all joints, each type is formed in a different way and it is this arrangement that leads to the different ways we can move.

Cervical vertebrae – there are seven of these which allow different movements at the top of the spline. The top two vertebrae, the atlas and the axis, allow you to nod and turn your head.

Thoracic curvature – the thoracic region has 12 vertebrae. Ten of these are attached to the ribs and help movement when breathing.

Lumbar curvature – the lumbar vertebrae are the most robust as they take a lot of weight. They are also large because they are in the area that allows the most movement.

Pelvic curvature – the sacrum has five vertebrae, which become fused together in adulthood. They make up part of the pelvic girdle.

At the end of the spine is the coccyx. There are four vertebrae here, all fused together.

The vertebrae.

Skiing involves a range of movements at different joints.

Task 2

Write out your own definition of the word joint.

The following are all **synovial joints**. These joints allow the greatest movement.

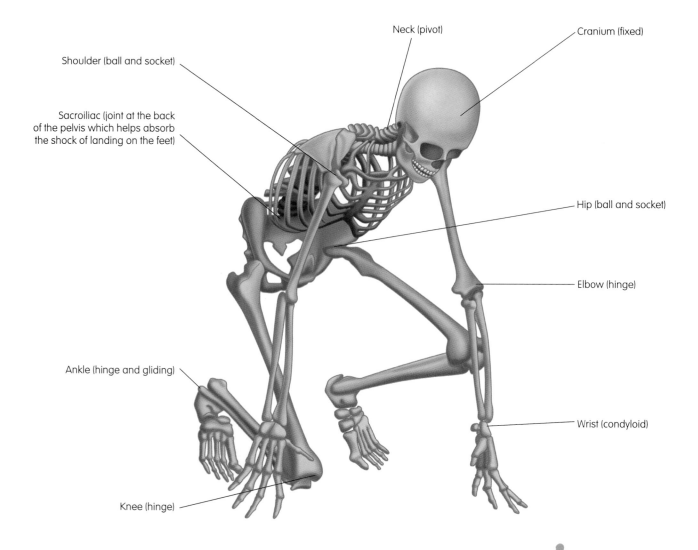

Neck (pivot)

Cranium (fixed)

Shoulder (ball and socket)

Sacroiliac (joint at the back of the pelvis which helps absorb the shock of landing on the feet)

Hip (ball and socket)

Elbow (hinge)

Ankle (hinge and gliding)

Wrist (condyloid)

Knee (hinge)

Task 3

1 – Make a table of the body's joints.

2 – State where the joints are in the body. Use neck, knee, hip, elbow and shoulder as headings.

3 – State the type of joint each is and the bones involved.

Key terms

Joint – a place where two or more bones meet

Fused – two or more bones knitted together so no movement occurs

Synovial joints – freely moveable joints with the ends covered in cartilage

Classification of the bones

There are four different **classifications** of bone: **long bones**, **short bones**, **flat bone** (or plate) and **irregular bones**. The way differently shaped bones are arranged in the body allows them to perform certain jobs. It would be hard to imagine an irregular bone, such as the pelvis, at the point between the elbow and the shoulder being as efficient there as the long bone of the humerus. The role that the bone has to perform determines its shape, size and density (compactness).

The following are a selection of bones from the human body. How should they be classified?

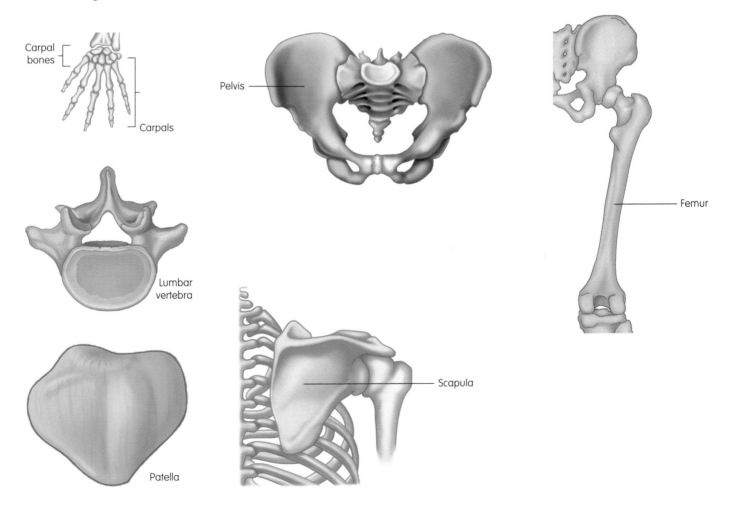

Carpal bones

Carpals

Pelvis

Femur

Lumbar vertebra

Scapula

Patella

How bones are grouped together

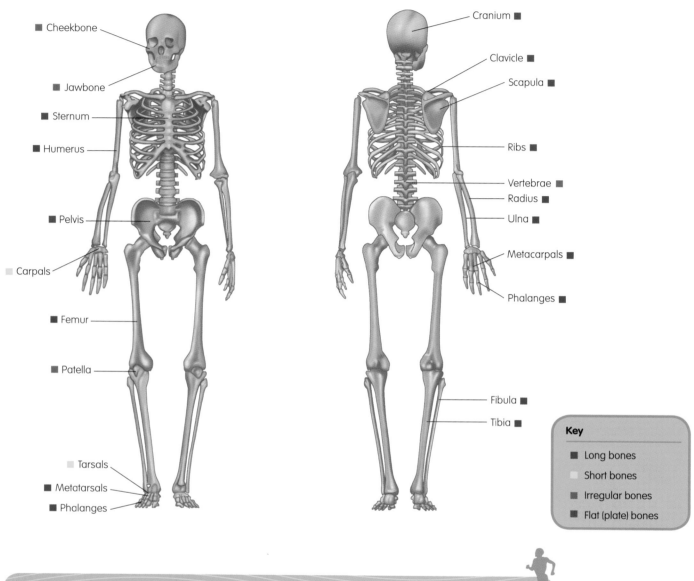

■ Cheekbone

■ Jawbone

■ Sternum

■ Humerus

■ Pelvis

■ Carpals

■ Femur

■ Patella

■ Tarsals

■ Metatarsals

■ Phalanges

Cranium ■

Clavicle ■

Scapula ■

Ribs ■

Vertebrae ■

Radius ■

Ulna ■

Metacarpals ■

Phalanges ■

Fibula ■

Tibia ■

Key

■ Long bones

■ Short bones

■ Irregular bones

■ Flat (plate) bones

Task 4

Make a list of all the bones in the following groups: long, short, irregular and flat.

How bones help the sportsperson

Whenever a sportsperson is in action, they are relying on their skeleton to play a supporting role in their performance; bones are also designed to help the action. Whatever a sportsperson does, bones are there, helping them to move efficiently.

Long bones, due to their length, create **leverage** when playing sport. Whether hitting a shuttlecock or bowling a ball, long bones play an important role in the performance of the player, helping to generate speed, force and power:

- When a bowler spins a cricket ball they are relying on the bones of their hand to help apply the spin, so the metacarpals and phalanges are important, as well as the carpals.
- Swinging a racket to play a forehand drive in tennis involves the bones of the arm. Therefore the humerus, radius and ulna help the swing action of the stroke, as well as the scapula.

Flat bones are tough and can withstand hard impact. The cranium takes a hard blow when heading a ball. When a rugby player is in a tackle his pelvis and ribcage can protect his internal organs owing to their strength.

Short bones are specialists for fine movements, especially those of the hand. Short bones are responsible for putting spin on a ball in cricket and rounders, and for helping a ball accurately hit a target. As these bones can make small adjustments they help keep the body balanced – important for the gymnast and golfer.

Irregular bones, like the vertebrae, work together and act as a shock absorber. When players land on their feet from a jump it is the vertebrae that help reduce the shock on their backs.

Different types of bones work together. Landing on their feet after playing a spike or smash, volleyball players require their legs to cushion the landing. Here the pelvis at the hip, the femur, patella, tibia and fibula in the legs, plus the tarsals, metatarsals and phalanges in the feet, are in play to make the landing safe and the body balanced and ready for the next movement.

Active challenge

Work with a partner. Point to different bones and ask your partner to say what class of bone they are. Take turns to link a sporting movement with the class of bone indicated.

Task 5

Give two examples of each bone type and link them with a sporting action. Use common names and proper names when describing areas of the body. For example, irregular bone, (lumbar vertebrae) in the lower back bending to field a ball in rounders.

Task 6

1 – Look carefully at the photos on page 202.

2 – Work out the action that they are performing and name the bones involved.

3 – Write a heading for each action that you see and give the names of the bones that are involved in the specific action.

Sporting actions use various bones for movement.

Classification of joints

Freely moveable synovial joints are common in the human body. The components of this type of joint have built-in safety factors to help guard against injury. These joints are designed to reduce wear and tear, absorb shock and reduce friction. These factors are especially important when performing skills at pace and with power. The classification of joints includes:

- ball and socket: located at the shoulder and the hip
- hinge: located at the elbow and the knee
- pivot: located at the neck (involving the atlas and axis bones) and the elbow (involving the radius and ulna bones).

Each type of synovial joint is different. This is due to where it is in the body, how many bones are located at the joint and the types of bones involved. Each variation will afford a different type of movement.

Whenever a sportsperson is involved in an activity they are relying on the joints of the body to help the action:

- In cricket the bowlers rely on the joints of the fingers to move forward and spin the ball.
- Playing a forehand drive in tennis involves the shoulder rotating as the racket is swung forward.
- Volleyball players rely on the joints of the leg to cushion their landing after performing a smash.

Swinging a racket/kicking a ball: hinge joint – long bones – legs and arms. In some shots there is a pivot action at the elbow involving the ulna and radius.

Spinning a ball in cricket: hinge joints – short bones – fingers – fine motor movements.

Throwing the ball in rugby: ball and socket – flat bone – scapula.

Task 7

Use the examples above to create your own movement/action chains using different types of bones.

Remember to include: type of joint, type of bone, location of the bone and the linked action relating to a sporting activity.

Key terms

Classification – a way of sorting or organizing groups

Long bones – those bones that are the longest in the body which make up the arms and legs

Short bone – smaller version of a long bone, found in the hands and feet

Flat bone – also known as plate bone, mainly linked with protection

Irregular bones – bones that have no uniform shape

Leverage – the use of force or effort (muscle power) to overcome resistance

Components of joints

Using the knee joint as an example, let's look at the components of joints. There are many parts to the knee joint. Its position demands that it can withstand hard pressure. This makes it a robust joint. The ligaments that hold the bones in place are called the cruciates. When footballers have serious knee injuries it is these ligaments that are often damaged.

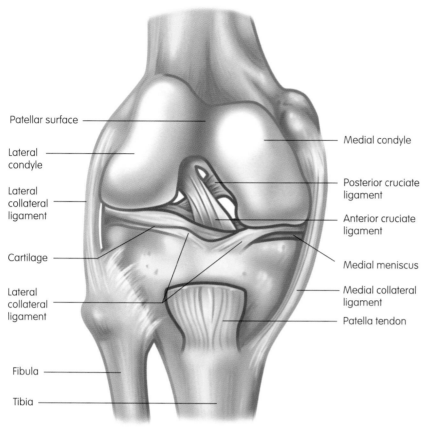

Patellar surface

Lateral condyle

Lateral collateral ligament

Cartilage

Lateral collateral ligament

Fibula

Tibia

Medial condyle

Posterior cruciate ligament

Anterior cruciate ligament

Medial meniscus

Medial collateral ligament

Patella tendon

The knee joint.

Between the femur (thigh bone) and the tibia (shin bone) is the semi-lunar **cartilage** that helps lubricate the joint. This is also the damaged or torn tissue that is in knee twisting injuries and cartilage problems. The synovial membrane may be affected and excess synovial fluid becomes present in the joint, resulting in inflammation.

Task 8

1 – Copy the diagram of a knee joint.

2 – Refer to work already studied on the skeleton and add three labels to your diagram.

3 – Pass your diagram to a partner and let them add three more labels, in pencil, without referring to their notes or the Student's Book.

4 – Pass back and complete the other labels.

5 – When you have finished, check your work.

Functions of different parts of a joint
Cartilage covers the ends of the bones where they meet and stops the bones touching each other. This is called hyaline cartilage. The cartilage acts as a cushion and creates a barrier

reducing the amount of **friction** that occurs when the bones are moving against each other. This stops the bones wearing each other away.

Synovial fluid lubricates the joint, like oiling the chain of a bike or putting oil in a car, allowing all the parts to move against each other smoothly. It also keeps the joint free from infection.

The **synovial capsule** is a tough fibre that surrounds the joint, holding the fluid in place.

The **synovial membrane** lies inside the capsule. It is here that the synovial fluid is produced.

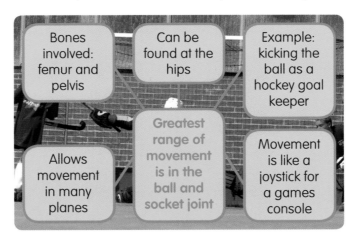

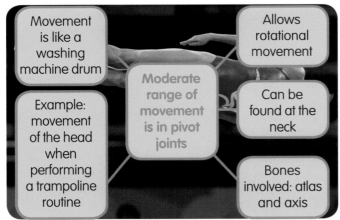 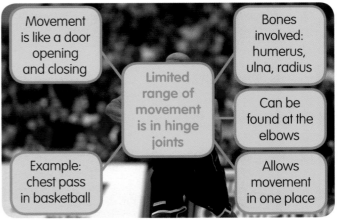

Range of movement at specific joints.

The importance of cartilage, tendons and ligaments in sport

Cartilage is a shock absorber. When running, the knee takes a lot of pounding. It is the cartilage that acts as a cushion so that the bones do not rub together and wear away. If the cartilage were not there, pain would occur at the joint due to the friction of the bones rubbing together. This is especially important in activities such as long-distance running, where there is continued use of the joint. Cartilage damage is common in sportspeople. Frayed cartilage decreases the efficiency of the joint and is extremely painful too.

Ligaments surround the sides of the joint and are made of tough elastic fibres. It is the ligaments that hold the bones in place, thus keeping the joint together. The stability of the joint relies on the strength of the ligaments and on the muscles supporting the joint. Ligaments attach bone to bone. As bones move a lot, ligaments have to be strong and elastic. If there were no ligaments the joint would be unstable. Running, stopping and changing direction all put pressure on the joint. When changing direction at speed it is the ligaments that keep the bones in the right place. If the ligaments are stretched too far the joint can **dislocate** and the ligaments can tear. After tearing it is unlikely that the ligaments will return to their former strength.

Tendons are not strictly part of the joint, although they play an important part in the joint's movement. Their job is to attach muscle to bone. Without tendons muscle would float around the bone and movement would be impossible. It is this attachment that creates an anchor for muscles to shorten and bring about different actions. Tendons are very strong because great exertion is required for some actions. As the muscle needs to be held firmly, the tendons act as a non-elastic anchor.

If a muscle is large or pulls in more than one direction, more than one tendon may be needed to anchor it. A weightlifter moving a maximum weight needs their tendons to hold firm and keep still.

Task 9

Use the words 'cartilage', 'synovial fluid', 'ligaments', and 'synovial capsule' as headings in your workbook. List the following words under the appropriate headings. Each word can be used only once.

- elastic
- stabilize
- helps move freely
- hyaline
- reduces friction
- tough
- lubricates
- tough fibre
- acts as a cushion
- barrier between the bones
- attach bone to bone
- surrounds the joint

> There are four groups to make. Use the text you have just read to find the links.

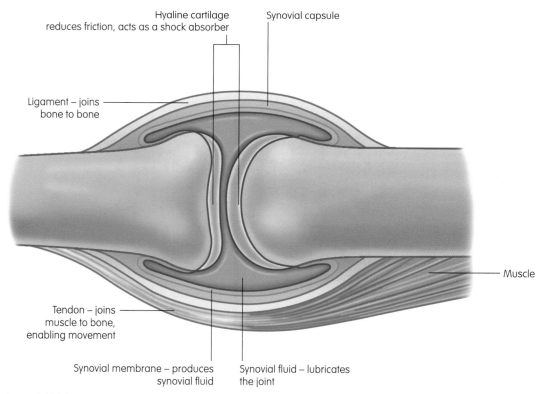

A synovial joint.

Task 10

1 – Study the information on cartilage, tendons and ligaments.

2 – Create a table of the information and include at least three differences between cartilage, tendons and ligaments.

> Construct your table using columns for the information using the headings: 'Cartilage', 'Ligaments' and 'Tendons'.

Key terms

Cartilage – tough, flexible tissue, can be found at the end of bones

Friction – action of two surfaces rubbing together creating heat

Synovial fluid – found in synovial joint

Synovial capsule – tough fibre surrounding the synovial joint

Synovial membrane – lining inside joint capsule where synovial fluid is produced

Ligaments – tough, rounded, elastic fibre attaching bone to bone at a joint

Dislocate – joints moved out of their normal arrangement

Tendons – strong, non-elastic tissue attaching bone to muscle

Summary

Bones and joints are classified into different groups. This shows that each type has a different composition and job to do. Where two bones meet a joint is formed. Synovial joints are the most important to the sportsperson. They allow a wide variety of actions necessary to be successful in an activity. Their design is complex and they are susceptible to injury, but this complexity provides the range of movement for the performer.

2 — How the skeletal system works

The skeletal system works by bones and tissues forming joints. Each type of joint allows a different type of movement range from a great range of movement that the sportsperson utilizes during the game, to a limited range of movement and a moderate range of movement.

If the centre of the body is where all movement comes from, then working out the different types of movement becomes simpler.

Adduction: this movement brings part of the body towards the centre. In the butterfly arm action in swimming, adduction takes place when the arms pull to the sides. **Add**uction is **add**ing to the body.

Jemma Lowe demonstrates adduction of the arms, as she brings her arms back to her torso.

Abduction: this is the opposite action to adduction. The limbs are abducted from the centre. A goalkeeper abducts their arms when reaching to make a save. A badminton player abducts their arm when preparing for an overhead clear. A way to remember this is that when someone is kidnapped, they are abducted – taken away.

Abduction of the arms happens as David James reaches to save the ball.

Flexion: closing the angle at a joint. When preparing to throw a ball the angle at the elbow decreases. This movement of flexion gives the arm space to create power in the throw. Catching a ball and bringing it to the body is flexion at the wrist, elbow and shoulder joints. Recovery phase of the sprint leg action is flexion at the knee.

Andrew Flintoff shows how flexion occurs as the angle at the joint of both elbows decrease, in preparation to throw.

Plantar flexion: is the action of the toes moving down when standing on your toes with the top of the foot moving away from the body. A high diver will use this action as the take-off is initiated.

Blake Aldridge and Tom Daley illustrate plantar flexion.

Dorsi flexion: the movement of the toes up when standing on heels with the top of the foot moving towards the body. A long jumper when planting their foot for take-off, at the heel first action, applies dorsi flexion.

Phillips Idowu strides forward with the toes of his left foot lifted towards his body showing dorsi flexion.

Extension: this is the opposite of flexion. It is when the angle increases between the bones at a joint. In the run up for a jump a long jumper takes off and extends the take-off leg to generate as much upward lift as possible. This is an example of extension at the hips. Striding the leg forward to take a pace is extension at the knee.

As Phillips Idowu's left leg pushes back during take-off, it extends.

Rotation: the angles do not change but the joint moves in a circular motion. The throwing action of the service in tennis, or the bowling action in cricket or rounders demonstrates this type of movement.

Roger Federer using a rotation movement to serve.

Task 11

1 – Order the following joints from the greatest amount of movement to the least:
- hip
- shoulder
- knee
- elbow
- neck

2 – Give your own example of a sporting movement for each.

3 – Give the correct joint type.

Active challenge

Point to a joint on your own body for your partner to tell you:

- the name of the joint
- the type of joint
- what movement happens there
- an example of the joint's use in sport.

Functions of the skeletal system

Healthy bones allow us to lead a pain-free life. Their size and condition can be improved through exercise, which can benefit a person's present and later life.

We take for granted having a skeleton, but have you ever thought what we would be like without one? A mass of muscle and tissue on the floor would not be a pretty sight! The bones of the skeleton have five important jobs to do. Some of these jobs are more obvious than others.

1 – Shape
The way bones are arranged gives us our general framework and shape. When someone is said to be of a large build it is partly because of the size of their skeleton. Certain builds are more suited to particular sports. When you look at different sportspeople you will be able to work out the general shape and size of their skeleton. Jockeys have a skeleton that is likely to be small and thin, a basketball player's skeleten is often long and thin with a sturdy frame may be better adapted to contact sports.

2 – Support
As bones are firm and rigid they can support the rest of the body and keep us upright. Part of the body is made up of muscle, which is held in place by being attached to the skeleton. The bones act as an anchor or framework upon which the rest of the body tissues, such as muscles, can hang.

3 – Help with movement
When the bones work with the muscles of the body they allow the body to move. The skeleton provides a series of 'anchor points' to which the muscles attach. When bones are made to work by muscles they work as levers and so allow a variety of movements in everyday life and when we play sports. When a sportsperson swings a racket to hit a tennis ball, for instance, the long bones of the arm help create the leverage necessary to apply force to the shot.

4 – Protection
Some bones help to protect the internal organs of the body. These are the bones and arrangements of bone that enclose other parts of the body. They act a little like a box. This is especially important to the sportsperson playing contact sports or team games. A volleyball player dives to make a dig, a footballer heads a ball and a rugby player takes a tackle. The vital organs of the body would not last long if they did not have certain bones to protect them. Examples of these protecting bones are: skull, pelvis, ribcage and vertebrae.

5 – Production of blood cells
In the long bones of the body, the production of red and white blood cells takes place. As blood cells keep wearing out it is important that new supplies are made. The job of white blood cells is to go to any source of infection to fight germs and bacteria. Cells need to be regenerating constantly so the body can be guarded from disease. Red blood cells transport oxygen from the lungs to the rest of the body.

1 — The skeleton gives us our general **shape** and determines whether we are tall or short, broad or narrow.

2 — The bones of the skeleton **support** the rest of the body.

3 — The skeleton helps the body to **move** by providing a framework onto which muscles attach.

4 — Some bones help to **protect** the internal organs of the body.

5 — What is not that obvious is that **production** of red and white blood cells takes place in long bones of the body.

The skeletal system.

Task 12

Using skull, pelvis, ribcage and vertebrae as headings, list the part of the body they protect.

Use these words to help you: brain, spinal cord, heart, lungs, spleen, stomach, bladder and liver.

Task 13

1 – Copy and complete the sentences below about each function of the skeleton.

a. Some people choose a particular sport because of their _____ owing to their skeleton size.

b. Red blood cells are constantly being _____ in the long bones of the skeleton.

c. We need our skeleton to work with the muscles to allow different _____.

d. The skeleton provides the _____ upon which muscles can hang.

e. When a player heads a ball their brain is _____ by part of their skeleton.

Study this photograph. It shows all of the functions of the skeleton.

Task 14

1 – Pick out the five different functions of the skeleton from this section: use the above photo to help start you off.

2 – When you have found them, copy the spider diagram below and put one function at the end of each line as a heading.

3 – Add the following information to each heading:
   • particular parts of the skeleton involved
   • location
   • effect.

Functions of the skeleton

Key terms

Shape – form or outline

Support – helping to take the weight

Move – a motion, could be an action like running or swinging a racket at a ball

Protect – guard against threat of injury

Production – making something

Summary

Bones perform seen and unseen functions. A person may choose a sport because their body shape suits that particular activity and so they can be successful. Bones protect vital organs of the body so the sportsperson relies on the strength of bones to withstand pressure and knocks in contact sports. A shot to beat a keeper or a passing shot in tennis needs the length of the long bones to bring leverage to the action. The long bones help movements to be powerful and forceful.

Athletes need their small bones to aid in small movements, such as in balance and agility, important when dodging around the opposition or changing direction in a gymnastic movement. The skeleton supports the muscles. It is this anchoring that enables the muscles to work and bring about movement.

Production of red and white blood cells occurs in some bones of the body. This is essential so that the body can function, as the cells transport oxygen and nutrients, and fight infection.

3 — A healthy, active lifestyle and the skeletal system

Diet

Bones store minerals such as calcium and phosphorus. About 98 per cent of the body's calcium is stored in bones. Calcium forms part of the structure of bones and teeth. It gives bone its strength to help it support and protect. The body readjusts its store of calcium in the blood constantly. If more calcium is taken in through the diet then more calcium is taken up by the bones. If calcium is low in the diet then the bones release calcium to redress the imbalance. Therefore, if calcium is missing from a diet over a long period of time this affects the quality of the bone structure and in the long-term can lead to osteoporosis.

The recommended daily allowance of calcium is:

- 800mg for adults
- 1200mg for young adults (11 to 14 years old)
- 800mg for young children (aged under 11).

Vitamin D is produced in the body by the action of sunlight on skin.

The main sources of calcium are milk, cheese, and other dairy products. Vitamin D also helps to maintain bone mass, and can help reduce the risk of osteoporosis. Vitamin D is produced in the body by the action of sunlight on skin. There are not many dietary sources of Vitamin D, but it can be found in only fish and eggs.

Exercise and physical activity

Immediate and short-term effects

Exercising in the right way increases bone size and strength. Resistance and weight bearing exercise is essential for bone health.

Aerobic work including walking and jogging (but not swimming or cycling as there is no impact) and weight lifting decrease and can even prevent bone loss in certain areas of the body.

Effects of regular and long-term participation

Exercising when young can result in a lifetime of increased bone size. With age, the inside surface of the bone is gradually lost; however, as a result of exercising when young, the layers of bone on the outside build up, helping them stay strong as you age. Long-term participation in activities such as running, tennis, aerobics and walking can prevent osteoporosis due to the impacting nature of the activities on the bones.

Exercise benefits the skeleton by:

* increasing bone density, offsetting the risks of osteoporosis
* slowing the loss of calcium, so fights bone deterioration
* increasing the flexibility of the joints as the tips of the long bones are conditioned
* strengthening tendons and ligaments, stabilizing joints.

For older people, exercise maintains bone mass and balance, reducing the risk of fracture.

Potential injuries

There are minor and major risks of injury involved with most sports. There is less risk of injury in sports where teams stay on their own side of a net, such as volleyball and badminton. The risks increase in contact sports where players invade the territory of the other team. The rules and nature of the sport may present safety problems. The weather may play a part in increasing the risk or technical problems may occur.

 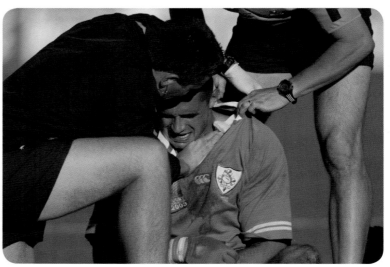

The risk of injury increases in sports such as football, where players tackle each other, and rugby, where players have contact with each other.

The following pages contain the procedures for dealing with a series of injuries. Only trained and qualified first aid and medical personnel should deal with serious injuries.

Fractures

Fractures are hard tissue injuries, which occur when an excessive impact or force is put on the bone. This can happen with a blow or a twist. When a bone is fractured, the limb becomes immobile and there is extreme pain. The area is tender and there may be swelling, leading to bruising. The fractured area immediately looks deformed. Fractures are difficult to avoid, as they are a result of spur-of-the-moment accidents. Keeping to the rules of the game and not tackling recklessly reduces the risk of injury.

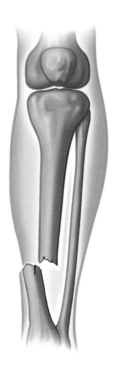

An compound/open fracture of the tibia.

A greenstick fracture of the tibia.

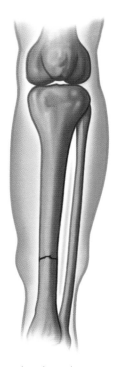

A closed/simple fracture of the tibia.

There are several types of fracture, each differing due to the bone and the type of impact, blow or pressure placed on it.

Compound/Open Fracture The broken end of a bone comes through the skin in a **compound/open fracture**. This causes complications, as there is a risk of infection from germs entering where the skin is damaged.

Greenstick Fracture Pressure or impact buckles or bends a bone but only partially breaks it. This fracture is common in the developing bones of young children, whose bones are quite springy.

Closed/Simple Fracture The break of the bone is under the skin in a **simple/closed fracture**.

In rugby, because of the upper body impact of tackling and falling on an outstretched hand, a fracture of the clavicle is a common injury. When this happens the casualty may automatically cradle the arm on the injured side under the elbow. They may also lean their head to the injured side too.

The impact of two legs meeting with force in a football tackle can cause a fracture. The tibia and fibula (lower leg bones) are the most common leg bones to fracture. If both are broken, the limb will rotate and have an angle at the point of the fracture. If the tibia (shin bone) is broken then there is a possibility that the fracture will be open.

Medical help should be sent for immediately and the casualty should be made comfortable and kept warm without moving the injured part.

STRESS FRACTURE   A stress fracture is an incomplete fracture of the bone. It is caused by unusual, repeated stress. As the bone withstands the constant pressure of impact it tries to remodel itself but fails, as the osteoblasts (bone-forming cells) become exhausted and unable to cope with the demand. As a result, small cracks are created in the weight-bearing bones, often referred to as hairline cracks. The tibia and metatarsals are often the most affected.

This is a common injury, most associated with long-distance running. During training or an event the muscles will help absorb the shock of running. When they become fatigued they lose their strength to absorb the shock and so the stress for the bones is increased, resulting in a fracture.

An athlete can look out for the following symptoms of a stress fracture:

- The area will be painful, tender and hurt when weight is applied.
- At the start of training or an event, acute pain will be felt.
- There will be medium pain during the middle of the run.
- Acute pain will carry on after the run has stopped.

The treatment for stress fractures is rest. Between four to eight weeks is necessary for recovery depending on the severity of the injury. After the recovery period, when training resumes, the first two weeks should be low-impact work, gradually building up the stress levels.

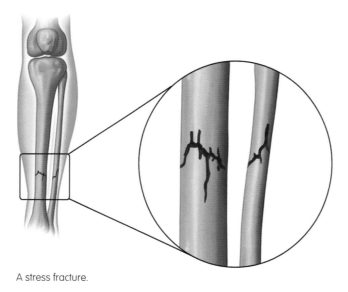

A stress fracture.

Active challenge

With a partner, think of sporting occasions where participation might result in each of the different fractures occurring.

Joint injuries

Although some joint injuries can be dealt with using basic first aid, some may need expert treatment. **Strains** and pulls affect the muscles of the body. **Sprains**, tennis or golf elbow affects the joints and the ligaments.

Use the RICE procedure to treat soft tissue injuries. Each initial stands for part of the treatment: Rest, Ice, Compression, Elevate.

Rest the injured part. 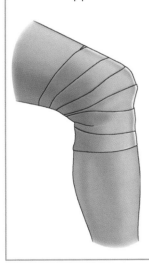 Rest prevents further injury.	Apply **Ice** to the injured part to stop the swelling and help the pain. 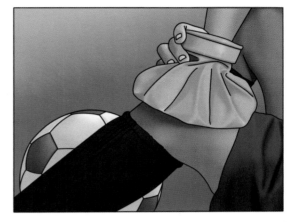 Ice applied for ten-minute periods stops swelling, pain and flow of blood to area.
Compression – put a bandage around the injured area for support and to stop swelling.  The bandage is just tight enough to reduce internal bleeding and swelling.	**Elevate** – lift the injured part to restrict the blood flow to the area and reduce swelling and painful throbbing. 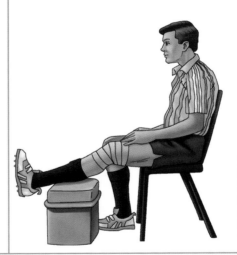 Raising the injured area above the level of the heart lowers internal bleeding and stops swelling and throbbing. In some instances raising an injured part slightly is enough to reduce any pressure on it.

DISLOCATION   This is a hard tissue injury. When the joint is moved outside its designed range and it **dislocates**. A forceful blow can move the joint out of position. All major joints are vulnerable. When it happens the joint looks deformed, it will be very painful and the person will have no control over the movement in that area. In these cases the person should be made comfortable, the joint immobilized and medical help found quickly – do not attempt to put the joint back into place. Strength training exercises for the muscles and tissues around the joints will help prevent this happening.

Participating in high-impact sports like rugby, skiing, gymnastics and football can cause dislocation.

An athlete would seek medical treatment, undergo physiotherapy or surgery depending on the severity of the dislocation.

Torn Cartilage   A torn cartilage is a soft tissue injury, it happens when a joint is twisted excessively. A player is prone to doing this when changing direction or pivoting at speed. A common area for this injury is at the knee joint. When it happens it is extremely painful for the joint to be moved. Treatment for this is RICE. An operation may be necessary in severe cases. Due to the nature of the game this injury is common for footballers. It is hard to avoid an injury of this kind, especially in competitive matches.

Task 15

Write a paragraph on elbow fractures and a paragraph on dislocation to explain them. Explain how and where they occur, and what treatment should be used.

Key terms

Compound/open fracture – the bone breaks and comes through the skin

Simple/closed fracture – break of the bone when the skin is not broken

Strain – pulled muscle as a result of overstretching

Sprain – injury involving joints and ligaments

Dislocate – joints moved out of their normal arrangement

Rest and work

As with all the systems of the body the skeleton needs time to recover from exercise. The skeletal system takes longer to recover than the cardiovascular, respiratory and muscular systems. Exercise may have caused stress injuries. Stress fractures occur with long-distance running events. Stopping the activity and resting can stop the pain.

Summary

There are many injuries that are caused by sport, some in training and some in the game itself. In general, soft tissue injuries, minor cuts and bruises happen frequently and, if treated early, clear up quickly, but if left they can become more serious. Such injuries can usually be treated immediately with basic first aid.

Hard tissue injuries – torn cartilage and broken bones – need specialized medical treatment and a period of rehabilitation so the injury is given time to heal fully and the body to return gradually to fitness.

Players or performers are sometimes not aware of an injury or condition gradually affecting their bodies, like heat and cold or stress fractures. Knowledge and experience of the event and the effects of the environment are crucial to the well-being of the performer so that preventative measures can be taken to counter the dangers.

Exam questions

Multiple-choice questions

1. (a) Which of the following is not a function of the skeleton?

    ☐ **A** Protects vital organs of the body

    ☐ **B** Stores minerals, essential to the good function of the body

    ☐ **C** Can be classified into groups

    ☐ **D** Provides the framework on which muscles attach to help movement

    (1)

    (b) Which of the following bones are linked with throwing a ball?

    ☐ **A** Humerus, ulna, fibula

    ☐ **B** Metacarpals, tibia, radius

    ☐ **C** Phalanges, humerus, carpals

    ☐ **D** Scapula, sternum, femur

    (1)

    (c) Which of the following best describes a joint?

    ☐ **A** A place where bones are close

    ☐ **B** Where several bones and muscles meet allowing movement

    ☐ **C** Where the production of movement occurs

    ☐ **D** Where two or more bones meet but where there is not necessarily movement

    (1)

    (d) Which statement best describes adduction?

    ☐ **A** Movement bringing the limbs of the body towards the centre

    ☐ **B** Where the angle of the joint decreases

    ☐ **C** Where the angle increases between the bones at a joint

    ☐ **D** The joint moves in a circular motion

    (1)

    (e) Which joint is mainly involved in the action of kicking a football?

    ☐ **A** Pivot joint

    ☐ **B** Hinge joint at the elbow

    ☐ **C** Ball and socket at the hip

    ☐ **D** Hinge joint at the knee

    (1)

Short-answer questions

2. Giving shape and support are two functions of the skeleton. What are the other three?

    (3)

3. What is the name of the movement at a joint used in the shoulder action in a tennis service?

    (1)

Longer-answer questions

4. This question refers to the range of movement at a joint.

    Simon's preferred stroke in swimming is butterfly. Part of his training is on flexibility and he wants to start with the joints giving greatest flexibility.

    (a) Which joint will he work on first?
    (b) What type of movement does this joint allow?
    (c) Describe the parts that make up this joint.

    (4)

5. This question refers to potential injuries resulting from participation.

    An athlete training for a marathon suffers pain in the lower leg as the foot impacts the ground. The athlete is concerned that it is some kind of fracture.

    (a) What type of fracture could it be?
    (b) How does this type of fracture occur?
    (c) What treatment should follow?

    (4)

2.2 ～ Analysis of performance

There are five components which form the analysis of performance:

2.2.1 — Rules, regulations and terminology
2.2.2 — Observe and analyse performance
2.2.3 — Evaluate performance
2.2.4 — Plan strategies, tactics and practices
2.2.5 — Plan a Personal Exercise Programme (PEP)

Analysis of performance forms part of Section 2.2 Analysis of practical performance. It presents the link between the theory in Unit 1 The theory of Physical Education and the practical work in Section 2.1. Any activity available for practical assessment can be analysed. Often, choosing a sport you already have in-depth knowledge of could be a good option, although choosing a sport that has simple, straightforward skills and tactics may suit better.

The analysis of performance will be based on one of the physical activities listed in the specification in the role of player/participant (not as an official or leader) in Section 2.1 Practical performance.

1 — Rules, regulations and terminology

You must be able to show your knowledge and understanding of the rules, regulations and terminology of a selected physical activity.

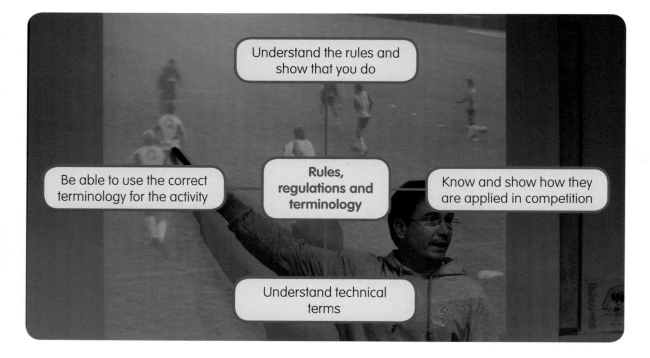

Understand the rules and show that you do

Be able to use the correct terminology for the activity

Rules, regulations and terminology

Know and show how they are applied in competition

Understand technical terms

It is important that you gain as much information as you can about the rules of your chosen sport. The following are ways to increase your knowledge and understanding of the rules:

- read governing bodies' publications
- watch sports events on television and listen to the commentary of the experts
- play your chosen sport to as high a standard as you can
- read coaching manuals and the rules of your sport
- discuss rules with your teacher
- practice refereeing or umpiring
- use the Internet to find information on rules.

Active challenge

For your chosen sport, find five books you can use to help with your knowledge of the rules. You could use the Internet to help find the titles of these publications.

2 — Observe and analyse performance

The **analysis of performance** part of the course requires candidates to recognize the strong and less strong parts of a performance and to understand and demonstrate ways to improve them by observing and analysing the performance.

To be successful in this area, use a variety of techniques to observe and analyse performance:

The following coaching model is useful when breaking down analysis, and linking performance to feedback:

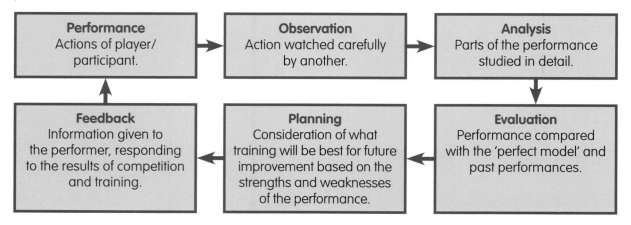

Performance Actions of player/ participant.	→ **Observation** Action watched carefully by another.	→ **Analysis** Parts of the performance studied in detail.
↑ **Feedback** Information given to the performer, responding to the results of competition and training.	← **Planning** Consideration of what training will be best for future improvement based on the strengths and weaknesses of the performance.	← **Evaluation** Performance compared with the 'perfect model' and past performances.

3 — Evaluate performance

To be successful in this area a full evaluation of strengths and limitations of performance should be made against a perfect model.

Complete feedback should be provided on all aspects of the evaluation in order to recognize strengths and areas for improvement.

In order to realize whether a sporting action is good or not, an understanding of how the action should look in its perfect state should be appreciated. This is the 'perfect model' you will mark any performance against. There are several ways you can observe the perfect model:

• World-class sports coverage.
• Training videos or coaching manuals.
• Action photos from magazines and books by top players.

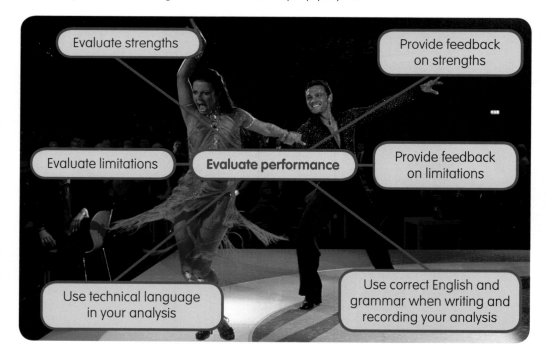

When developing an understanding of the perfect model it is useful to use video recordings of the best performers. This allows replays and pauses in the action to be made, giving time for you to appreciate the performance in question.

When looking at a performance, the shape of the body in action will indicate how close it is to the perfect model. Some areas to look for are the head position, where the centre of gravity is, a balanced body position and how the weight is distributed.

Rafael Nadal serves in the French Open Tennis Championships.

A young girl practises her tennis serve.

Task 1

Look at the two photos above and compare the differences in the following:

* head position
* centre of gravity
* balance of the body
* weight distribution.

Knowledge of skill-related fitness

What you have learnt about skill-related fitness and its application to different sports will help with your observations. You will now know which components to look out for in your chosen activity.

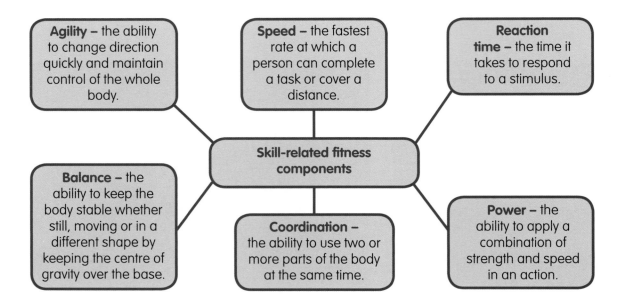

Agility – the ability to change direction quickly and maintain control of the whole body.

Speed – the fastest rate at which a person can complete a task or cover a distance.

Reaction time – the time it takes to respond to a stimulus.

Skill-related fitness components

Balance – the ability to keep the body stable whether still, moving or in a different shape by keeping the centre of gravity over the base.

Coordination – the ability to use two or more parts of the body at the same time.

Power – the ability to apply a combination of strength and speed in an action.

Characteristics of a skilful performance

There are a number of skill types that can be identified in a performance:

- Basic skills can be simple, closed skills, such as a set shot in basketball.
- Intermediate skills can be skills performed in sequence with other skills, such as dribble to a position to play a set shot.
- Advanced skills can be performing linked skills with the opposition, such as dribble past a defender or making a set shot avoiding a block from another defender.

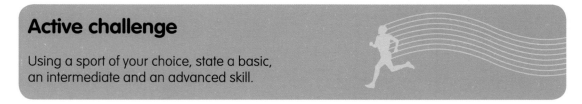

Active challenge

Using a sport of your choice, state a basic, an intermediate and an advanced skill.

When you watch a skilful performance it looks great. A skilful team player looks as though they have lots of time, create powerful shots with seemingly little effort and their attempts are often successful. The following information gives examples of skilful play:

- Shots make the target – this shows that the skill is being performed with accuracy.
- A kick, serve, stroke, pitch of the ball all go where the player intended.
- A good cricketer, specializing in bowling, can place the ball on a chosen target by pitching the ball consistently around a chosen spot.

- The action often has a successful outcome, showing consistency. Hitting a target or completing a pass regularly requires skill. Making a pass in netball regularly from the Centre to the Goal Attack gives the team a goal shooting opportunity.
- All parts of the body work in unison to affect the skill. This relies on coordination.
- When executing skills, a performer maintains smoothness to the technique even when responding to different and difficult situations.
- The correct weight/strength is put on a pass or hit, needing control. A tennis player can still play a winning shot despite having been defending, running across the baseline for the ball and being late in the game.
- The action performed looks good and is aesthetically pleasing.
- The skill is performed with smoothness.
- The specific physical components appropriate to the skill are applied: power, strength, agility, reaction time, balance and speed.
- The technique used to perform the skill follows the correct technical model.

Germany's Amelie Kober demonstrates a perfect execution of skills.

- The skill is performed with the maximum output but with minimum outlay of energy and time – this shows timing and coordination. A golfer may strike the ball with ease but it travels further than usual, possibly making the next shot much easier.
- A skilled performer can easily adapt to changing circumstances and be successful. An attacking footballer may need to run back to make a tackle and then dribble out of trouble in a deeper position on the pitch than normal.
- A player is confident that their play will be successful and plays as such.

Task 2

1 – Give six examples where you have witnessed skilled performance.

2 – Develop four of these examples into sentences.

Many factors can influence a performance. These are sometimes in the control of the performer and sometimes not. When observing an activity a distinction should be made between the two, and comments and feedback given should be adapted accordingly. For instance, a player may well have shown success or great skill in an activity in the past, but changes in the weather could cause the skill to break down. For example, the ball toss for the serve in tennis might be a problem on a very windy day but at no other time.

The following are factors influencing the expectations and reactions of the observer:

Always have the perfect model in mind

Factors affecting the perfect model

Reaction and comments made appropriately

Rules
May be complex and competition strong so mistakes are made.

Skills may be good but broken in performance.

Fitness
The performer may drop in standard due to lack of fitness.

Experience
Player may be relatively new to the game.

Weather
May make surface slippery.

Standard of game
A player's own skills may be fair but those of the other players may be poor.

Degree of difficulty of skill
The skill being performed may be complex and difficult to complete.

Open skills
Skills performed with many variables. May be affected by the actions of others in the environment.

Closed skills
Basic skills performed in isolation with no variables.

These should not be influenced by the people and conditions around the performer.

Comment on good aspects of performance.

Comment on poor aspects of performance.

Have knowledge of how the bad points can be improved.

Suggest ways to improve.

Make allowances for difficult circumstances.

Characteristics of an unskilled performer

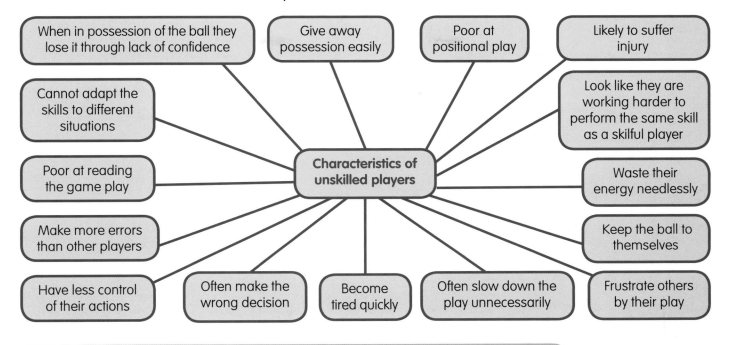

When in possession of the ball they lose it through lack of confidence

Give away possession easily

Poor at positional play

Likely to suffer injury

Cannot adapt the skills to different situations

Look like they are working harder to perform the same skill as a skilful player

Poor at reading the game play

Characteristics of unskilled players

Waste their energy needlessly

Make more errors than other players

Keep the ball to themselves

Have less control of their actions

Often make the wrong decision

Become tired quickly

Often slow down the play unnecessarily

Frustrate others by their play

Active challenge

With a partner, link the information in this section with a single chosen activity and describe good execution of three skills.

4 — Plan strategies, tactics and practices

Strategy is a pre-planned scheme to outplay the opposition. A strategy makes the most of the person's strengths and exploits weaknesses of the opponent in order to improve skills and performance. Tactics are short-term or immediate actions to outplay the opposition.

Know the practices to improve performance

Plan complex strategies to improve

Correct technical language should be used

Explain advanced tactics to improve performance

Plan strategies, tactics and practices

Use correct English and grammar when writing your analysis

Have good, clear documentation for the analysis

Be able to evaluate evidence and be able to suggest ways to improve accordingly

Tennis example

Strategies

Baseline play will show power control and accuracy, and serve-and-volley will show speed at the net and fine touch.

The strategies used may depend on both the surface and the shots played in the rally. Baseline play can work better on slower surfaces such as clay, whereas serve-and-volley play works on the quicker surfaces of hard courts. Good players will mix up the shots they play and bring the element of surprise into operation to beat the opponent.

Active challenge

Using a sport of your choice, state strategies that could be applied to the activity.

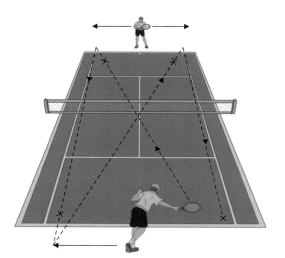

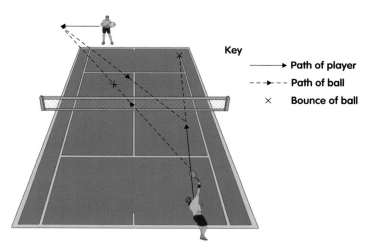

Key

→ Path of player

- - ▸ - - Path of ball

× Bounce of ball

Attacking baseline play – plays the ball deep, side to side of the court.

Net play – serve and volley – move from back to front of court – almost always attacking – when receiving will chip the ball over the net and charge forward to gain control of the net again ('chip and charge').

Tactics

For a tennis singles player the tactics will come about by the amount and type of spin applied to the shot and the speed and depth at which the ball is hit. In doubles there are other additions to tactical play:

Serving tactics:

- Who should serve first?
- Where should they serve from?
- Where should the serve be placed?

Returning serve tactics:

- Where should you stand?
- Where should your partner stand?
- Where should the return be placed?

Poaching tactics – interception played, often at the net:

- Committing only to a certain space to poach a shot.
- The player will cross the width of the court to play the shot.

Active challenge

Using a sport of your choice, state tactics that could be applied to the activity.

Practices

Practices often involve contrived situations that may occur in a game situation repeated in a controlled environment. This helps a performer to prepare for any eventuality in the game. In tennis this may include ground stroke drills, volleying, returning serve, and so on.

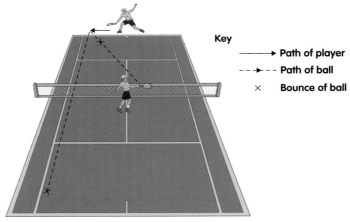

Key

→ **Path of player**

--→-- **Path of ball**

× **Bounce of ball**

Ground strokes for baseline play. Hand feed to player on forehand.

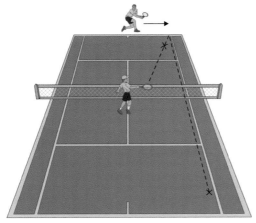

Hand feed to player on backhand.

The pressure can then be increased further by:

- racket feeding; and
- moment prior to feed, call direction of feed to prepare player to move either side.

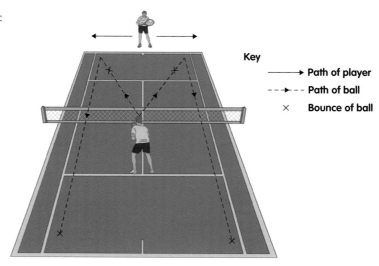

Key

→ Path of player

--▶-- Path of ball

× Bounce of ball

Hand feed to player alternately on forehand and backhand.

Active challenge

Using a sport of your choice, state a basic, an intermediate and an advanced practice that could be applied to the activity.

5 — Plan a Personal Exercise Programme (PEP)

Your Personal Exercise Programme (PEP) must be based on an activity undertaken in the role of player/participant in Section 2.1 Practical performance.

Planning a Personal Exercise Programme involves a great deal of preparation and understanding of the needs of the individual. If exercising with a specific sport in mind, then understanding the requirements of that activity is essential if the programme is to be worthwhile to improve your fitness and performance.

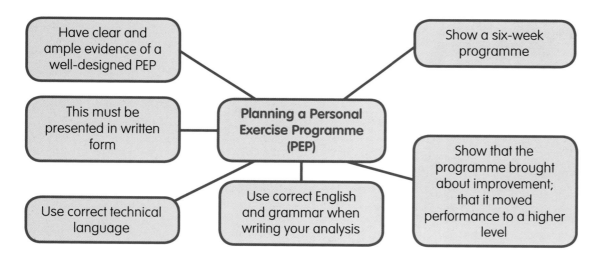

Have clear and ample evidence of a well-designed PEP

Show a six-week programme

This must be presented in written form

Planning a Personal Exercise Programme (PEP)

Use correct technical language

Use correct English and grammar when writing your analysis

Show that the programme brought about improvement; that it moved performance to a higher level

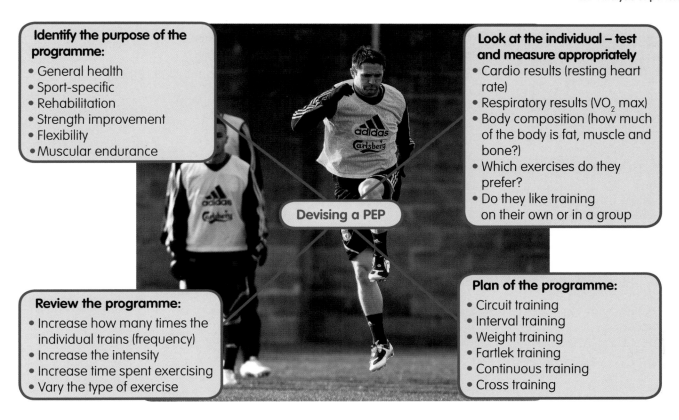

Identify the purpose of the programme:
- General health
- Sport-specific
- Rehabilitation
- Strength improvement
- Flexibility
- Muscular endurance

Look at the individual – test and measure appropriately
- Cardio results (resting heart rate)
- Respiratory results (VO_2 max)
- Body composition (how much of the body is fat, muscle and bone?)
- Which exercises do they prefer?
- Do they like training on their own or in a group

Devising a PEP

Review the programme:
- Increase how many times the individual trains (frequency)
- Increase the intensity
- Increase time spent exercising
- Vary the type of exercise

Plan of the programme:
- Circuit training
- Interval training
- Weight training
- Fartlek training
- Continuous training
- Cross training

Summary checklist

- Analysis of performance provides a link between the theory and the practical work.
- Analyse any activities that are offered in your school.
- Always be aware in the practical lessons of how you can and what you can analyse.
- Always look for a way to improve a performance.
- Look for strengths of a performance.
- Look for areas of a performance to be improved.
- You may not base analysis on officials or leaders, it must be based on a player/participant.

There are five key areas for analysis:

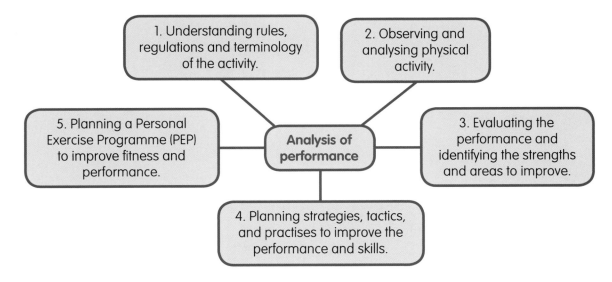

1. Understanding rules, regulations and terminology of the activity.

2. Observing and analysing physical activity.

5. Planning a Personal Exercise Programme (PEP) to improve fitness and performance.

Analysis of performance

3. Evaluating the performance and identifying the strengths and areas to improve.

4. Planning strategies, tactics, and practises to improve the performance and skills.

You should present the PEP for assessment in written form. All the other areas for analysis (understanding rules, regulations and terminology, observing and analysing performance, evaluating performance, and planning strategies, tactics and practises) can be completed using the most appropriate of the following formats:

- question and answer sessions
- written reports
- a presentation.

The main examination rules to follow are:

- Authenticity – all work in this section must be completed under some supervision.
- Feedback – your teacher may support the preparation of the assessment, but not in the production of the final assessment.
- Time – all work should be compiled using a minimum of nine hours. Remember, written reports may take longer than a question and answer session.
- Collaboration – you can work with other people, but you must have your own individual response.
- Resources – you must choose the format of presentation that suits the resources available in your school.

Useful websites

The following are a selection of useful websites to help you increase your PE and sports-related knowledge.

BBC GCSE Bitesize: a BBC run website with useful information, revision tips and example questions: www.bbc.co.uk/schools/gcsebitesize/pe/

BBC Sport Academy: a BBC run website for up-to-date news on sport: www.bbc.co.uk/sportacademy

Brain MacSports Coach: information on coaching, sports, nutrition and more: www.brianmac.co.uk

British Bottled Water Producers: information about water and health: www.britishbottledwater.org

British Olympic Association: everything you need to know about the Olympics: www.britisholympicassociation.co.uk

Bupa: details about general health: www.bupa.co.uk

Interactive Resources for GCSE PE: GCSE PE questions answered: www.interactivepe.co.uk

International Paralympic Committee: everything you need to know about the Paralympics: www.paralympic.org

Leisure Connection: information about national sports centres: www.leisureconnection.co.uk

National Health Service (NHS): information about various health and body matters: www.nhs.uk

Peak Performance: all about sporting performance: www.pponline.co.uk

Rugby Fitness Training: tips on how to improve your rugby performance: www.rugbyfitnesstraining.com

Sport England: information on sport in England: www.sportengland.org

sports coach UK: the agency for development of the UK coaching system: www.sportscoachuk.org

Sports Injury Clinic: sports injuries and their treatments: www.sportsinjuryclinic.net

Sports Search: information on all sports for 11 to 17 year olds: www.sportssearch.org

Try My Sport: information on all types of sport and how to get involved: www.trymysport.co.uk

UK Sport: up-to-date information on UK sport: www.uksport.gov.uk

Women's Sport and Fitness Foundation (WSFF): about women in sport: www.wsf.org.uk

Youth Sport Trust: information on TOP and Active Kids Programmes: www.youthsporttrust.org

Glossary

A

Aerobic 'with oxygen'. If exercise is not too fast and is steady, the heart can supply all the oxygen muscles need.

Aesthetic appreciation recognition of beauty.

Agility the ability to change the position of the body quickly and to control the movement of the whole body.

Alveoli air sacs where gaseous exchange takes place.

Anabolic steroids drugs that mimic the male sex hormone testosterone and promote bone and muscle growth.

Anaerobic 'without oxygen'. If exercise is done in short, fast bursts, the heart cannot supply blood and oxygen to muscles as fast as the cells use them.

Anorexic someone who suffers from anorexia nervosa, a prolonged weight loss eating disorder due to obsessive control of food intake, leading to loss of appetite.

Antagonist relaxing muscle allowing movement.

Aorta main blood vessel leaving the heart.

Arterioles blood vessels that are sub-divisions of arteries.

Atrophy when muscle loses its size because of lack of exercise.

B

Balance the ability to retain the body's centre of mass (gravity) above the base of support with reference to static (stationary), or dynamic (changing), conditions of movement, shape and orientation.

Balanced competition grouping based on size, age or experience for an even match.

Balanced diet a diet which contains an optimal ratio of nutrients.

Basal metabolic rate (BMR) the level at which energy is used without exercise.

Beta-blockers drugs that are used to control heart rate and that have a calming and relaxing effect.

Blood doping is a banned method of improving performance that does not involve the use of drugs.

Blood pressure the force exerted by circulating blood on the walls of the blood vessels.

Body composition the percentage of body weight that is fat, muscle and bone.

C

Carbohydrate loading building up carbohydrates in the body to use in endurance events.

Cardiac muscle only found in the heart, never tires.

Cardiac output the amount of blood ejected from the heart in one minute.

Cardiorespiratory to do with the heart and lungs.

Cardiovascular fitness the ability to exercise the entire body for long periods of time.

Cartilage tough, flexible tissue, can be found at the end of bones.

Centres of Excellence centres offering use of facilities to all levels in a variety of sports but also concentrating on one sport taking it to the highest level.

Circuit training a series of exercises completed in order and for a certain time.

Circulatory system transports blood using the heart and blood vessels.

Classification a way of sorting or organizing groups.

Competence the relationship between: skill, the selection and application of skills, tactics, strategies and compositional ideas; and the readiness of the body and mind to cope with the activity. It requires an understanding of how these combine to produce effective performances in different activities and contexts.

Compound/open fracture the bone breaks and comes through the skin.

Continuous training aerobic exercising, at a moderate to high level, with no rests.

Coordination the ability to use two or more body parts together.

Cross training using different training methods in the same session.

Cultural influences established way of living of a particular group.

D

Detoxify removing poison from.

Diaphragm muscle that divides the chest cavity from the abdominal cavity.

Dislocate joints moved out of their normal arrangement.

Diuretics drugs that elevate the rate of bodily urine excretion.

Drug substance (other than food) that has a physiological effect when taken into the body.

E

Ectomorph a somatotype, individuals with narrow shoulders and narrow hips, characterized by thinness.

Endomorph a somatotype, individuals with wide hips and narrow shoulders, characterized by fatness.

Endorphins hormones released during exercise.

Endothelium internal space of the blood vessels; in arteries this changes according to the amount of blood to be transported.

Energy drinks fluids containing carbohydrates.

Erythropoietin (EPO) a type of peptide hormone that increases the red blood cell count.

Etiquette unwritten and unofficial codes of practice followed in an activity.

Exercise a form of physical activity done to maintain or improve health and/or physical fitness, it is not a competitive sport.

Expiration breathing out, exhalation.

F

Fartlek training 'speed play', changing speed, distances and times of exercise in the same session.

Fast twitch muscle fibres muscle fibres used in events requiring quick reactions and power.

Fatigue the body's inability to complete a task.

Fibrinogen a protein found in blood that helps clotting.

Fitness the ability to meet the demands of the environment.

FITT Frequency, Intensity, Time, Type (used to increase the amount of work the body does, in order to achieve overload).

Flat bone can be called plate bone, mainly linked with protection.

Flexibility the range of movement possible at a joint.

Forced breathing breathing during exercise when requirements increase.

Friction action of two surfaces rubbing together creating heat.

Fused two or more bones knitted together so no movement occurs.

G

Gender male or female.

Goal setting series of phases setting out achievable targets for progress.

H

Haemoglobin found in red blood cells, transports oxygen to body tissue.

Health a state of complete mental, physical and social well-being, and not merely the absence of disease and infirmity.

Health-related exercise activity undertaken with specific focus on improving the bodily systems.

Healthy, active lifestyle a lifestyle that contributes positively to physical, mental and social well-being, and which includes regular exercise and physical activity.

Heart rate the number of times the heartbeats each minute.

Hypertrophy when muscle increases in size because of exercise.

I

Individual differences/needs matching training to the requirements of an individual.

Insertion the point where a tendon attaches a muscle to bone where there is movement.

Inspiration breathing in, inhalation.

Interval training mixing periods of hard exercise with rest periods.

Introspective thoughtful or meditative.

Involuntary muscles work automatically, controlled by the involuntary nervous system.

Irregular bones bones that have no uniform shape.

Isometric contraction muscle contraction which results in increased tension but the length does not alter; for example, when pressing against a stationary object.

Isotonic contraction muscle contraction that results in limb movement.

J

Joint a place where two or more bones meet.

L

Lactic acid chemical built up in the muscles during anaerobic exercise.

Leverage the use of force or effort (muscle power) to overcome resistance.

Ligament tough, rounded, elastic fibre attaching bone to bone at a joint.

Long bones those bones that are the longest in the body which make up the arms and legs.

M

Masking agent a legal substance for a sport, hiding the presence of an illegal one.

Maximum heart rate calculated as 220 minus age.

Mental of the mind.

Mesomorph a somatotype, individuals with wide shoulders and narrow hips, characterized by muscularity.

Methods of training interval training, continuous training, circuit training, weight training, Fartlek training, cross training.

Minimum level of fitness the resulting fitness level when someone exercises over a period of weeks including five sessions of 20 minutes, raising the heart rate to 60 to 80 per cent of its maximum.

Move a motion, could be an action like running or swinging a racket at a ball.

Muscle tone muscles' state of slight tension and readiness to work.

Muscular endurance the ability to use voluntary muscles many times without getting tired.

Muscular strength the amount of force a muscle can exert against a resistance.

N

Narcotic analgesics drugs that can be used to reduce the feeling of pain.

National Sports Centres headquarters for particular sports, providing facilities for public, aiming to provide best facilities for the success of elite athletes.

Newton a unit of force.

O

Obese a term used to describe people who are very overfat.

Optimum weight ideal weight for a person, giving them the best chance of success in an activity.

Origin the end of a muscle that is attached to a fixed bone.

Overfat a way of saying you have more body fat than you should have.

Overload fitness can only be improved through training more than you normally do.

Overweight having weight in excess of normal (not harmful unless accompanied by overfatness).

Oxygen debt the amount of oxygen consumed during recovery above that which would have ordinarily been consumed in the same time at rest (this results in a shortfall in the oxygen available).

P

PAR-Q Physical Activity Readiness Questionnaire.

PEP Personal Exercise Programme.

Peptide hormones drugs that cause the production of other hormones.

Performance how well a task is completed.

Performance-enhancing drug substance that artificially enhances personal characteristics and performance.

PESSCL PE, School Sport and Club Links.

Physical of the body.

Physical activity any form of exercise or movement; physical activity may be planned and structured or unplanned and unstructured (in PE we are concerned with planned and structured physical activity, such as a fitness class).

Posture the way the muscles hold the body when still or in motion.

Power the ability to do strength performances quickly (power = strength × speed).

Prime mover contracting muscle, causing movement.

Production making something.

Progressive overload to gradually increase the amount of overload so that fitness gains occur, but without potential for injury.

Protect guard against threat of injury.

Pulmonary circuit transports blood from the heart to the lungs and back again.

Q

QCA Qualifications and Curriculum Authority developing and modernizing curriculum, assessments, examinations and qualifications.

R

Reaction time the time between the presentation of a stimulus and the onset of a movement.

Recovery the time required for the repair of damage to the body caused by training or competition.

Recovery rate the time it takes for the heart to return to resting rate after exercise.

Rehabilitate recovery from injury.

Release of energy amount and type of energy release used at different stages in different kinds of activity.

Residual volume the amount of air left in the lungs after a maximal exhalation.

Rest the period of time allotted to recovery.

Resting heart rate amount of heart beats per minute when the body is at rest.

Reversibility any adaptation that takes place as a consequence of training will be reversed when you stop training.

RICE Rest, Ice, Compression, Elevation (a method of treating injuries).

Role model a person looked to by others as an example to follow.

S

Self-esteem respect for, or a favourable opinion of, oneself.

Septum wall of muscle dividing the left and right sides of the heart.

Shape form or outline.

Short bone smaller version of a long bone, found in the hands and feet.

Simple/closed fracture break of the bone when the skin is not broken.

Skill-related fitness physical motor abilities of the body adapted to specific sports.

Skin-fold calliper a device that measures the thickness of a fold of skin with its underlying layer of fat.

Slow twitch muscle fibres muscle fibres required in endurance events.

SMART Specific, Measurable, Achievable, Realistic, Time-bound.

Social to do with the community and society.

Somatotypes classification of body type.

Specificity matching training to the requirements of an activity.

Speed the differential rate at which an individual is able to perform a movement or cover a distance in a period of time.

Sport centres providing sport facilities for the community.

Sport England non-departmental public body, operating under Royal Charter, responsible for sport in England.

Spotters trained and alert people surrounding the trampoline prepared to prevent the performer coming off dangerously.

Sprain injury involving joints and ligaments.

Stimulants drugs that have an effect on the central nervous system, such as increased mental and/or physical alertness.

Strain pulled muscle as a result of overstretching.

Stroke volume the volume of blood pumped out of the heart by each ventricle during one contraction.

Superior vena cava blood vessel transporting deoxygenated blood back to the heart.

Support helping to take the weight.

Synovial capsule tough fibre surrounding the synovial joint.

Synovial fluid found in synovial joint.

Synovial joints freely moveable joints with the ends covered in cartilage.

Synovial membrane lining inside joint capsule where synovial fluid is produced.

Systematic training planning a programme for an individual as a result of the effect of previous training.

Systemic circuit transports blood from the heart to the body and back to the heart again.

T

Target zone the range within which an individual needs to work for aerobic training to take place (60 to 80 per cent of maximum heart rate).

Technique way in which a skill is performed.

Tendons strong, non-elastic tissue attaching bone to muscle.

Tension mental and emotional strain.

Tidal volume amount of air breathed in or out during normal breathing.

Training a well-planned programme which uses scientific principles to improve performance, skill, game ability and motor and physical fitness.

Training threshold the boundaries of the target zone.

Trend fad or fashion of the moment.

U

Underweight weighing less than is normal, healthy or required.

V

Valve openings allowing blood flow in one direction only, found in the heart and veins.

Vital capacity amount of air that can be breathed out, after a deep breath in.

VO$_2$ maximum the maximum amount of oxygen used in one minute per kilogram of body weight.

Voluntary muscles skeletal muscles attached to the skeleton, can be made to work consciously.

W

Weight training progressively lifting heavier weights or lifting weights more often to improve strength.

Index